To the Bryant Blasters, my little Barça.

"The reason we do things the way we do them is because we love the ball"
Xavi Hernàndez, midfielder, FC Barcelona.

TABLE OF CONTENTS

Preface

"We can discover more about a person in an hour of play than in a year of conversation"

Plato (428 – 348 B.C)

Why do we love sports and why is soccer the most popular sport?

Why do so many people love soccer, and for that matter so many other sports? "There is a truth to sport, a purity, a drama, an intensity, a spirit that makes it irresistible to take part in, and irresistible to watch", said the legendary British runner Sebastian Coe in the Opening Ceremony of the London 2012 Olympic Games. Perhaps in that regard we are not very different from many animals, ranging from dogs to birds and dolphins, who are often observed to take pleasure in – and also learn through – what appears to be gratuitous physical activity. Contrary to animals, however, we are capable of structuring our games with complex rules and adorning them with colorful uniforms and arousing anthems. There is something tribal, even territorial about how fans assemble to support their teams. Music is also a mode of communication between humans that universally helps generate a sense of communion, like sport. Later in the Opening Ceremony, thousands of happy athletes improvised beautiful dances to the tune of "Hey, Jude", sung live by ex-Beatle Paul McCartney. Tens of thousands of people sang cheerfully in a giant, spontaneous chorus as their high-tech arm-rests lit up and became the pixels of a stadium-size screen, the backstage of the most magnificent discotheque ever built by humankind. Perhaps sport and music are biologically connected in that they are both deeply appealing to a primitive part of our brain that deals with feelings and sensations. The traditional view of sport as a competitive, and thus aggressive, activity, is not easily reconciled with sports' immense popularity at the amateur level: most of the participants lose and the winners are always in minority, so the unlikely reward for winning cannot explain why so many people love sports. Most people are clearly in it for participating with fellow humans and friends, certainly inspired by the godly skills of the best athletes, but always for the fun of improving one's fitness or one's abilities. "Hey, Jude, Take a sad song and make it better".

But why is soccer, among all the sports, the most popular one? It has been argued that soccer is the only ball game that can be practiced on almost any surface, and with almost any ball: we have all seen kids play soccer with tennis balls, basketballs, even with home-made tape balls or oranges, on cement parking lots, on dirt streets, on the beach, on snow, on mud fields, on top of buildings and inside houses. A friend of mine who was visiting Guatemala once witnessed a scene that was as surreal as it was a violation of all the standards of modern safety: an eleven-year-old girl playing soccer while carrying in her back an eight-month-old baby (who, apparently, looked rather habituated to the jerky outings). Soccer is played in the midst of all sorts of human conflicts, in peace and in war, perhaps to evade despair. Since 2005, when Israel (evoking self-defense) erected a 100 km-long, 8 meter-tall cement wall that splits Palestinian land into two – effectively cutting Cisjordania from Gaza –, Palestine is the only country in the world that is forced to hold two separate leagues. Soccer enthusiasts are not easily stopped from playing it. It is being played right now by children in bare feet on the African savannah, all day long, it was played in prison by Mandela with other life-term inmates in South Africa during the *Apartheid*, and there are records of it being played in 1914 by the twenty-seven explorers of Shackleton's expedition that was trapped near the South Pole for almost two years.

One of my favorite sports journalists, John Carlin, has said that one of the reasons that soccer is so popular is the "injustice factor" – it is often decided by errors, since it is played with an imprecise part of our body, and the field is so huge that the referee's eyes cannot cover it all. This,

Carlin argues, coupled to the fact that the errors get exposed to mass audiences through television, amplifies their magnitude and generate endless debate and more media revenue. Nobody argues about who the just winner is in basketball, American football, or baseball.

Men from the 1914 Shackleton expedition to the South Pole playing a soccer game on snow. The ship on the background was trapped by ice for almost two years.

However, as a player and a coach, I refuse to believe that Carlin's "injustice factor" is fundamentally important in explaining why soccer is so popular. Who is drawn to a game of errors? That surely cannot be the *essence* of soccer. People were joining this game in growing numbers way before the arrival of television. Soccer (*foot*ball!) has been born as a sport several times in different corners of our planet thousands of years ago. Give a ball to a one-year-old child, and he or she will kick it. There is a basic attraction in trying to control the ball with your feet, rather than with your hands: what's the challenge, with your hands? That's why

7

other sports have added hoops, rackets, and bats – to add a *challenge*. What is so uniquely alluring about soccer is that the main challenge is presented by an imprecise part of the human body. If you have never done it, you'll see that the challenge of controlling the ball with your feet is *a lot of fun*. Try it. Then get together with friends to practice it, on a parking lot, on the beach, or on a meadow in the middle of the mountains, and you've become one of us. A *billion* of us, uniting people across the Americas, Oceania, Asia, Europe, and Africa.

Because all it takes is your foot and a ball, soccer is a great social equalizer, and that also has contributed to making it so popular. You don't need to be rich, or tall, or strong, or fast; if you are one of those, it might help you a bit, but you will soon find yourself outwitted by a player that has other advantages, such as technical ability or positional wisdom. In a couple of weekly pick-up games we have in Seattle, dating back to the 1980s and now organized via email (Val Landicho keeps more than 100 subscribers and it is not uncommon to have 50 people show up), there are players encompassing 7 to 87 years old from about a dozen countries and all professional extracts – ranging from a surgeon to a car salesman, from an elementary student to a retired Wall Street analyst, money and looks rendered irrelevant for the purpose of this game, like unaware naked boys splashing in the water.

What is this book about?
Much has been said already about how FC Barcelona players, mostly raised in their youth academy, pass the ball between each other at great speed while they execute choreography-like movements to deceive their opponents. Why is the youth academy so successful and who devised its coaching methods? Why aren't they copied everywhere? What is more cost-efficient, to run a youth academy or to buy already-formed soccer stars? Are American clubs implementing these coaching methods, and if so, is their performance improving? Did you know that there is already an American player being formed at the FC Barcelona youth academy?

This book answers these and other questions related to the educational process that raises FC Barcelona players, how it was conceived, and analyzes why it is more successful in some scenarios than others. As an educator myself, I became interested in the FC Barcelona coaching methodology when I realized that the very reason for its appeal to kids is its logical simplicity. Indeed, I believe that FC Barcelona's greatest legacy will not be the record-breaking 2009 string of six titles or even its Argentine-born star player Lionel Messi but rather that its soccer style based on "Possession Soccer" is now, due to the success of a first team fueled by its youth academy, being taught in youth academies everywhere.

In the last five years, FC Barcelona – no doubt fueled by Messi's presence in its team – exploded like a firework as the symbol of *attractive soccer*. First of all, there is the *women factor*: a recent poll among women in Barcelona (50% of the population!) showed that a large percentage of them never used to watch soccer but now they would watch an important match such as a FC Barcelona final or a Barça-Madrid game. Women now form a good percentage of the FC Barcelona fan base – why would they want to miss the fun? I know this to be true because both my sister *and my mom* (who never watched games as I was growing up) are counted in this poll. Second, women, specially the U.S. women team, but also the Brazilians and the Germans, have shown great skill and their games are now watched by increasing numbers of both men and women. Third, the FC Barcelona "brand" seems to have spread like a virus, no doubt propelled through satellite TV by Ronaldinho and Messi's deeds. The three biggest present stars of the NBA (Kobe Bryant, LeBron James and Kevin Durant) confess that "we do not watch whole [soccer] games" but they can tell "Leo Messi is the best". Barça shirts are reportedly seen in all the continents, even in remote places like deserts and Amazon tribes.

This book is the story of how FC Barcelona's youth academy has fueled one of the most successful soccer clubs in the world in present times. I purposely waited until the exploits of the team would start to taper down in order to bring a bit of perspective which time always affords. I emphasize here that the success was not built by purchasing players (as other clubs built their supremacy periods in the past) but rather by methodically building a productive educational program. I am not the first one to tell the story. It has been told many times before in the form of Catalan and Spanish newspaper articles, books, or web publications – but I do not expect you (an English-only reader) to have been able to read them. Here I have synthesized all those materials in a comprehensive format and added some of my own. In the United States, *The New York Times* and other major newspapers have run stories on "Barça" (pronounced "Barsa" and often misspelled and mispronounced "Barca") every time the team has won major competitions such as the *Champions League*. Journalists like to ask why the latest winning streak has been so spectacular and most of the times those articles did get it right – but the short format was not conducive to explaining all the details. Indeed, the majority of my American soccer friends do not know those details (as told in this book) because most people don't read the *New York Times* every day. If you do not know that it was all engineered by the genius mind of Johan Cruyff – legendary Dutch player who brought "Total Football" to FC Barcelona in the 1970s *and* legendary coach in the 1990s, who coached a recent coach! – then you need to read this book. (There is more to it, of course, so even if you know that much, you might find it interesting.)

I have also added an appendix to explain my own soccer coaching experience, both as the coach of a team of elementary school-age kids here in Seattle, the *Bryant Blasters,* for over four years, and as a guest coach for a FC Barcelona summer camp in Seattle. I wrote the appendix because I obtained about half of those tips from staff at the FC Barcelona youth academy and I then applied them to my kids' team with great success. I do not claim that the methods described are the only way to teach soccer effectively, but since the methods are relevant to the overall theme of this book (soccer education), I decided to include them here in case they can be of practical use to parent coaches.

Why did I write this book?

Once every twenty years or so, the natural selection of soccer produces one great team somewhere on Earth by mere chance. When that happens, a great deal is written about that team. In fact, the formation process of the team is usually not that interesting, or only interesting to its own fans, because it almost always happens by an accumulation of random circumstances that result in the accumulation of great players in one team – typically money and birthdays. Presently, there is wide consensus that FC Barcelona managed to build one such "great team" starting 2008 – and we will see in the book that Barça is neither the richest club in the world nor it is a matter of "luck" that the club accumulated so many good players. If we take a look at their performance in the *Champions League*, arguably the most competitive competition in the world, FC Barcelona has won it three times (in 2006, 2009, and 2011) in the period 2006-2013 and has reached the semifinals for a record six years in a row. The fame of the team has grown well beyond these dry statistics into popular culture status: even in the United States, where soccer gets relatively little media attention, my FC Barcelona jacket, sweatshirt or backpack (on any given day, I can be seen wearing one of these items for sure) prompts friendly comments from a clerk one moment, or a person waiting in a bus line later. All this is a set of happy circumstances for people from Barcelona like me, but it would not have been enough to motivate me to write a book. (I have a busy professional life outside of writing, you see.)

What compelled me to write this book was that someone suggested that the making of this great team had been due to *chance*. It was not just *someone*, actually. And it did not happen just once. Twice within a month's time and in seemingly independent occasions, *two* of the greatest players of all time, Zinedine Zidane and Diego Armando Maradona (my childhood hero, who slept inside a poster above my bed for almost ten years!) both said that FC Barcelona was "lucky" to have accumulated stars such as Xavi, Iniesta and Messi on the same team. Now, if you just landed from Mars and watched a Barça game for the first time, you might reach the same conclusion. But FC Barcelona fans and people from Spain in general know very well this not to be true: there is a great deal of planning – and very little chance – in FC Barcelona's success, and that's why the tale is worth telling to people outside of the FC Barcelona fans' circle.

It took more than 30 years of planning, including the drafting of a soccer style or "FC Barcelona soccer language", the coaching of kids of all ages according to the same style, and a highly selective scouting that fitted that style. How can one explain, otherwise, that parents from all over the world that want to see their kids succeed in soccer are asking if they can bring them to Barça's youth academy? (For that reason the club does not hold tryouts anymore; it has a sophisticated network of scouts, as we will see.) It was crucial that everyone in the club fell in love with that style, which had as its primary postulate to always seek the possession of the ball. I know the intricate details of the story because I was born in Barcelona, I was raised into a family of FC Barcelona fans, I'm an avid reader of everything that concerns the club, and I've been acquainted with some of the coaching staff of the youth academy. Hearing Zidane and Maradona and talking to my many American soccer friends, I realized that the story was not as well-known as I had assumed. It has never been published in English, for starters. Furthermore, the methods employed to create the present FC Barcelona team were applied with scientific rigor, which is why (as a scientist) I find them so interesting and I would like to share them with you.

Due to a serious injury, I had to be away from the fields for over a year. This gave me some extra time to write on weekends. However, this was a period of hardship for me, since I usually spend weekends playing as much soccer with my friends and kids as I can. Our pick-up games (still visited by fantastic ex-professional players like Danny Machado, Lee Eckmann, or Fred Hamel) have an unwritten rule that we have to show up with two shirts, a color one and a white one, so that when you arrive you can always join the team that has less players by putting on the appropriate color jersey. For many years I'd say I forgot my white jersey, but given that I always showed up with a Barça one, the real reason (a quirky "allergy" to Real Madrid colors) became quite obvious. I will always cherish how this group silently – or humorously – indulged my eccentric transgression of the rule.

Enjoy!

European soccer nomenclature

For the most part, European soccer teams compete in organizations called "clubs", a word that has a different meaning than the family-supported soccer clubs in which American kids play soccer. The European clubs are typically owned by its members, who pay a monthly or yearly fee (independently of the price of the season ticket that buys them a seat) and have voting rights, typically to vote for the President or the Board of Directors. The members of a club thus have a feeling that they own a piece of the club, which encourages them to get involved in its governance using democratic mechanisms and to participate in social gatherings organized by the club. (Recently some top clubs have been acquired by financial groups or millionaires and are no longer owned by its members, but note that those are a very small fraction of the total number of soccer clubs that exist in Europe.) The club always competes in many divisions, with a youth academy, and often even in several sports (basketball, hockey, etc.). FC Barcelona is one of the soccer clubs in the world with more subscribing members, counting 176,058 registered members in the 2010-2011 season; Arsenal and Benfica also have similar numbers.

Soccer teams can be formed by clubs, normally one or two for every big city (i.e. FC Barcelona, Arsenal, Roma, etc.), or by countries (only one "national team" for every country). As most of this book refers to club life, very little in this book deals with international competitions between national teams such as the World Cup (organized every four years, e.g. 2006, 2010, 2014, etc.) or the *EuroCup* (also organized every four years, but 2008, 2012, 2016, etc.).

In European club soccer, every country has two main national competitions. The most prestigious one is always the "league", where everyone plays twice against everyone (once at home, once away). In Spain, the league is called *Liga*, in Germany *Bundesliga*, in England the *Premier League*, etc. The other major national competition is usually called the Cup, which has an elimination format: the teams (including some second- and even third-division teams to make up to an exact power of two) are paired at the beginning of the season, also play twice, and the best team of the two games passes to the next round (usually 16 or 32 rounds). In Spain, the Cup is called *Copa del Rey*, in Holland the *KNVB Cup*, in England the *FA Cup*, etc. In most countries, the winner of the League and the winner of the Cup play a single match at the beginning of the following year called the *Super Cup*; in England this match is called the *FA Community Shield*.

The leagues are typically organized in "divisions". By default we usually refer to the "first division" when we speak of any given top league: *Liga* (Spain), *Bundesliga* (Germany), *Premier League* (England), etc. However, all these leagues have a second division, a third division, and so on. In all cases there is a system of relegations and promotions such that the top teams (usually three) of a given division exchange places with the bottom places of the division just above it. In England the format is somewhat different, because the *Premier League* formed in 1992 as the result of a break-away of the 20 top clubs from another competition, the *Football League*. The *Football League* was founded in 1888 and is the oldest league in the world. Since 1992, it is the league to which clubs relegate when they end at the bottom of the table in the *Premier League*, so in essence the *Football League* plays the role of England's (and Wales') second division; it is divided in three tiers of 24 teams each (in Spain, for ex., there are only two tiers: Second Division A and B). The seven levels below the *Football League* are known as the *National League System* – the equivalent of third and lower divisions in most other countries. To make matters more confusing, every year in

England there is a short, 7-round competition named *Football League Cup*, which gathers all the 20 teams of the *Premier League* and all the 72 teams of the *Football League* and in a Cup (single elimination) format.

Even more confusion arises with the international competitions, which have been changing over the years. Many years ago, when Europe was smaller, the one team that won the league of every country would play the *European Cup*, and the team (in every country) that won the Cup would participate in a separate *Cup Winners' Cup* competition. Real Madrid, which had a powerful squad in the 1950s, won the first five editions of the *European Cup* as well as the 1965-66 editions. Both competitions were organized by the *Union of European of Football Associations* (UEFA). The first editions of the *European Cup* were entered by just 16 teams (later 32; the previous champion would qualify automatically for the 16-team second round). UEFA decided to change all that in 1992 by introducing the *Champions League*, an extremely competitive cup with 77 participants and an appetizing prize (e.g., in 2011, FC Barcelona, the winner, was awarded €30.7M in addition to the €20.3M in TV revenues). Since 1992, never a team has repeated the crown two consecutive years.

FC Barcelona won a (32-team) *European Cup* in 1992, before it changed to the new format. Since 1992, FC Barcelona, AC Milan and Real Madrid have won three *Champions Leagues* each. To this day, Real Madrid's management adds the six small-format early *European Cups* to the newer three *Champions League* titles and contends (using easily-manipulated sources such as Wikipedia) that they have won "nine *Champions*", a clear fallacy that is an insult to the intelligence of all soccer fans. To avoid controversy, I prefer to conserve the old designation ("*European Cup*") when referring collectively to both *Champions League* and *European Cups*, as most serious journalists now use: for example, it is perfectly correct to say that "Real Madrid has won nine *European Cups*".

Acknowledgments

This book would have never existed if my son Jordi had not asked me to coach his kindergarten team about five years ago. Together with my scientist friend Mehrdad Jazayeri, now an M.I.T. professor, we took upon the task of teaching a group of ten or so kids the very basics of soccer. What soccer teaching method could we choose that was easily comprehended by kids? Total Football! I soon realized that everything I knew or experienced as a FC Barcelona fan – in Catalan or Spanish – was not readily available in English, so the idea to communicate my ideas to a wider audience slowly grew in me. Hence my deepest gratitude goes to the *Bryant Blasters* soccer team, a group of fun kindergarteners and their lovely families from the Bryant Elementary School. I will always cherish my memories of teaching them to properly kick a ball, to pass it or stop it, to think about their position and their opponent, to love the game and to love the ball. Now that my son has joined a local club, Seattle United, I find myself "parent-coaching" all the time – an activity that is strictly forbidden by the club (I too hated it when I was a coach!) and that we parents only do stealthily as a function of which direction the wind is blowing. Above all, I enjoy watching my son running like a devil after the ball, wanting it like a puppy, feeling with him the pleasure of a perfect control, a nice pass, learning to cherish the game with his friends.

I specially want to acknowledge my wife Lisa and my daughter Tàlia, who have always dealt with my (and now my son's, for it is inheritable and contagious) soccer obsession with infinite patience and a great sense of humor. We are fortunate that there are two ball-neutral people in our household that compensate for the other two ball-crazy ones – without them, we would be having dinner all the time in front of the TV, sitting on soccer balls and watching re-runs of Barça games like pathetic soccer gollums. Thanks to them we are not mad, only mad *about* soccer. And when that obsession runs too high in my thermometer – as when I was finishing this book –, the voices of my wife and my daughter come to the rescue with the same wisdom that the president of Holland used to remind his country when the Dutch National Team lost the 2010 World Cup final against Spain: "It's just a game".

I could not have been able to initiate this project without the help of key people at the FC Barcelona youth academy. I like how everyone I've ever met at the FC Barcelona academy has always been extremely helpful and nice to me. Albert Puig, then coach of the *alevins* and now coordinator of youth soccer, who has authored an influential book about the youth academy (*La força d'un somni – Els camins de l'èxit*; translated title: "*The strength of a dream – The paths of success*"), agreed to meet with me in a Barcelona coffee shop when this book was a most uncertain project. The book might have never seen the light if he had not generously, patiently, and passionately explained his coaching methods to me. I will not reproduce them here because this is not a coaching book and the diagrams were rather technical, but the information is public (Barça offers coaching courses) and opened my eyes about how Barça goes about divulging information. Xevi Marcé, the director and founder of the *FCBEscola*, was kind enough to spend time with me to make sure I understood all the intricacies of the *FCBEscola* and differences of philosophy between the Escola and the youth academy. I had the fortune of coaching in an *FCBEscola*-organized soccer camp in Seattle and was able to learn practical Barça methods from *FCBEscola* coaches Jordi Molà and Toni Claveria, whom I'm fortunate to count among my friends. All these people are always a joy to spend time with because they are extremely passionate about their work.

Last but not least, my final words of thanks go to the various friends that helped edit, grow, polish, trim, and shape this book into its definitive form: David Yanez (Professor of Biostatistics at the University of Washington and expert at the art of fooling defenders by passing while looking the other way, *à la Ronaldinho*), Tim Hargrave (Professor of Business School at the University of Washington-Bothell, a fantastic midfielder that knows how to control the pace of the game), Anna Gilabert (who gave me a personal tour of the Barça museum, which provided for a truly unique *Camp Nou Experience*), and Kyle Rodeheaver (ex-player of the MLS and U-10 coach director at Seattle United, who taught me how the MLS youth system operates).

Except where stated, all the images (including the cover) and figures contained in this book are copyright-free and can be re-used without permission to promote, advertise, or critique this book. The watercolor of a soccer field used as the background for the cover image was made by my son Jordi when he was six years old. Images of historical characters were obtained from free web resources. The photos of *La Masia* and of the *Ciutat Esportiva Joan Gamper* were taken by me. To protect the anonymity of background subjects in certain photos, or to enhance a desired effect, some images where processed with artistic filters in Adobe Photoshop CS6.

This book was finished 8,708 kilometers away from the *Camp Nou* stadium exactly 47 years after I was born.

Seattle, September 25th, 2013.

Chapter 1: An American boy in FC Barcelona

Ben Lederman in action, in a position that captures Ben's fine technique and elegant style.

Watching a Barça game, one might be tempted to conclude that the FC Barcelona youth academy uses dancers and choreographers to train its players; such is the grace with which the players synchronize their moves across the pitch. The distinctive feature of this ballet company is the incredible velocity and precision with which they pass the ball to each other; they seem to achieve this ability not by physical strength – they are rather weaker and smaller than most other top teams – but by superior body speed and mental coordination. They have been doing it together for ages so it seems as if they are able to execute this spontaneous choreography by communicating telepathically. "Our level of understanding is so high that we do not need words to move on the field", says Xavi about Iniesta. "When he goes up, I come down; when he has the ball, I go to an unmarked position; when I receive the ball, he goes to the open space. It's a simple dance."

They do it with such accuracy that they can afford to do most passes not in the vertical direction – towards the goal, where passes are theoretically more lethal – but in the horizontal direction – where the risk of an interception would hardly seem to pay off. They perform these risky horizontal circulations simply *to keep possession of the ball*, a procedure that tires the defenders and makes them lose their focus. The ball swings back and forth, back and forth, patiently, until suddenly a defender, as if hypnotized by the rhythmic motion of the ball or by the pendulum of Barça players swinging in accord, makes a mistake – then suddenly everything unfolds with lightning speed: midfielder Xavi, Iniesta or Busquets swiftly sends the ball into the small sliver of space created by the defender's error, while Messi, Pedro, or one of the midfielders runs for it, and the ball pierces the net. The great English defender John Terry described very well how, as a defender, he had to suffer possession soccer: "I don't like playing against teams that touch and touch. You spend the whole game running after them and it's very frustrating. You must stay much focused all the time. You make one mistake and they score a goal."

If you saw a goal by FC Barcelona that did not go as I just described, it is an uncommon Barça goal. "Soccer is a game that is won by the team that makes the least number of mistakes", has said ex-Barça Dutch soccer legend Johan Cruyff, pointing out a seemingly obvious truth that underlines a deep teaching and a founding pillar of the academy: this sport is played with the feet, an imprecise part of our body, and therefore it is a sport where quick thinking, clever positioning, and cooperation (moving to space or passing) are paramount elements for success. Hence the academy emphasizes that the most important part of your body for playing soccer is not your foot but your brain – another favorite teaching of Cruyff. Consequently, Barça's coaching methodology is geared towards raising fast-thinking footballers, tactically focused on smart positioning, with extremely precise control and passing abilities. While most other academies start by teaching the kids essentials such as how to dribble, the FC Barcelona youth academy starts by teaching them how to position themselves on the field – they will learn how to dribble later, most likely on the streets, on their own time.

But how did it all come to be? Understanding the process is just as important as knowing how the present youth academy functions, because each youth academy should be tailored to the historical needs and style of a club. That is the main question that this book strives to answer, in an effort to offer some hints to soccer educators everywhere that are trying to improve their programs. *Scouting the best youth players – in your area or beyond – is not enough.* There are other clubs in Spain with very powerful youth academies, such as Real Madrid and Espanyol, whose teams typically compete at about the same level as those of FC Barcelona's. The main difference is that at Barça the best players are methodologically scouted to match a playing style and then groomed with the utmost care, as one would grow a garden tree: an average player at the Barça academy fulfills as many as 5,600 hours of practice before reaching the first team. Before I delve into the history of the youth academy, I will first explain the process of how a young boy ends up being selected for entering the academy, a brief history of the club to put things into context (Chapter 2), and how the present-day academy is structured (Chapter 3).

The young boy I want to tell you about is a real boy. Ben Lederman, then an 11-year-old boy from Los Angeles, was accepted in 2011 into the FC Barcelona youth academy – the equivalent of Harvard for kids' soccer education, with the only *small* difference that tuition is free. This must have come as a welcome surprise to Ben's parents, since in the United States soccer is a rather elitist sport sustained by the families: once a kid is accepted by an American club, the families must pay all the team fees and the coaches' salaries, which amounts to at least $2,000/year, as well as any cost incurred in traveling if the team participates in tournaments (upwards of thousands of dollars if they are out of state). Many U.S. clubs offer fellowships, but it is widely recognized that the American system does not encourage participation from poor communities. Ben's parents decided to move to Barcelona and seize the opportunity, despite being informed that, given the unpredictability of athletic growth patterns, the chances that he makes it to the first team are as great as any of the other eighty-odd kids accepted in the same year – which means: slim. Typically only two or three players every year (2-4% of the initial ~80) are issued a first-team contract, and even those players will not play every game. If Ben makes it to the first team, he will play for at most ten years before he is forced to transition to lesser teams or to consider other, even more uncertain career options. I would never advise my own son to attempt to climb that steep and shaky pyramid: his prospects of building a successful lifelong career as a lawyer, writer, doctor, or whatever he chooses to be are much, much brighter than this scary 4%.

Ben was the best player of a Los Angeles children's team that took a trip to Europe to play an international tournament in 2008. What caught the attention of the FC Barcelona scouts is that Ben's team beat the Barça squad that participated in the same tournament, with a great performance by Ben. FC Barcelona decided to invite Ben and his family for a more detailed inspection of his talents in 2010. These are, in fact, standard procedures for capturing promising players in soccer, not only at FC Barcelona. The aspiring kid is placed in a team that matches his age and/or physique and he may be asked to play in various positions on the field. This inspection can take two or three days, with participation in training sessions and a couple of games per day. The coaches take very detailed notes about the kid, such as his control with both feet and both sides of the feet, his passing abilities, his shot, etc. At the end, the coaches combine the notes and elaborate a final report that is used to accept or reject the candidate.

There has been a lot of talk about Ben and whether his enrolment at FC Barcelona's youth academy is the sign of an inflexion in American youth soccer itself. Is soccer coming of age in the United States, finally? American soccer seems to have been gaining momentum since the men's National team reached the quarterfinals of the Japan/Korea World Cup in

2002. (The fantastic success of American women at soccer, superior to any of the men's teams in all soccer history – winners of 1991 and 1999 World Cups, sub-champions in 2011, and third place in 1995, 2003 and 2007 World Cups, as well as gold medalists in the 1996, 2004 and 2008 Olympics, and silver medalists in the 2000 Olympics! – is an entirely different story and deserves to be the subject of a whole other book.) As we shall see in the last chapter, whether Ben's case is the sign of something great or not for American (boys') soccer remains to be seen: it depends on how U.S. soccer education evolves. Ben's being found by FC Barcelona scouters could also reflect improvements in the scouting techniques by FC Barcelona.

The Barça scouting procedures

FC Barcelona invests heavily on this part of the process. The club cooperates – and at the same time competes – with about 30 other clubs all over Catalonia to train youth players. Satellite clubs such as Espanyol, Damm, Gramenet, Sant Gabriel, and Cornellà, all with excellent youth programs, use very similar coaching methodologies so the best children in these clubs end up being adept at the "FC Barcelona style". When attracted by Barça, they adapt quickly. It is interesting to note that this model (unlike in Holland, where the youth system is highly coordinated by the Royal Dutch Football Association or KNVB) was not imposed by any Federation – the clubs converged to it by symbiosis: most of the clubs operate in divisions separate from Barça and benefit in the long term from this cooperation (clubs that contribute kids to FC Barcelona receive percentages of their future contracts and transfers as part of "formation rights"). The exception is Espanyol (a team most Barça fans would like to see in Second Division), which competes in the same division in *La Liga*. Per a 2009 statistic by an Espanyol coach, Barça has snatched 40 Espanyol youth players in the last 10 years – for free –, and you can bet they are the best of the crop. While the children in smaller clubs usually do want to be noticed by Barça scouts, logically the clubs do not always cooperate: it is well known that when Cesc Fàbregas used to play in the *infantil* (U13) of Club Esportiu Mataró, the coaches wouldn't field him if they were visited by a Barça scout to prevent the scout from reporting on their best player. (While the free movement of youth players from club to club will always be protected by the European Union's labor laws, in my opinion FIFA should establish rules that – somehow – protect the smaller youth academies from the predatory behavior of the larger clubs' youth academies: indeed, the difference in performance between the largest clubs and the smaller clubs only keeps on increasing in all the countries.)

FC Barcelona has permanently 21 scouts all over Spain (7 in Catalonia and 14 in the rest of Spain), and 6 additional people elsewhere in Europe and the rest of the world who send reports. The scouts are full-time club employees to allow for targeting Barça-specific searches and to avoid conflicts of interest (many years ago, scouts used to work as free lancers for various clubs simultaneously). Travel within Spain is always by road, covering several games per weekend. The 6 international scouters have to travel extensively to cover 26 countries, separated by areas (one area per scouter). The areas are unfathomably huge: Area 1 covers Brasil, Holland, Germany, Mexico, Paraguay, and Uruguay; Area 2 comprises France, Slovenia, Bosnia, Serbia, Croatia, Denmark, Sweden, and Norway; Area 3 encompasses Argentina, Italy, England, Belgium, Greece, and Turkey; Area 4 reaches Portugal, Ukraine, Russia, Sweden, Chili, and Colombia; Area 5 is Spain; Area 6 covers Catalonia, Aragon, and Balearic Islands. Asia is notoriously absent. Africa is somewhat covered through the task of ex-Barça player Eto'o's foundation *Fundesport*, which selects players from Cameroon and other parts of Africa to come to FC Barcelona. These African kids, of which there are typically two per team in each squad at the youth academy, have exquisite technique and have a privileged physique for their age, so they do very well at the academy.

At least twice a year all the scouts are brought to Barcelona for a meeting. In 2010, for example, the scouts drove more than 350,000 km to watch 5,254 games during 10 months and produced reports for 4,763 players between 7 and 23 years of age. Barça scouts look primarily for technical talent, tactical intelligence, ability to adapt to the Barça style of play, and even the parents' behavior (which is a predictor of future conflicts: that's right, if you are that obnoxious parent that insults the referee all the time, you might be the reason why FC Barcelona didn't pick your kid, so you better behave from now on in case the scout comes back). Note that, contrary to what was routine procedure 30-40 years ago, in the screening process the scouts do not take into consideration physical parameters such as height or strength. As we will see, this change in screening emphasis from physical to fast/technical was pioneered in the 1970s by FC Barcelona youth academy coaches and has resulted in a spectacular change in the biotype of the soccer player, in particular the midfielder and even the defender – we now see lots of good small players (a biotype traditionally reserved to forwards), typically swift as a mouse, smart, and quick-footed. Sometimes the scouts are looking specifically for, say, a left defender, but end up finding a great right forward. Of these 4,763 kids (in 2010), a total of 943 (19.8%) passed the first set of technical, tactical and emotional criteria. The reports were sent to the club, where after some discussions with the scouts the final 221 (4.6%) "Barça profile" candidates were chosen.

From these the club built the list of new admissions to the youth academy (80 in 2010 or 1.7% of the initial 4,763 candidates). The number of players in the youth academy stays constant, so be certain that, sadly, around the same number of players had to be dismissed. As a policy, to avoid judging mistakes that are not too infrequent in developing talent – even Albert Benaiges, one of the great youth coaches of the club, acknowledges that he missed Sergio Busquets and let him go as a little kid –, the club only displaces a player by an outsider if the outsider is "two or three levels" better: the goal is to improve the overall technical level of the academy every year. Accordingly, the renewal has a pyramidal structure: the *pre-benjamin* (youngest) team obviously needs to be re-filled from scratch every year; about half of the *benjamin* team is renewed (43% in 2009); the *alevin* team by about a third (28% in 2009), the *infantil* team by 18%, the *cadet* team by 13% and the *juvenil* team by 6% (in 2009). Most of the players were from the Catalonia area (74% in 2010), and six were foreigners, of which one (Ben Lederman) was an American. In 2009, there were a total of 15 foreign kids counting all years (under 18 years of age).

Ben Lederman's case is atypical because it does not follow the pattern of most kids that are found by the scouting network. Ben lived in the U.S. and became within the scouts' range only because his team made a trip to Europe. He is not the only case. When FC Barcelona organized a soccer summer camp in Yokohama, Japan, the coaches discovered an incredibly talented 8-year old named Takefusa Kubo and alerted the club for a follow-up. (These summer camps, co-sponsored by Nike, are not really targeted for scouting, and the club does not generate much revenue from them. Rather, they are targeted to project the club's training philosophy beyond Spain's borders. The club sees them as a form of marketing targeted to kids, since these kids later buy FC Barcelona Nike products such as shirts and cleats and generate TV and advertising revenues because they want to watch Barça games.) Takefusa was invited to play a tournament next year in Belgium and, luckily, the year after his mom found a job in Barcelona. "Take" is one of the six foreigners that entered the academy in 2011 and he is now one of its rising stars. For very young kids such as Ben and Take that are discovered at ages when they cannot yet join the academy, the scouts and coaches follow their evolution for years if needed (two years in Ben and Take's case). The story of Takefusa highlights that, while the FC Barcelona scouting network does not regularly scan Japan or any other Asian country, it will not let go of a good kid once it spots one.

There are also two Koreans (Lee Seung Woo and Jang Gyeolhee) in a team three years older than Take's, and one more (Seung-Ho Paik) in the next team up. Lee's dribbling skills, like Take's, are raising high hopes. In sum, there are a handful of Asians, several Europeans, and quite a few Africans. These international kids are usually exceptional, as FC Barcelona wants to make sure that all the uncertainties associated with uprooting a child and giving him a new home at Barça are compensated by his outstanding potential. The presence of these international kids reminds us that the FC Barcelona youth academy is now considered worldwide as providing the best soccer education in the world, and FC Barcelona takes advantage of it to attract – as if it were the only magnetic pole of soccer – the best kids from each continent.

Ben Lederman, now a left midfielder at *La Masia*, is proudly signaled as the first American to ever join the FC Barcelona youth academy. Provided he has the aptitude, it will take him 8-10 years to learn to play soccer like Xavi, Iniesta, or Messi. He has already been called to join the U14 U.S. soccer national team (despite being born in 2000!). It costs around €20 M/year to run all the teams and programs of the youth academy, including the salaries of the coaches and of the oldest players. In the end, this investment is justified only by the projected market value of the players that make it to the first team and by the actual market value of those that are sold to other teams. Xavi, Iniesta, Messi, Busquets, Thiago, and many others, are now each worth several times more than one year of running the whole youth academy. Since the main goal of the academy is not to sell its talent but to produce players for the first team, the real measure of success for Ben will be his first contract as a professional player.

Chapter 2: A brief history of the club

It is impossible to fully grasp the history of FC Barcelona's youth academy without quickly reviewing the club's history, in particular analyzing the origins of Barça's rivalry with Real Madrid. I decided to include this section here because my American friends are appalled to learn these things from me and I'm surprised that they did not already know about them. You should be appalled by what you will learn here, and I invite you to question it; these historical facts can be easily double-checked with web resources.

As a general rule, club soccer has managed to stay politically neutral in Europe. If you take two great teams with historic rivalries from any given country, say Manchester United and Liverpool in England, Bayern Munich and Schalke 04 in Germany, or Milan and Juventus in Italy, passions are fierce and as ancient as the clubs – but there are little politics involved at the club level. Mussolini, for example, used sports as a propaganda tool for his nationalistic fascism, but was too busy to favor Lazio (his favorite club). Between 1929 and 1948, the Italian national team managed by Vittorio Pozzo won 66 out of 80 games, including the 1934 World Cup, which fueled Mussolini's agenda. Lazio forward Paolo Di Canio celebrated his goals against Roma and Livorno (clubs inclined to left-wing politics) with the fascist salute. To this day, a loud group of right-wing Lazio fans, tolerated by the club, still waves swastika flags at matches, chants anti-semitic anthems, shout racist insults against black players, and yells Mussolini's favorite cheer ("Boia chi molla" – *execution for those who abandon*), but these pressure groups have never really influenced the outcome of the games. Hitler was not a soccer fan, although the German Soccer Federation (the DFB) enthusiastically supported the Nazi regime and its philosophy of the superiority of the Aryan race. The dominant team of the Nazi era was Schalke 04, which won six German leagues in the period 1933-1942, so naturally many Germans were Schalke fans. However, the rumor that Schalke 04 benefitted from administrative Nazi favors has been discredited, since the team had many players that were descendants of Polish immigrants, including their two stars.

One rare case of soccer rivalry that has intermingled with politics is the rivalry between Celtic and Rangers, both based in Glasgow; Celtic has an association with Scots of Irish descent, who are Roman Catholic, and the Rangers traditionally come from Scottish or Northern Ireland Protestant backgrounds. Some Celtic fans express this religious opposition by chanting songs of support for the Irish Republican Army at matches. Another unique case of soccer rivalry that has been influenced by a political conflict is the rivalry between Barça and Real Madrid. The rivalry was influenced by the Spanish Civil War (1936-39) and the ensuing fascist dictatorship (1940-1975) by General Francisco Franco which was particularly repressive in the Catalonia region. Franco was a fervent Real Madrid supporter.

What you are about to read is an account that pictures the Real Madrid directors – never its players or fans! – in a historically negative light. (I am friends with Real Madrid fans who are just as critical with these directors as I am, so I know who is to blame; being a Barça fan, I have admired many Real Madrid players such as Juanito, Butragueño, Míchel, Zidane, Laudrup, Cristiano Ronaldo, Buyo, Casillas, and many others, and still watch most of their games.) This account is well known to people in Spain and you can verify it in multiple sources. If you are, say, a Real Madrid fan that has lived all your life in the United States, then some of it might come as a surprise to you. For decades, people at FC Barcelona were also shocked by how Real Madrid obtained an unfair advantage by flirting with the central government.

The Gamper era
FC Barcelona was founded in 1899 by a 22 yr-old Swiss sugar trader named Hans Kamper. Kamper was a highly regarded football player in

Switzerland, where he had been captain of FC Basel and a player and co-founder of FC Zürich. The FC Barcelona shirt was designed with colors similar to that of FC Basel, with blue and dark-red stripes. At FC Barcelona, he played 48 games between 1899 and 1903 and scored over 103 goals. Kamper later learned Catalan, catalanized his name to Joan Gamper, and became the president of the club in 1908. The club's crest was designed in 1910 by a Barça player and then Medicine student (later orthopedic surgeon) and cartoonist Carles Comamala. (The present crest is a design of 2002.) Gamper signed legendary player Paulino Alcántara, the club's all-time top scorer with 369 goals in 357 matches. During the Gamper era, FC Barcelona won eleven *Campionats de Catalunya*, six *Copas del Rey*, and four *Pyrenees Cups*. Gamper was instrumental in expanding the club member base from 20,000 to 60,000, which allowed for financing the move from a small 8,000-seat stadium to a remodeled *Les Corts* stadium with a final capacity of 60,000. Gamper committed suicide in 1930 due to depression after business and personal problems. Since 1966, every year a tournament, named *Joan Gamper Trophy*, is played at the end of summer to honor his memory and to unveil the upcoming season's team.

Joan Gamper (1877-1930).   The 1910 crest.   The 2002 (present) crest.

A 40-year handicap

Catalonia stands alone in the geopolitical map of Spain for two characteristic features: it is the richest region of Spain and it has evolved its own Latin-origin language (Catalan) with a strong literature, being widely spoken to the present day. Since the foundation of Spain in the 15th century, Spanish governments have repeatedly attempted to suppress the use of the Catalan language in Catalonia in order to preserve a centralist administration. The present Government of Spain does not recognize Catalan as the main language of Catalonia – granting it a "co-official status" with Spanish –, despite the fact that it was the original language and it is the majority language.

FC Barcelona is deeply rooted in – and trusted by – Catalan society precisely because as an institution it has consistently stood up firm and loud against Madrid's oppression. On June 14th 1925, fans at the stadium protested against Miguel Primo de Rivera's dictatorship by booing the Spanish national anthem and by giving a defiant ovation to *God Save the King*. As retaliation, Gamper was forced to resign as president and the stadium was closed for six months. On August 6th 1936, during the Spanish Civil War, Josep Sunyol (28th club president and representative of a pro-independence political party) was murdered by a pro-Franco firing squad near Guadarrama. In the summer of 1937, when the team went on tour around Mexico and the United States, half the team sought asylum in Mexico and France. On March 16th 1938, when the city of Barcelona came under aerial bombardment by Franco's air force (resulting in over 3,000 deaths), one of the bombs hit Barça's offices. As Catalonia became occupied a few months later, the club membership dropped to just 3,486 members (making finances extremely difficult) and faced a number of restrictions. (Real Madrid faced none.) At the end of the Civil War, in 1939, Franco banned the Catalan flag (so the club crest had to be changed), and football clubs were prohibited from using non-Spanish names (which forced the club to change its name to *Club de Fútbol Barcelona* until late 1974, as the dictatorship was languishing; Franco died on November 20, 1975).

Franco had a real impact in the performance of FC Barcelona simply because its biggest rival, Real Madrid, benefitted in many ways from being his favored club. There is abundant footage of Franco at the Real Madrid stadium hugging and socializing with Real Madrid president Santiago Bernabéu (who had fought with the fascists during the war) and the other directors. During the dictatorship, Real Madrid's membership and financial status only increased. Franco reigned over soccer with utterly whimsical manners, like a dictator of a banana republic. He re-named the Cup as *Copa del Generalísimo Franco* ("Generalísimo" is a title that he invented for himself and, were it not for the cruelty of the character, it's grammatically comical: it means "very General"). In 1968, Barça had to play the Cup final against Real Madrid (initially scheduled to be played at a neutral stadium) in Real Madrid's *Santiago Bernabéu* stadium because "his excellency" did not deign to move from Madrid. (Barça won 0-1.)

The best documented scandal (because of the impact it had in the history of Spanish soccer) was without a doubt the signing of Argentinian star Alfredo Di Stéfano, the "Messi of the 1950s". In 1953, after Di Stéfano had already agreed to sign for FC Barcelona, Franco intervened and forced the Spanish Football Federation to null the transfer and obliged FC Barcelona to share Di Stéfano with Real Madrid (one year each). Di Stéfano finally decided to sign for Real Madrid and stay there, probably to make his life simpler. Di Stéfano has said that he was not coerced to do so, but the bottom line is that if Franco had not intervened, Di Stéfano would have been a Barça player – happily so, unless proven otherwise. Real Madrid, which had only won two leagues until that day (in its first 51 years of history), went on to win eight Spanish leagues in the "Di Stéfano period" (1954-1964) and the first five editions of the *European Cup* (1956-1960) with Di Stéfano scoring in all five finals. It can hardly be argued that he would not have made a difference had he played for Barça: in the 1960 edition he scored two goals in the semifinal against Barça that ended with 3-1 victory for Real Madrid. In almost 40 years of dictatorship Real Madrid won 21 domestic titles (14 *Liga*s and 7 *Copa*s). Despite the handicap, FC

Barcelona still managed to win 17 titles (8 *Liga*s and 9 *Copa*s) during the same period. After the dictatorship (in 37 years), Barça has won 21 domestic titles (12 *Liga*s and 9 *Copa*s), the same number as Real Madrid (16 *Liga*s and 5 *Copa*s).

Interestingly, the collective Barça fan memory never quite registered the Di Stéfano theft episode – which had an enormous impact on the trophies that went to Real Madrid when they could have been won by Barça – and focused instead on the referees and political manipulations, which had much less effect on the number of trophies. Instances of games where the referees were suspect of corruption or the players were directly coerced abound in the 40 years that Franco was in power. Here I will just give the two most famous examples of match fixing (in favor of Real Madrid) that reside in the memory of every good Barça fan. The most infamous one is the visit by the director of state security to the locker room in the second leg of a Cup semi-final against Real Madrid in 1943, which "surprisingly" resulted in a loss by Barça 11-1 despite fielding a better team (they had won the first leg by 0-3, which was precisely the reason for the visit). To understand how real the threat of such a visit was in the minds of a group of impressionable young players, on top of the ongoing political repression and memories of the Barcelona bombing five years before the game, it suffices to remind the reader that the last Barça president, Josep Sunyol, had been executed by the fascists just seven years prior to the game and half of the team was in exile.

The second most-famous instance occurred in 1970, during a Barça-Real Madrid *Copa* game. Barça player Quimet Rifé pushed Real Madrid player Velázquez several meters away from the penalty area. It was not a mistake: referee Emilio Carlos Guruceta purposely called a penalty so that FC Barcelona could be eliminated. The fans reacted with such unusual violence that the police had to intervene. From then on, and until his death, Guruceta was not allowed to referee a Barça game ever again – and, what is perhaps most humiliating, "Guruceta" became an entry in the dictionary as an insult: whenever *any* referee would make outrageously bad calls, the *Camp Nou* would start chanting "*Guruceta,*

Guruceta!" He was a narcissist referee that spawned a school of referees after him for whom the authoritarian image was more important than adherence to the soccer rules. Although the *Copa* elimination was never investigated, Barça fans felt that justice was done when in 1997, ten years after Guruceta's death, a Belgian court proved that Guruceta had pocketed 4 million pesetas to favor Anderlecht in the 1984 UEFA Cup semi-final between Anderlecht and Nottingham (he disallowed a Nottingham goal and called a penalty for Anderlecht). It looks like the crook, used to impunity, had repeated the crime.

If the abuse had ended after Franco's death, time would have slowly erased the memory of newer generations who did not suffer any insult and now all this would be water under the bridge. But the National Committee of Referees (which designates the referees for every game and establishes sanctions when there are red cards and other incidents) has been presided by 26 different men; of these, 16 were ex-players, ex-upper-management, ex-club-members, or fans of Real Madrid. Until now, never a Catalan or a referee with any Barça affiliation has been appointed to the National Committee of Referees in its approximate 100 years of existence.

Real Madrid prides itself in being the club with the most honors in the history of soccer. I would be the first to clap if the titles had been won without external help. But using the influence of a bloody dictator to inflate the club's shelves with trophies at the expense of its rivals places Real Madrid's track record under suspicion, to say the least. Real Madrid owes soccer fans, in particular Spanish fans, a historical apology for unfairly distorting the honors landscape forever.

The end of victimization

FC Barcelona also had its share of heroes during Franco's dictatorship. In fact, Barça had a fantastic team in the 1950s – starting by the Catalan goalkeeper, Antoni Ramallets, nicknamed the *Cat of Maracaná* after a legendary performance with Spain's National team in the 1950 Brazil World Cup. The great and attractive Hungarian László Kubala, who played at FC Barcelona for 10 years between 1951-1961, was admired by men and women alike, and the resulting increase in fans' attendance made it possible to build a larger, 100,000-fan stadium (the present all-seater *Camp Nou* has exactly 99,354 seats). Kubala introduced the curved ball, never seen in Spanish soccer before. Later, in 1959, Kubala convinced two fellow soccer players and Hungarian refugees, Sándor Kocsis and Zoltán Czibor, to join him at Barça. The Spanish player Luis Suárez joined in 1955 and Brazilian forward Evaristo in 1957, forming a magnificent team coached by Helenio Herrera that won a *Liga/Copa* "double" in 1959 and a La *Liga*/Fairs Cup double in 1960. In total, that team won 4 *Ligas* and 5 *Copas* in the 1950s.

Real Madrid won almost all the Leagues through the 1960s, 1970s, and 1980s. Barça won only in 1960, 1974 (with Johan Cruyff as the star player), and in 1985. The past history of Barça as the "victim" of Franco created a sense of "victimization" in both the fans, the players and the management that was not helping the morale of the team. Even if Real Madrid had cheated by getting unfair help from Franco's officials at various levels, by the late 80s – when Franco was long gone – Real Madrid had a fantastic team that was again the envy of Europe. I remember growing up admiring *La Quinta del Buitre*, because they had the elegant midfielder Michel, who could pass long balls with the precision of a tennis player, the fast forward Butragueño, always wise and elusive, and the winger Martín Vázquez, who had a powerful kick and could read the minds of their fellow teammates because he had played with them since he was a teenager. They were not only a pleasure to watch, but also (for a Barça fan) painfully *better at soccer*, independently of whether Franco had existed or not.

In 1985, FC Barcelona fell into a deep crisis that, paradoxically, would change the club forever. The loss of the *European Cup* final against lesser rival Steaua of Bucarest (on penalty kicks) triggered the anger of the fans. By 1988, President Josep Lluís Núñez's popularity fell very low, because in his first 10 years of presidency he had signed eight different coaches and the club had only won one *Liga*, two *Copas*, and two *Recopas*. After winning the *Copa* in 1988, the players tried to leverage Núñez's low popularity and demanded his resignation. However, it soon emerged that the real reason for the now-known as "Hesperia mutiny" was a dispute between the club and the players over who should pay the taxes of their image contracts. Fourteen players (out of 26) were fired and a whole new squad (11 players) was purchased. What really changed the club forever is that a new coach was brought to manage this new team. Núñez signed the only man in the world that would appease the wrath of the fans: Johan Cruyff.

Johan Cruyff came back in 1988 to coach the club and made it a winning club for the first time in thirty years. Since that day (until the end of the 2012-2013 season), Barça has won 12 of 24 *Ligas*, 5 *Copas*, 4 *European Cups* (3 of them *Champions League* format), and two *FIFA Club World Cups*. (Real Madrid, by comparison, has won 8 *Ligas*, 3 *Copas*, and 3 *Champions Leagues* in the same period.) Cruyff had soccer knowledge, and luckily for the club his teachings were followed like those of a Messiah. As we will see, he instilled optimism at all levels and reversed a decades-long historical situation by re-structuring the whole club, by propelling the talent from the youth academy, and, well, by beating the eternal rival. There is only room for one at the top. Finally, in the 1990s, the victim was Real Madrid – they were losing and, for the first time, they started complaining about referees' decisions. For Barça's fans, seeing the Real Madrid management protesting against referees was a catharsis, the realization that they were not *really* in power (at least, not anymore). Therefore, Barça could be at the top also, simply by doing what soccer is about: playing better than the opponent. If you visit the FC Barcelona museum, you will notice that it only irradiates positive values, like the constitution of a new country. Floating by on a colorful video with happy people and celebrating soccer players are displayed the words "Commitment to society ... Sport as a means of training, sport as a means of social integration, sport as a means of teaching values ... Responsibility. Solidarity. Respect. Equality. Honesty ... Passion. Effort. Perseverance. Self-improvement. Commitment. Team work. Cooperation. The ability to share. Comradeship. Respect for one's opponents. Dialogue. Fair play. Knowing how to win with humility. Knowing how to lose with dignity. Democracy. Racial and sexual equality." The end message from the club is crystal clear, one that is incompatible with victimization and with complaining about referees' decisions every weekend: "We teach and foster sporting values in children and young people".

The rest of the history of FC Barcelona is, in fact, what this book is about: how the youth academy was able to shape the present glory of the team that you have been enjoying over and over.

Chapter 3: The present-day structure of the FC Barcelona youth academy

The new La Masia, *the residence for the youth academy players within the* Ciutat Esportiva Joan Gamper.

If you picked up this book, I am sure that you know at least this much: that FC Barcelona (nicknamed "Barça" by its fans) is one of the best football teams in the world and that Lionel Messi is its star forward. Hopefully you also know that Messi, who was born in Argentina, has been in the FC Barcelona youth academy since age 13, which is one of the reasons why his teammates Xavi and Iniesta, from the academy as well, are able to read his moves so well – they have been playing together for over a decade, actually.

How do they accomplish this level of team-playing that looks like a dance performance? How were they coached to do that? We will see here that it is all reduced to the notion that they "speak" the same "soccer language", a repertoire of tactical moves that only them can accomplish at that speed.

I will explain all that in the following chapters and, historically, how it all came to be, but for clarity, I first need to explain how the youth academy is presently organized.

I will begin by telling you that nobody calls it "youth academy" in Catalan (our native language) or Spanish. Everybody calls it indistinguishably "cantera", the Spanish word for quarry, the place from which stones are extracted in a mountain, or "planter", the Catalan word for a botanic nursery. In English, "youth academy" has undertones of military discipline, which the Barça academy does not adhere to. When we refer to the "youth academy" as "cantera", we are constantly reminded that these young players are being chiseled from stone and converted into diamonds by expert educators; when we use the word "planter" we are fond of picturing our players as trees that we care for every day in our garden until they grow to adulthood. However, as these subtleties are lost in translation, I will continue using the expression "youth academy" from now on.

The FC Barcelona youth academy program is generically dubbed *La Masia* (a "masia" is a rural house associated with family farming in Catalonia) after an ancient country house named Can Planes built in 1702 that is next to the *Camp Nou* stadium. When the *Camp Nou* was inaugurated in 1957, the Can Planes grounds were acquired shortly after and the building was remodeled into a building for social gatherings in 1966. In 1979, President Josep Lluís Núñez converted it into a youth residence for young footballers from out of town. The original two-story, 610-m² building had a kitchen, a living room, an administration room, restrooms, showers, four bedrooms (12-bed capacity) and a locker room; an additional 48 beds inside the *Camp Nou* stadium allowed for a 60-player capacity.

The Can Planes building is no longer being used. The new youth academy's training ground and offices, named the *Ciutat Esportiva Joan Gamper* (which opened in June 1st, 2006) are physically located 4.5 km away from the *Camp Nou*, in nearby Sant Joan Despí. The training grounds include five grass pitches, four artificial grass pitches, a training area for goalkeepers, one multi-sport pavilion, three gymnasiums, and pool and sauna areas. Water canons next to the artificial grass fields remind the visitor that Barça likes to keep the pitch wet to increase the speed of the ball and develop good ball handling technique. All the training sessions are (or can be) recorded from elevated cameras for improvement of the youth players.

A detail of the Ciutat Esportiva Joan Gamper. *To the left are a set of locker rooms. To the right is the grass field where Barça B trains. All the fields (except the first team field) are accessible to visitors.*

One of the buildings inside the *Ciutat Esportiva* is the new, glass-façade 6,000 m² *Masia* residence that hosts up to 83 players. Most rooms are for 2 or 4 residents and have a bathroom and desks. There are also rooms with special beds for basketball and handball players. The ground floor contains the kitchens, a self-service restaurant, administrative offices, classrooms, and a large living room to relax; this living room includes a very large flat-screen TV with a set of seats (in a mini-theatre configuration) facing a nice grassy courtyard with a barbeque pit, just above the dining room area. For all these aspiring sportsmen, *La Masia* would be the closest thing to heaven, except for a poignant detail: most of them have to be away from their parents to live their dream – an unbearable price to pay for any kid. Over the last 30 years (until 2010), *La Masia* has hosted 514 youth players, 458 (89%) from Spain (217 or 42% from Catalonia and 241 or 47% from the rest of Spain) and 56 (11%) foreigners.

The main goal – but not the only one – of the FC Barcelona youth academy is to create players for the first team. "We have to educate them as people and as players", says Guillermo Amor, ex-Barça player, the first graduate of *La Masia* and present director of the youth academy. "What matters the most are not the titles won by the youth categories but to bring the kids all the way up to the top". The €20 M/yr invested in a youth football program might seem like a lot of money, but in the end this investment turns out to be a money-saver, and it is the only chapter in which there are never cuts: in effect, the youth academy provides the coal to run the club's steam engine – the first team.

The FC Barcelona youth academy follows the same organization of youth soccer as elsewhere in Spain, adopting five categories for children: *pre-benjamins* (7 year-olds), *benjamins* (8-9 year-olds), *alevins* (10-11), *infantils* (12-13), and *cadets* (14-15). *Pre-benjamins* to *alevins* (7-11 year-olds) play Football-7 (6 on the side plus goalie) with ball size 4. From *infantil* on, they play on FIFA-size fields with ball size 5. Each category takes two years to complete (except for the youngest, who take one year), so each one consists of two levels ("first-year" and "second-year"). At Barça, most categories have two squads (A and B) for each category (generally separating younger, B, and older, A, kids; the *benjamins* have a C squad and the *alevins* a C and a D squad because they play with smaller teams, on Football-7 format). From age 16 on (if they make it), they are *juvenils* (ages 16 – 18) and they are then under the administrative umbrella of

Barça B (the second-division team of Barça, which has no limit of age and where they start interacting directly with the first-team coaches and players). There are presently a total of 15 boys teams (including Barça B) and 4 girls teams in the Barça youth academy. Kids that are too advanced for their category and are not challenged by their peers are usually advanced one category up (or even two, in exceptional cases), sometimes for only part of the year to try it out. Every team has a coach and an assistant coach, several of them retired FC Barcelona (or Barça B) players. This in-breeding is very similar to the technique used to improve cattle and pigeons, where the size of the gene pool is kept small to prevent the diffusion of advantageous traits into the genome. Since the coaches are also raised in-house, it is easier for the tactical concepts to get transmitted with continuity from generation to generation.

Barça does not charge to teach football in its youth academy. (Note: the *FCBEscola* is administratively disconnected from the youth academy.) The kids (between 19-21 per squad) get free schooling, free boarding if they are from out of town and, if needed, free transportation to make it to practice after school. A fleet of about 15 taxis takes the kids from door to door, with several kids per taxi, serving the whole Catalonia region. Most of the kids go to the same school, which is used to making special arrangements, but the parents are free to choose another school.

The *FCBEscola*
A brainchild of Xevi Marcé, the *FCBEscola* targets 6-12 year olds and follows a more school-like, less competitive philosophy than the youth academy. It also organizes the famous FC Barcelona camps around the world that are used to spread the club's coaching philosophy and style of play. Most age groups (except the 6-year-olds) overlap with those in the youth academy. Unlike at the youth academy, here the girls (amounting to 10% of the kids) are not separated from the boys. The *FCBEscola* is a separate entity from the youth academy, in the sense that graduation from the *FCBEscola* does not secure you a spot in the youth academy. In fact, the vast majority of kids at the *FCBEscola* never make it into the

academy – as they compete with the highly efficient scouting network described above –, although the *FCBEscola* coaches do communicate with the youth academy coaches about the quality of their players and a few players end up being transferred. Of the present batch of *FCBEscola* graduates, Sergi Samper, born in 1995, shines with great strength and might well be the first one to reach the *Camp Nou* one day, but he is the exception to the rule. The *FCBEscola's* official stated mission is not to train future soccer players but "to learn while playing". While the youth academy trains next to the first team at the *Ciutat Esportiva* (far away from the *Camp Nou*), the club has kept the location of the *FCBEscola* separate from that of the youth academy to detach both programs. The *FCBEscola* offices are physically located inside the *Miniestadi* (the smaller stadium that was built next to *Camp Nou* for Barça B games), and the kids train on artificial grass fields south of the *Miniestadi*.

A training session of the FCBEscola *inside the* Ciutat Esportiva *during a Christmas soccer camp, when the youth academy is not in session. Usually the* FCBEscola *holds its training sessions at a set of fields next to* Camp Nou.

Admission into the *FCBEscola* is by a tryout and, once a kid has been admitted, he or she is never rejected by the school (unlike in the academy, where continuation is not guaranteed because competition from incoming students is fierce). In 2012, for example, about 2,000 kids attended the tryouts to enter the *FCBEscola*. The tryouts are a 3-day process (on three consecutive weekends), in which each kid is asked to come on one of the days and perform a set of simple routines (juggling, control, passing) and play a 40-min game, all in about 1 hour. About 60 kids were admitted in 2012, mostly to fill up the 6-7 year-old teams, since most of the older kids stay. The *FCBEscola* does not play in external competitions, a policy designed to engage kids into developing Barça-style of play and to prevent them from getting obsessed about winning. The training methods (in the school and in the camps) are virtually identical to those adopted and developed by the youth academy.

Survival of the fittest

At the youth academy, on the other hand, competition is fierce. Of the 514 kids that have lived in *La Masia* at some point in the last 30 years (until the end of 2010), only 60 (11.7%) have made a debut with the first team in official games (the percentage rises to 14% if we consider also friendly games). In addition to this internal competition, there is external competition from kids who are trying to enter the academy. The club uses this competition for entering the academy to screen for better and better kids every year. The least gifted are replaced by kids who are detected by the network of scouts all over the Spanish geography and the world. To be accepted (and thus displace a kid already in the academy), an incoming kid must be two or three levels above the displaced outgoing kid. These techniques for selecting the most technically-competent kids are not unlike the techniques that Charles Darwin first used to select pigeons in his custom-built loft to prove his theory of the *Origin of Species* about 150 years ago. While Barça obviously does not genetically cross-breed its "pigeons", it does manage to improve, by a simpler procedure of replacement or "artificial selection", the quality of the pigeons in the "loft" (the youth academy) as a whole – thus it guarantees the "survival of the fittest".

What happens to all the kids that do not make it into FC Barcelona's youth academy, and those that are rejected by the academy after a few years of development? I've never heard of a player who, after being at the academy for a few years and having been rejected, has been re-accepted. There are a number of youth academies that are happy to take a good look at these "Harvard rejects" knowing that many of them are still excellent and that FC Barcelona's screening system sometimes also makes mistakes. Neighboring club Espanyol is the best example of a top-notch youth academy, rivaling in quality with that of FC Barcelona at almost every division up until the professional level. L'Hospitalet plays in Second Division B and the Europa and the Terrassa in Third Division. It is fair to say that their coaches are so good that, were it not for the constant bleeding of talent towards FC Barcelona, these clubs would be in much better shape. Then there are the kids – the large majority of them – who are rejected by most First Division clubs. What happens to them? There are still plenty of options: below First Division there is Second Division, and Second Division B (with several groups each), then Third Division, then Regional Soccer. Most clubs have at least one team in one of these divisions, and they offer low-price soccer training for kids. In general, clubs that compete in Second and Third Division can afford to hold tryouts (a selection process) every year and still charge a fee (typically, the kid or one parent has to be club member, etc.). These kids often have the dream of making it into First Division, and as they develop they might attract the attention of a FC Barcelona scout, but as a whole the success rate here is even lower than the kids that are already inside FC Barcelona's youth academy. In fact, most kids are not likely to make a living out of soccer (or barely, if they play in Second Division) and we will not follow their fate any further in this book.

Ben Lederman, on the other hand, is following in the footsteps of the greatest players that Barça has had. Andrés Iniesta (from Albacete), for example, was first watched in a tournament in Plasencia (in central west

Spain) at the tender age of 10 and the scouter sent a most favorable report of him to the club to keep following him. One year later, in another tournament in Brunete (Madrid) that was televised, Iniesta was awarded Best Player of the tournament and youth coach Albert Benaiges phoned him to offer him to join the club "without further tryouts" at age 11; after some deliberations – he had offers from most major clubs and his dad was a Real Madrid fan, but his mom and himself were convinced after visiting the excellent facilities of *La Masia* –, at 12 he landed at the club. The rush to sign Iniesta was not due to Real Madrid's competition, as you might be tempted to think; Barça had just signed another 12 year old (Jorge Troitero, from Mérida), the youngest occupant ever at *La Masia* until then, and the club was worried that Troitero might feel lonely or homesick.

Xavi Hernández arrived from the nearby Terrassa, also at age 11, although the scouters knew about him (through his father, also a soccer player) since age ... 6! It took three trials for Josep Guardiola, from Santpedor, to get accepted at 13, as his frailty generated some doubts. Luis Milla (from Teruel) entered exceptionally late, at 17, spending only three years at Barça B before Cruyff called him to the first team in 1988. Messi was signed from Newell's Old Boys of Rosario, Argentina, at 13, including an expensive treatment for growth hormone – it is molecular biology that cured the defect of this pigeon in the loft and gave him wings to fly to the top of the football heavens. Each of them has displaced another player less gifted. Everything is for the improvement of the species.

The reader should realize that this literary analogy with Darwin's pigeon loft trivializes the youth academy as a bunch of clever scouters that cherry-pick the best kids around the world; the analogy might induce you to infer that these players would have become good soccer players *anywhere*. I'm sure they would have become good soccer players, but they might not all have become world class and they certainly would not have learned the "Barça style". That is precisely the mission of the youth academy. The youth academy operates like a Football University that teaches young players to play soccer in the same style as the first team.

As it turns out, this notion was not invented at FC Barcelona, so now we have to travel far away from Barcelona, and far back in time.

Chapter 4: The birth of *La Masia*

The original La Masia, *now a Barça administrative building.*

The Ajax connection: a genius called Jack Reynolds

It all started about 100 years ago, nearly a thousand miles from Barcelona. It was likely on a rainy day in Amsterdam, when a Brit named Jack Reynolds was coaching then-amateur team Ajax every day from 8 am till 10 pm. He had a key vision, one that would influence countless generations of coaches and players: he insisted on coaching himself all age groups with the same style. He also defined the style that until very recently has been an exclusive trademark of Ajax: quick-passing, attacking football played with wingers, resulting in a youth academy that continuously produces talented players with a "signature style" imprinted in their brains and legs. Reynolds coached Ajax for 25 years (interrupted by World War II), until he retired in 1947, during which he won the Dutch League eight times and the Dutch Cup once.

The legacy of Jack Reynolds at Ajax still endures. After Reynolds' retirement, Ajax won the Dutch League and Cup an additional 21 and 16 times, respectively (37 national titles in the period 1947-2010, or a title every 1.7 years, a substantial improvement over the average performance during Reynolds' tenure), and won the *European Cup* four times, among other important trophies. Reynolds' most famous quote, "The attack is and remains the best defense", remains an unrenounceable principle of the Ajax school. Jany van der Veen, the legendary youth coach that discovered Johan Cruyff and many others (Hulshoff, Suurbier, Van Eijden) at Ajax, always considered Jack Reynolds the greatest trainer that Ajax has had. By building on Jack Reynolds' legacy and teaching to Ajax youth a style of play based on attacking football of high intensity, van der Veen is thought to have set all the foundations for Total Football. Another Englishman, Vic Buckingham, coached the team in the periods from 1959-1961 and 1964-1965 and saw the ascent of the young Johan Cruyff, the most talented Dutch player of all times.

Rinus Michels and Total Football

Fortunately for FC Barcelona, Jack Reynolds had had a very good apprentice. His striker after World War II, Rinus Michels, a technically mediocre player but effective scorer, became his best follower twenty years later when he became coach of Ajax in 1965-70 and 1975-76, of the Netherlands team in the 1974 World Cup, and of FC Barcelona (1971-75 and 1976-78). Unfortunately, Michels, who obviously learned much from Reynolds (as well as from van der Veen), also showed a great deal of ingratitude because he later described Reynolds' methods as "old-fashioned". Michels has been historically credited with inventing the "Total Football" style of Ajax and of the Dutch national team and was named "coach of the century" in 1999 by FIFA. However, that FIFA decision might have been a bit rushed. The historical records now speak in favor of Reynolds and van der Veen as the pioneers of the foundational ideas of Total Football and place Michels more appropriately as one of the great Ajax coaches that coincided with the best generation of players that ever came out of the Ajax school. Without the talent of the players, and most particularly Johan Cruyff, it's very unlikely that Michels would have done anything revolutionary. Many people still say that the best Ajax was the one that was trained by Stefan Kovacs, Michels' successor, in the short period 1971-1973 (and won all the five existing competitions in 1972). Further, Michels is not without blame for the loss of the 1974 World Cup final against Germany, because he let his players relax too much in the days before the game (they were throwing pool parties with naked girls) and neglected to scout the semi-final game between Germany and Poland. This indulgence was unusual in Michels, for he was known to be otherwise very strict and methodical, which did not always go well with his players.

How do we know that Michels would not have done anything revolutionary without Cruyff? Was the proper experiment ever done? Did Michels try to teach Total Football methods to any other team without Johan Cruyff, and then Cruyff was added to see if the team improved dramatically? Yes, actually, the experiment was done ... at FC Barcelona! In the early 70s, the board of FC Barcelona (which had not won a Spanish *Liga* since 1960) correctly understood that the best soccer in the world was being played by Ajax and were determined to hire their best star *and* their coach, but it was not possible to hire them both at once. (Ex-Ajax coach Vic Buckingham had been hired in 1970-1971, with poor results, although the team did win a *Copa del Rey*. Buckingham requested to then-President Agustí Montal to dismantle the youth academy in order to save money for signing up players for the first team, but Montal, who was determined to build a good youth academy, fired Buckingham instead.) Michels was signed as Buckingham's replacement in the middle of 1971, just after winning the first *European Cup* final with Ajax. Michels talked the Barça players into new training methods but Total Football was nowhere to be seen. In 1973 (after Ajax had won their third *European Cup* in a row), when Cruyff arrived, FC Barcelona was at the bottom of the table, and by the end of the competition year they had won the 1974 *Liga*. I will offer later a testimony from a key player from that squad, Charly Rexach, to reinforce the notion that the crucial addition that deployed Total Football at FC Barcelona was that of Johan Cruyff, not Michels.

However, for the purposes of this book, the debate of whether Michels or Cruyff was the soul-bearer of Total Football is not as important as Michels' key contribution to the budding FC Barcelona youth academy. From Ajax, Michels brought the famous *rondos* and Reynolds' concept that the youth teams should play with the same tactical schemes as the first team. Barça was already a club that believed strongly in its youth teams (we remember the Ramallets, Fusté, ...), but there was no coaching methodology. From that rich, tiny, Northern, rainy country called Holland that was revolutionizing soccer, Michels brought something that nobody in our poor, Southern, sunny country knew it even existed: the science of coaching. Michels restructured the Barça youth football and in the summer of 1972 put a young and bright coach, Laureano Ruiz (b. 1937), in charge of the *"juvenils"* (pre-professionals) and Oriol Tort (1929-1999, previously in charge of the *"benjamins"*, the youngest kids) as director of the youth academy.

The combination of Michels, Ruiz and Tort was explosive: those early 70s mark the beginning of the dominance of *La Masia* in youth competitions, as will be explained in detail later. Since then, the youth academy has not fundamentally changed its coaching principles – most of the improvements have come from technology, resources, and the ages being targeted. (At that time, the youngest kids accepted into *La Masia* were 15 or 16 years old.) Michels and Cruyff would leave FC Barcelona in 1978, leaving a permanent "Ajax imprint" at Barça. Michels, despite all his defects, was a fervent believer in the power of soccer education because he had seen what it can do at Ajax. Even though he knew that he would not collect the fruits of these seedlings, he insisted in creating a coaching structure mirroring that of Ajax that would empower a continuous creation of talent. FC Barcelona owes this much to Michels.

Laureano Ruiz and Oriol Tort: the end of the "fury"

In the 1970s, the culture of youth soccer programs was very different from now. Players that developed physically at an early age had an edge and that was considered an advantage for soccer, so they were selected in favor of weaker, even if more able players. The result was that Spanish soccer players were tough and strong, but rarely, with occasional exceptions, swift and agile. As I grew up, I remember TV commentators cheering for Spain with names such as "fury" and "race". These heroic terms only made Spain's multiple defeats all the more ridiculous, since it became obvious that someone did not understand the very basics of this game – it is not about fighting and running as it is about passing and thinking.

Something that would change the fate of FC Barcelona forever happened on the 15th of April of 1972. Then-President Agustí Montal was watching the final of the Catalonia Cup of the *juvenil* team in the company of first-team coach Rinus Michels. The Barça *juvenil* A side got beaten 3-2 by the reigning champion, the Damm team. Montal was furious and decided right there that something should be done to put an end to Damm's supremacy. With his decision, the FC Barcelona youth academy took an orthogonal turn, one that projected it into a level of excellence for the first time. Montal immediately signed Laureano Ruiz, a young youth coach that had worked with Racing Santander, Torrelavega and Langreo. Upon arrival, Ruiz changed the coaching methodology – then based on increasing physical strength – and started a program centered on ball handling and fine technique. Laureano Ruiz is credited with seeding into Barça his highly fertile philosophy that the development of a player should focus on technique, speed, and intelligence, disbanding the notion that players should be screened according to their physical condition: on the first day at work, he took down an ad from the club that read "If you come to offer a *juvenil* who is less than 180 cm tall, don't even bother". Ruiz's thinking was based on a simple premise that is now the predominant criterion for scouting in almost every youth academy in the world. Kids should be screened primarily based on technique and speed.

Even if they are small. It now seems so obvious: they have time to grow, they are just kids. And so what, if they don't grow? The ball is played on the ground and they will be closer to the ground. As with all good educational programs, it was a triumph of patience.

Ruiz's results were spectacular. Under him, between 1973-1977 the *juvenils* won five consecutive Spanish championships (note that each year Ruiz had to work with a different group of kids, so it's hardly attributable to one year's luck). Appointed by Michels, Oriol Tort became in charge of the youth academy initially, then later Ruiz. The Barça youth academy went into a slump when, for disagreements with the board of President Josep Lluís Núñez, Laureano Ruiz – who was covering for Michels' absence as first team coach for only one year – left for his native Santander, where he still leads a very prestigious football training school. He has trained more than 30,000 soccer players, of which about 1,000 have become professionals and almost 50 internationals. At FC Barcelona, the method persisted because Oriol Tort (and many others) stayed with the children.

At the end of the 80s, when Charly Rexach (who had already absorbed Total Football playing with Johan Cruyff) took over the *juvenils*, they won two successive championships and one runner-up. In this team there was Amor, Milla, Tito Vilanova, Jordi Roura, Busquets (Sergio Busquets' father), and Najim, among others. With the exception of Amor, none of them would have fit the traditional biotype of the tall and strong Spanish soccer player – but they were quick thinkers, could pass the ball at first touch and with great precision so they could elude contact with bigger, slower players. Almost all of them ended up playing in First Division (a rare occurrence), and several of them even struck luck because, as it was time for them to debut in First Division, Johan Cruyff was hired to coach FC Barcelona (in 1988). That team would be called the *Dream Team*.

Ruiz's efforts effectively abolished the "fury" in the long term, when Cruyff's pupils started populating the Spanish National team. Both Guardiola and Xavi give a lot of credit to Luis Aragonés, who coached *La*

Roja from 2004-2008 and won the *EuroCup* 2008 with Puyol, Xavi, Cesc and Iniesta in the starting lineup and a playing style based on Barça's possession soccer ideas. Aragonés was smart enough to ride the Barça wave, but he often gave the impression of being crudely ill-bred and unprepared for the dignity of a job that projects the ambitions of a whole country. He disgraced himself when the TV cameras caught him instructing a player to "tell that shitty negro that you are better than him ... tell him I said so". As most racist comments, it was also plain stupid: the black player in question was none other than Arsenal's Thierry Henry, one of the top players of the moment. In a controversial decision that cost the Spanish Federation an $87,000 fine, Aragonés was allowed to stay until the *EuroCup* because the players adored him, but was replaced by the suave Vicente del Bosque afterwards. Del Bosque added two more Barça players to the starting lineup – Pedro and Busquets – and won the *World Cup* 2010 and the *EuroCup* 2012.

The first *rondos*

The *rondo* (or "piggy in the middle"), where a circle of players try to keep the ball away from one or two players in the middle, is the stellar exercise of the FC Barcelona youth academy. It is not obvious for a non-expert why this seemingly childish routine would prepare you to beat the greatest teams in Europe. The *rondo* is a laboratory concept that incarnates the bare essentials of soccer: it isolates soccer from the noise that contact and running bring into the game. Pure touch. The youth coaches recognized a long time ago that the *rondo* helps focus on developing *at once* two of the most important skills of soccer: the first touch and the ability to make lightning-quick decisions. In this artificial setting, the brain can concentrate – without distractions – on the instant where the foot impacts the ball. Hence it was adopted as part of the method (both at FC Barcelona and at Ajax), and generations of players have spent more than 10,000 hours in training positional games and *rondos* before reaching the first team. Personally, I find very few things more spectacular in soccer than a *rondo* with stars from *La Masia*. The ball moves and ricochets at a billiard-like speed while the feet play swift tricks of difficult execution and – what's more important – unbelievably quick thinking. (You can find plenty of Barça *rondos* on YouTube by searching under "FC Barcelona training session rondo" or "tiki-taka".)

Ruiz claims that he devised the *rondo* in 1957 and introduced it to the youth academy in 1972. First-team players of the time such as Rexach have reported that the *rondos* were brought by Michels from Ajax, but the two accounts are not necessarily in conflict: the *rondo* is, after all, a rather simple exercise, so it might have been invented more than once by different people that had similar coaching philosophies. When Cruyff returned as a coach in 1988, and forever thereafter, all the training sessions (of the first team and all the youth teams) would start with a *rondo* as part of the new coaching methodology. Independently of who invented and who emphasized it, these two moments are historical: in time, the *rondo* has become the most famous and most practiced exercise of the FC Barcelona youth academy. In soccer, there are fundamentally two ways of passing an opponent: you either dribble him, or you first pass it to a teammate, who passes it back to you – a "one-two" or a "triangulation", since the ball's trajectory and your run form a triangular shape around the defender. Rondos were designed to make players visualize triangulations very quickly (the defender is the "piggy in the middle"). The ability to excel at rondos helps players resolve situations of numerical superiority. Barça players advance through enemy lines by summoning small rondos here and there against outnumbered rivals. It's a simple matter of counting, yet the other teams fall for it because the *rondo* is resolved too quickly in FC Barcelona's favor before numbers can be counteracted. As Barça's style of play is based on long possessions and continuous ball circulations, visualizing favorable triangulations through numerical superiority is key to maintaining possession and, ultimately, cutting through the opponent's lines. As Xavi has said: "Some youth academies worry about winning, we worry about education. You see a kid who lifts his head up, who plays the pass first time, pum, and you think, 'Yep, he'll do.' Bring him in, coach him. [Our model] is all about rondos. Rondo, rondo, rondo. Every. Single. Day. It's the best exercise there is. You learn responsibility and not to lose the ball. If you lose the ball, you go in the middle. Pum-pum-pum-pum, always one touch. If you go in the middle, it's humiliating, the rest applaud and laugh at you."

Núñez's imprint

FC Barcelona's longest-serving president has been Josep Lluís Núñez, from 1978 until 2000. His tenure can be summarized by highlighting that in 1979 he established *La Masia* next to the *Camp Nou* as a residence for young players from outside Barcelona. In 1982, Núñez built the *Miniestadi*, also next to the *Camp Nou*, to give a home to the Barça B and the *juvenils*. Núñez is also remembered for signing Maradona in 1982 (he was sold to Napoli in 1984), for signing Cruyff as a coach in 1988, and for firing him in 1996.

Most Barça fans do not remember Núñez as a particularly visionary or smart president. Most comediants made fun of his intelligence and his most famous quote is "Barcelona, this city that bears the name of our club ..." In 22 years the team only won 7 *Liga* titles, 6 *Copas*, and a *European Cup* (plus four *UEFA Cup Winners' Cup* and a few more trophies), and the fans attribute them mostly to Maradona's foot skills (the 1982 *UEFA Cup Winners' Cup* and the 1983 *Copa*) and to Cruyff's coaching (specially the string of four 1991-1994 *Ligas* and the 1992 *European Cup*), not to Núñez's vision. When he signed the Dutch coach, Núñez did not foresee that Cruyff would revolutionize the club, changing its style forever and taking the youth academy to a new level of excellence. The signing of Cruyff was a savvy political maneuver to attract votes and save an election that Núñez was about to lose, but left to his own devices he would have never signed Cruyff: Cruyff publicly repudiated and humiliated Núñez all the time. Many fans despised Núñez for being primarily a construction millionaire who kept the club in healthy financial status and who also happened to be a soccer fan, but with no specially helpful soccer expertise. In 2011 he was convicted with a six-year prison sentence for tax crimes in his personal business.

Yet, since this is a book about the FC Barcelona youth academy, I would like to put in a good word for his pioneering idea in the foundation of *La Masia*. Núñez has explained that from the beginning he envisioned the academy to be an educational center, where the boys would learn not only soccer but also all other aspects of life. This vision is still imprinted and strictly enforced to this day: the coaches have observed that, unless the boys are normally schooled, they do not succeed in soccer. For example, when they are issued their first soccer contract, their earnings can easily jump from about 5,000 €/year to 200,000 €/year, and this can happen when they are 17 or 18, with no expenses (the club still pays their housing and studies); money from sponsors such as Nike starts pouring in too. The temptation to spend it all on parties and cars to impress girls is too strong at this age, and the only shield that the club can offer to prevent temptation from biting is education, education, and education. The whole Spanish and Dutch soccer youth systems have largely accepted this premise, but it was not an obvious premise back in 1979, at least in soccer circles. This vision that soccer education at Barça should be tied to the overall's education of the player as an individual is a legacy from Josep Lluís Núñez.

Cruyff and "Total Football" arrive at FC Barcelona

Johan Cruyff is arguably the most remarkable and influential man in the history of soccer: the history of soccer took a very different turn after he started playing soccer, and *another sharp turn* after he started coaching. The first time I saw him in Barcelona I was an impressionable seven-year old boy and he came into the shoe store next to our house where my mom had taken me to buy shoes; when we left, there was a long line of people waiting outside for autographs. Later, at the time when I was a Physics student at the University of Barcelona, he became FC Barcelona coach. A whole soccer style – universally known as Total Football – was born around his figure and he helped it evolve into a coaching method.

In the World Cup of Germany '74, Holland beat Argentina 4-0, with two goals by its star captain Johan Cruyff. This famous picture immortalized the instant before Cruyff score the 1-0 in the 12th minute, as he dribbled goalkeeper Daniel Carnevali with one of his characteristic jumps while Ramón Heredia watches in a frightened stare. Dutch players Johan Neeskens and Wim Jansen, in the background, are about to come hug Cruyff.

For those that have not seen Johan Cruyff play, I will only quote here the most memorable descriptions I have read over the years. Cruyff had fantastic skills with both feet (he was ambidextrous), a lightning start and a deadly stop, and he invented the back-heeled "Cruyff turn", but above all, he was a tactical genius. When David Miller of *The Times* first saw Cruyff play, he marveled at a "Pythagoras in boots". Indeed, like a mathematician, he added another dimension to the game. He had the authority and knowledge of a coach on the pitch, ordering the players around. Ajax defender Barry Hulshoff and Cruyff teammate from the legendary team that won three consecutive *European Cups* (1971-1973), recalls discussing space the whole time: "Johan Cruyff always talked about where people should run and where they should stand, and where they should not move". Marco Van Basten, who trained under him and who is one of the only four all-time triple-winners of the *FIFA Ballon d'Or* (together with Cruyff, Michel Platini and Messi), said: "Johan is technically so perfect that even as a child he stopped being interested in the technique. He sees the football situations with such clarity that it was always him who decided how the game should be played". If you have not seen Cruyff play, it will be almost impossible for me to describe in words how graceful his moves were, and how much intelligence they irradiated; he didn't just dribble the defenders: he *outwitted* them by some clever touch or unexpected change of pace or course. (In that regard, he was similar to Iniesta.) Even Nureyev, the famous ballet dancer, is said to have been fascinated by Cruyff, "intrigued by his movements, his virtuosity, the way he could suddenly switch directions and leave everyone behind, and do it all with perfect control and balance and grace". Nureyev was "amazed that Cruyff's mind was so swift, you could see he was thinking so fast ahead, like a chess player".

Carles Rexach was one of the most talented homegrown players in that squad; *el noi de Pedralbes* ("the lad of Pedralbes", in reference to his family home's affluent neighborhood) had an extraordinary technique: never again another player at the *Camp Nou* has been seen scoring free kicks with both legs – with this all is said. Perhaps for that reason, he established the closest relationship with Cruyff both inside and outside of the soccer pitch in those years and in the future, and from him he absorbed the essence of Total Football tactics. This connection between Cruyff and Rexach as players would become essential to form the first stellar generation of players at the youth academy when Rexach became a youth coach. "Charly" – the English nickname invented by Johan and that stuck forever – remembers in his memoirs that what stimulated the team were not the instructions and theories of Michels but Cruyff's motions on the pitch. When it comes to explaining the success of Michels at Barça, where Rexach was a central protagonist, he subtracts credits to Michels and adds them to Cruyff: "When Michels came he introduced the new 4-3-3 system and novelties such as the study of the opponent or the positional game, but they did not catch on until Cruyff's arrival at Barça two years later". When Cruyff arrived, "seeing how well Johan played made the others want to be at his level". The Catalan version of Total Football. The team nicknamed Michels "Mister Mármol" (translated as "Mr. Marble"), for his difficulty in expressing his feelings, whereas Johan Cruyff instantly acquired a legendary status (*"The Flying Dutchman"*) after beating arch-rival Real Madrid in their own turf 0-5. Cruyff had already won a FIFA *Ballon d'Or* in 1971 while at Ajax; he won two more in 1973 and 1974 while at FC Barcelona.

Insisting on education

Soccer education has become one of the foundational pillars of the club. The club's motto, "More than a club", used to recall the collective memory of the club's social and political struggle against the central Madrid administration – at a time when staying united in the face of a powerful Real Madrid squad was more important than ever. Now that those struggles are one generation behind and the enemy is recognized by the world as performing one notch below FC Barcelona, the "More than a club" motto has acquired a new significance: it reminds us that FC Barcelona doesn't just play soccer – it also educates the soccer players of tomorrow. In 2010, an unprecedented number (11!) of players of Barça B were college students: one (goalie Miño) was studying the third year of Law School (a B.S. degree in Spain), five (Montoya, Bartra, Romeu, Gómez, and Planas) were studying Physical Education, one was studying for a Teaching Degree (Fontàs), and four were studying an MBA (Sergi Roberto, Muniesa, Sánchez, and Riverola). Montoya, Bartra and Sergi Roberto have made it to the first team and are now the first professional Barça players in college. (I find it unbelievable that the club does not advertise the great effort of these three players more prominently.) In the afternoon, tutors paid by the club help struggling students at the classrooms on the first floor of *La Masia*. Kids that do not pass a certain level at school are benched and prevented from coming to practice (usually at parents' request) until they improve at their studies. Similarly, for college students, the club pays all the university fees, except for flunked courses. (They all improve, instantly, motivated by what they love the most.) As a result, about 90% of the kids finish high-school and, of those that go to college, 100% pass the college-entry test ("selectivitat"), a better outcome than just about any other high school in Barcelona. (I'm fully aware that the studies chosen by Barça players are not as challenging as Physics, Medicine, and so on, but to the credit of *La Masia* kids, the non-*Masia* kids that choose Physics and Medicine do not have to spend half of their lives learning soccer.)

In addition, FC Barcelona coaches insist on education almost to a Victorian perseverance. The kids must shake the hands of the coaches every time they see them in the morning and say a courteous "Bon dia" ("Have a good day"). The tone is the opposite of the firm military tone, but the discipline is the same. It's a serious matter that the kids take very seriously, as a way of life, if they want to stay in the academy. If they insult or start a fight with an opponent – never mind a referee – they sit on the bench for a game or two. The parents must follow example: you will never see parents protesting the referee's decisions in a FC Barcelona youth game. The result of all this is that FC Barcelona-raised players are an example of behavior. They have been educated to behave well because they know they bear the responsibility to project FC Barcelona's image to the world every time they play. By several measures, FC Barcelona has already succeeded in projecting that image. When the ex-Real Madrid defender Fernando Hierro worked with the youth teams of Spain's National team, he observed: "If you stand at the entrance of the cafeteria without knowing which player comes from which team, you will soon identify the ones that are from FC Barcelona, because they stand out by the way they sit, by the way they serve themselves, and by the way they talk. Thus, you can imagine how easy it is to identify them by the way they play on the field." Messi, Xavi and Iniesta are the perfect image of "good boys" – several studies have shown that their immense popularity is due not only to their foot skills but also to the fact that parents (both fathers *and* mothers) point to them as examples for their children. Busquets, perhaps the most cerebral of all – a player that the club has protected with a monster buyout clause of €150M –, avoids the limelight of Facebook and Twitter and declines juicy advertising contracts; "I earn enough", he tells his agent. As Pablo Picasso once said, "It's not what the artist does that counts, but what he is".

Chapter 5: Cruyff's return as a coach

Cruyff's coaching career did not start in FC Barcelona. He started by coaching Ajax during 1985-1988, when he won the Dutch Cup in 1986 and 1987 and the *UEFA Cup Winner's Cup* in 1987. His pupils from that era became top stars: Marco van Basten, Frank Rijkaard, and Dennis Bergkamp, to name a few. In 1988 he moved to FC Barcelona.

The Dream Team and Cruyff's "luck" with *La Masia*

Cruyff came to FC Barcelona prepared to dazzle the fans with attacking football. "I want my team to play well even if only because I have to watch all the games and I don't want to get bored", he said once. Cruyff remembered bringing joy to the fans as a player and made it also his goal as a coach. Cruyff brought from the Ajax school his firm belief in the principles of ball possession, but he had to start by assembling an entirely new squad (the team from the previous season had been virtually dismantled). So the first thing he did upon arriving was to dig in the Barça B. Luckily for Cruyff, the youth team had been properly coached with the legacy of Total Football techniques by the hand of his former teammate Rexach, as well as Oriol Tort and Laureano Ruiz, so the upcoming players understood all the important concepts right away.

Cruyff's "luck" finding a youth academy that was ready for his larger project is relative. First of all, it was he who had brought that new mode of soccer thinking as a player and influenced a whole generation of people (Rexach, Tort, Ruiz) that stayed behind when he left. Second, we can safely speculate that Cruyff obtained all the information he could about the state of *La Masia* before accepting to coach FC Barcelona. He was good friends with Rexach, so when he considered his job offer to coach FC Barcelona, he must have had conversations with his former teammate – who was then in charge of coaching the *juvenils*, the last stage of the youth academy. Rexach must have reassured him that they had a youth academy in full steam, and I would be surprised if Cruyff didn't visit a practice session himself (following common standards of job interviews). Cruyff knew very well what he was facing because from the first day at the job he knew what needed to be done.

The second thing that Cruyff did was to use the money wisely to bring in stars that would make a difference and fill the stadium – the "sacred cows", Cruyff called them humorously). Among these, the best remembered are Ronald Koeman, a Dutch defender with an exceptional tactical sophistication and a shot of super-human strength and precision (he scored 102 goals in 345 games, an unheard-of record for a defender); Michael Laudrup, the best Danish player of all times, a player with a gift for inventing the impossible pass and with a graceful dribble that allowed him to drift unscathed like a dancer between defenders; the Brazilian Romario, "a player from the cartoons", as the Argentinian ex-player Jorge Valdano vividly described him, so unreal was the speed of his movements and his economy of touches inside the goal area; and Stoichkov, the Bulgarian forward who had a fine technique but, above all, the speed of a 100-meter Olympian. These players, and all the youngsters led by a teenager Guardiola, constituted the team that became known as the *Dream Team*. It would win a UEFA Cup Winner's Cup in 1988, four Spanish *Liga*s in a row (1991-1994), and a *European Cup* in 1994 (the year before the tournament was re-baptized as *Champions League*), among other titles.

A reversal of fortune

Barça's history is, for better and for worse, eternally linked to that of its arch-rival, Real Madrid. If Barça is up, Real Madrid is down, and when Real Madrid is up, Barça is down: there is only room for one winner at the top and second place tastes like defeat. Until Cruyff's arrival as a coach, Barça's glory seemed (and it was) definitely smaller than that of Real Madrid, even after editing out the handicaps inflicted by Franco's administration. Then suddenly, Cruyff's *Dream Team* appeared in the TV sets of every football lover in the world and was admired by sports commentators, writers, singers, and women. The soccer chat of the moment was about Koeman's superpower kicks, Laudrup's fantasy passes, Stoichkov's dashing sprints, and Romario's *cola de vaca* electric dribble. And all of a sudden the referees' mistakes – of which there continued to be plenty – stopped amounting to a conspiracy and became anecdotal: since then Barça has never had to blame the referees anymore for its losses. Cruyff, like a returning Messiah, changed the wheel of fortune once again, as he had done when he was a player.

But this time it was different – this change was much more powerful. It was not that the percentage of victories won by Cruyff as a coach (58.13%) had improved a tiny bit since the times of Michels, when Cruyff was a player (50.75%). It was not the "sacred cows" that brought us hope. It was the *children*, as Barça fans called the young players that come out of *La Masia*: this team was powered by an infinite factory that seemed to have found some sort of magic cloning *method*. Barça could be better than Real Madrid *forever*.

Cruyff's legacy

Cruyff's Spanish pupils from that team also became international stars: Luis Milla, Josep Guardiola, Albert Ferrer, Sergi Barjuán, Iván de la Peña. Again, these were players that did not fit the traditional Spanish warrior-player biotype: Milla was small and quick, Guardiola was slim and slow (but both could pass at first touch with spectacular accuracy), Ferrer and Barjuán were short but lightning-fast, and de la Peña was short, swift, and had Laudrup's passing imagination. *La Masia* had broken the soccer player's mold and produced a new biotype, more adaptable to a new style of soccer: smaller, quick on the turn, a biotype where the physique is unaccounted for as long as you can pass the ball quickly and precisely.

The biggest legacy that Cruyff has taught us is that the style of a team arises from the boots of its creative midfielders, the chief postulate of FC Barcelona football style. It is an almost sacred position in the club. "The barometer in football is the center of the field", Cruyff has said. There are many ways to bet on attacking football, and many can be very boring: Manchester United and Real Madrid also bet on attacking football, but not with the exquisite movement and crushing possession of the ball that characterizes FC Barcelona: on these other teams the ball is often rushed from defense to forwards, flying crazily over the heads of the midfield. For this reason, it has been more than 25 years since Barça has bought a player to fill a midfielder position. Barça prefers to educate them according to its own mold. (Disclaimer: Mascherano, who was a Liverpool midfielder and captain of Argentina, and Cameroonian Alex Song from Arsenal, both excellent defensive midfielders, signed for FC Barcelona knowing that they would not be on the starting squad; indeed, they have been superb substitute players.)

Cruyff's legacy has extended beyond FC Barcelona. Cruyff's *Dream Team* changed the Spanish League by showing to defensive-minded soccer coaches that it was possible to play attack soccer and win. "In soccer, you only need to score one more goal than your opponent", was Cruyff's response to critics of his daring (for lack of) defensive tactics. Guardiola inherited the best virtues of the *Dream Team* and polished out its defects. Guardiola's team, with Xavi and Iniesta as the "brain" midfielders, with Puyol and Piqué as the main defenders, with Busquets as "pivot" (connecting defense and midfield), and Pedro up front, was the skeleton of the Spanish national team that won the World Cup in South Africa in 2010. It is unquestionable that the Spanish national team plays in a recognizable "Barça-style". They do not quite reach the fluidity levels of Barça's midfield because the national coach, Vicente del Bosque, has rather defensive theories and insists on fielding an additional, unnecessary defensive midfielder that only slows down the midfield combinations between Busquets-Xavi-Iniesta: the result is that del Bosque's Spain has very little punch and didn't score much during the 2010 World Cup.

Cruyff must have been proud to see Holland and Spain reach the final: all his "football grandchildren" were on the field, all his wisdom of team-playing, attacking football praised by the fans and the press of both sides.

Never before in the history of soccer so many teachings and disciples had pointed to one same man. As the game started, I could not help but think that FIFA's award to Michels as best coach of the century had been a rushed decision, to say the least.

Cruyff the cultural icon

What has always distinguished Johan Cruyff is that he is not only cleverer than any footballer, but also than *just about anyone*, and it shows in the way he attracts attention. He was a media and cultural icon in Holland, a sort of *Beattle* (he looked like one), when he came to Barcelona to play for Barça in 1973, but he was not a celebrity in Spain. Once when I was a nine year-old kid, my mom took me to the shoe store next to our house and Cruyff came in soon after us to buy shoes for his children; when we came out there were a few kids lining up to get his autograph outside the store. This scene would be unthinkable 15 years later: a hazardous swarm of hundreds of people would form around him and follow him wherever he would go. He instantly endeared himself amongst Catalans when he declared that he had not signed for Real Madrid because he would not play for a team so close to the regime of dictator Francisco Franco. (And he named his son Jordi, a quintessential Catalan name.) When policemen showed up to escort him out of a game, he talked *down* to them with the authority of an untouchable, showing them that a soccer pitch was no place for *them*. I was seven years old at the time, and I remember very intensely this strange mixture of politics and soccer caused by the arrival of the new soccer star, because my father was imprisoned for a couple of months for his participation in student protests at the university. A friend of my father's who was a journalist contacted Cruyff and asked if he would autograph his picture to lighten up my father's days in prison, which he did generously, so the prison guards were quite impressed with this prisoner who was befriending the biggest soccer star of the moment. Due to bureaucratic reasons, Cruyff missed the first eight games of *La Liga*, and Barça – which had not won a title for 14 years – was next to last at the bottom of the table. After Cruyff's arrival, the team didn't lose another game until they won the

1973-1974 *Liga* and, notoriously, Barça beat Real Madrid 0-5 at the Bernabéu. A new Barça star was born – rather a supernova, whose bright light reached into the most unsuspecting corners of the world. Writer Jordi Soler has vividly explained how, deep in the Mexican jungle where his grandfather had ended up in exile during Franco's dictatorship, the news of that 1974 championship arrived via a biweekly bulletin with a black and white picture of Cruyff. That picture and an autograph of Cruyff were framed and worshipped by the natives in an altar next to various and colorful religious objects. A few kids in surrounding tribes were named "Cruyff".

This picture was autographed by Cruyff for my father in Catalan and reads "For Xavier, hoping that he'll soon be able to watch Barça play". My father was in prison for protesting against Franco's dictatorship at the time. Cruyff's public dissent against the dictator made him an instant hero amongst Catalans.

During Franco's dictatorship, policemen were sometimes called to remove non-compliant red-carded players from the field. Cruyff had never seen this and, in an occasion when he was red-carded, he refused to be escorted by the policemen. This photograph made Cruyff very popular amongst FC Barcelona fans and amongst opponents to the Franco regime in general: very few people in Spain had the courage to talk to a policeman with this defiant look.

Cruyff's fame grew to grotesque proportions during and after his coach tenure (1988-1996). It might be hard to grasp this in America: in at least two countries (Spain and Holland), Cruyff's ability to generate media attention is far above even that of a president. In one occasion, Cruyff arrived at *Catalunya Ràdio* for an unannounced interview the day (coincidentally) before an election, where one of the large rooms was packed full with a hundred journalists for a press conference by a right wing party's presidential candidate. Then, suddenly, someone noticed that Cruyff was in the building and, as he entered his interview room, *all* the reporters in the large press conference room left to hear what Cruyff had to say. The press conference of the presidential candidate had to be cancelled: Cruyff's words are more newsworthy than a presidential election in Barcelona. I obtained a first-hand account of this whole scene from my brother, who witnessed it with great amusement while sitting next to Cruyff as he was also waiting for an interview, and was able to thank him for my father's picture many years ago.

God's demise

At times, Cruyff's management style was tough on the players, partly due to his dominant character and also to his peculiar use of the language – a characteristic that has earned him fame both in Holland and Spain and has been subject of study of linguists and sociologists. (When a journalist once mentioned to his wife Danny how come Johan had not been able to master Spanish in more than 20 years of living in Spain, she said: "You have not heard him speak Dutch"; we will see several examples of his idioms in this book.) Once to "welcome" a new player from a team he organized a *rondo* with himself, Rexach, Guardiola, Laudrup, and Koeman (the best first-touch players) outside the circle, and the new-comer inside. The new player, who was the star in his old team, spent one hour fruitlessly chasing the ball around; Cruyff did the exercise to teach him a humility lesson. In another occasion, he gladly accepted a bet with a cocky Hristo Stoichkov, who defied him to hit the cross bar from the penalty box line; first went Stoichkov, who hit the cross bar a few times out of 10 attempts (very impressive!), but Cruyff didn't miss a single hit. In his memoirs he explains that he organized games at the end of the training session with a tiny field so that he could play and have a technical advantage, since he was less physically fit than them but had more technique. He always seemed to avoid any fraternization or friendship with the players – he enjoyed being Johan Cruyff the legend in their eyes, so he could tell them who the boss was. He even used to call the players "idiots" if the situation called for it. Johan Cruyff lost his father at age 9, so the boy undoubtedly had to toughen up and find his way to express his dominance. He never realized that respect and love, which he was surrounded by tons of it at FC Barcelona, were more than enough to lead the way – forever.

With the benefit of historical hindsight, Cruyff, who might have been the greatest coach that FC Barcelona ever had, clearly had a weakness: the towering presence of his own greatness, which he was always too ready to impose on his players, as a constant management tool, even at the cost of public humiliation. His greatness was indeed a convenient tool in the sense that his legendary status as a player and superior tactical knowledge as a coach always erected him as the natural alpha male of the group and kept the stars' egos in check. His team won everything for several years: four *Liga*s in a row and a *European Cup* at the end of the fourth year. Nobody blamed him for having won two of the leagues *in extremis* – literally, at the last minute, and thanks, twice, to unbelievable defeats of Real Madrid and Deportivo de la Coruña who were ahead until the last day of the competition. I remember being at the *Camp Nou* in 1993 watching the last game of the season. Barça secured the game fairly early, but they still needed Real Madrid to lose to Tenerife, so many fans were listening to their portable radios. I vividly recall this man one row behind us who was explaining the Real Madrid game to people around him. Tenerife was fighting for a UEFA Cup spot and Real Madrid players were nervous because the year before they had lost the league the last day of the season also against Tenerife. Tenerife scored a goal, and the whole stadium erupted, as if the goal had been scored at the *Camp Nou*. Still, we were nervous because an equalizer goal could mean the end of our dreams. Then suddenly, the radio man behind me started screaming "GOAL!" while jumping up and down. My dad and I started hugging this total unknown who was making us so happy. In a split second, the radio-less portion of the stadium understood and followed with a "goal" roar. I remember that Laudrup had the ball at that moment, and got so confused that he stopped to look around and lost the ball. If I had to describe the most incredible experience I have ever lived in a soccer stadium, this is it.

The last-minute euphoria of those championships, I believe, is what ultimately led Barça fans to forget that Cruyff *almost lost* those two leagues – in the 1991-1992 *Liga* alone, he accumulated three losses by 0-4 and one by 0-6 (!), while Real Madrid was slowly adding up points. In the end, the collective memory only registered that the team played the best attack football we had seen in ages, and he was using many kids from the youth academy. He was playing a new soccer style with a new generation of players.

But what surprised all of us blindfolded Barça fans – unaware of the deficiencies of the team – is that the *Dream Team* didn't die slowly, as one would expect from stars retiring from old age, one by one. It crumbled like a deck of cards, rather unexpectedly. After having won four *Liga*s in a row and one *European Cup*, the *Dream Team* made it again to the final of the *Champions League*. This time the final seemed a piece of cake. The rival was an aged Milan and the press presented reigning European champions FC Barcelona as the clear favorites. The final was in Athens and Cruyff arrogantly gave the whole team permission to go shopping the day before to relax, as if they had already won the game. But as in many ball sports, skill in soccer is only one half of the equation for winning – running and fitness is the other half. Milan's experienced players came onto the pitch decided to fight for their lives. Barça lost 4-0.

In fact, that *Champions League* final announced the end of the *Dream Team* precisely because it exposed so vividly before the world all of its flaws at once – Cruyff's arrogance and the weak defense. Also, this was a team that, after winning too many things, did not have the same thirst for victory. We have seen it over and over in soccer and many other sports. Suddenly so vulnerable: a more humble Cruyff might have lasted decades, but as it turns out, the one and only Cruyff was destined for self-destruction. Most coaches would have concluded that the only thing that those super-stars needed was group therapy, but he decided (against all common sense) that a punishment would be more productive, and proceeded to dismantle the team. The tension became unbearable when he fielded a mediocre goalie who happened to be his son-in-law, Angoy. Cruyff, who had won a record of 11 trophies in the period 1988-1994, was finally fired in 1996 after two seasons without winning a single trophy. (Assistant coach Charly Rexach took over to save the team.) To add to the tragedy, the Dane Michael Laudrup, one of the most elegant players and intelligent passers in the history of the club (and, in my memory, of soccer), left for Real Madrid.

But, if it seems obvious that teams have a cycle – after all, players age –, it did not seem obvious at the time that Cruyff, the God of FC Barcelona, had to go. Who could ever replace him? What would become of the youth academy? Cruyff seemed so perfect for FC Barcelona, except for this little defect of his – the egotism – that it seemed impossible to find a better candidate for the job. It was Cruyff's arrogance that made him unsuitable for rebuilding a *Dream Team* 2.0 – nothing else. Arrogance, alas, can cloud the brightest minds. When the team was working in synchrony and trophies were pouring into to the club, nobody noticed that this would be Cruyff's demise: he seemed brighter than everyone, too bright to fall for this one. But as Mourinho said once, "in almost every soccer club, success is everyone's success but failure is the coach's failure". This universal truth applies very well to Cruyff's success, shared with the *Dream Team*. When the team's precision machinery was slowed down by their internal clock, Cruyff reacted with sanctions instead of with incentives – but it was entirely his choice, his failure to make better choices. Cruyff's Achilles' heel, it turns out, is that he was incapable of love.

It all makes sense now. We can see clearly that Cruyff had been elevated to a Pope-like status by the Barça religion and been given a sort of credit of infallibility. But infallible he was not. He also made mistakes, and some rather big. In 1988 he signed Paraguayan Julio César Romero ("Romerito"), who only played seven games before returning to his country. When his son Jordi was a player in Barça B, the presence of Cruyff (or his wife Danny, secretly referred to by the technical staff as "Marilyn") during games was not revered but feared, because it meant that his son had to play. (Clarification: including Jordi Cruyff in a roster would not have hurt the team, as he was an excellent player. I'm referring to the fact that Johan Cruyff was incapable of noticing that his and Danny's presences were inappropriate, and that this conflict of interest was damaging his relationship with *La Masia*, the well-oiled engine upon whose good functioning he was relying to fuel his team.) In 2010, Sandro Rosell, newly elected president of FC Barcelona and long-time fan of Johan Cruyff, was devastated to learn that the club had been paying Johan Cruyff, by then Honorary President, a large sum (€2 M/year according to Sandro Rosell) to act as an intermediary between the previous Barça president, Joan Laporta, and Jaume Roures, the president of MediaPro, the company that handled all the TV rights for FC Barcelona: the position was completely unnecessary, since Laporta, Roures and Cruyff are all best buddies who don't need an intermediary. With good judgment, the position was cancelled. Cruyff resigned as Honorary President, saying it was in protest of the fact that the title of Honorary President is not recognized by the club (a simple administrative loophole that Rosell says he was meaning to fix; Rosell was unfairly attacked by the press for seemingly causing the cancellation of Cruyff's Honorary Presidency because he had the tact of not publicizing Cruyff's shady deal, but it was Cruyff's own choice to cancel his well-deserved presidency). But perhaps the biggest mistake in Cruyff's career is when he expressed doubts about Guardiola being able to coach the first team in front of the FC Barcelona board: "I don't know if, as a Catalan, he will be able to make the right decisions". Guardiola would later beat every coaching record won by Cruyff. Sometimes, as it happens sooner or later to all those who think they are touched by The Truth, the Pope spoke nonsense.

In my professional life, in the field of science and engineering, I have had the fortune of meeting Nobel Prize laureates and other men and women endowed with immense intellects. Highly revered when speaking about their specialty subject, I have met them later at informal gatherings where, for some reason, many of them discourse buoyantly on all sorts of subjects, as if their knowledge in a small branch of science extended magically to politics, art, and sports – and just about any area of science. I usually pretend to listen and smile from within. How can such bright minds lack so much common sense? I often think of Cruyff. After a while, people lose interest in egotistical individuals. When they die, nobody feels the need to build them a statue because they already sculpted their own: it's called their big ego. We are social animals, programmed to be more interested in people that create bonds of respect and friendship than in people that create links of admiration or fear.

Guardiola would later change the club with his fresh, frank attitude and friendly managerial style. "In the end, everything is reduced to feeling loved", he has stated. I met Guardiola when FC Barcelona came to Seattle for a summer U.S. tour in 2010 and I was able to access one of the training sessions, which took place on the University of Washington grounds. After introducing myself for the first time, Pep gave me a big friendly smile (he is a friendly type *and* he is friends with my dad), then he had one urging question: "How is life in Seattle?" It was not just a polite question. He really wanted to know: he was looking beyond, at the tall, lush green trees, probably sensing the differences with the stout pine trees of his native Santpedor, close to the dry mountains of Montserrat. Before answering, I pondered for a second that I was looking at the most loved person in all Catalonia – a living statue.

Chapter 6: Guardiola: the era of love

Pep Guardiola and the "Pep Team" celebrating the 2011 Champions League *final 3-1 victory against Manchester United at Wembley Stadium in London. Ian Chadband, Chief Sports Correspondent of* The Telegraph, *wrote that "Guardiola's side played football from the gods".*

A number of coaches came after Cruyff departed the club, with variable success, and two of them Dutch too: Robson (1996-97), Van Gaal (1998-2003), and Rijkaard (2004-2008). They all respected the basic postulate of Cruyff (using a creative midfielder from the youth team: Iván de la Peña, then Xavi), but Van Gaal's "BarcAjax" (as Ajax fans dubbed the FC

Barcelona squad full of Ajax players that subtracted more than added quality to the game) did not go well with Barça fans. Van Gaal, however, must be credited for his strong commitment to bringing up players from *La Masia* – he understood the process and believed in it strongly from his times at Ajax. He wanted to monitor the up-bringing so closely that often he would send his assistant coach (a then-unknown guy named José Mourinho) to coach the Barça B side. Guardiola and Xavi speak very highly of Van Gaal in terms of his understanding of the game, although he clearly did not have the necessary leadership skills to make himself respected. The team went through a long period of low self-esteem and poor results. In the seven years following Cruyff's traumatic sacking, the coach had been changed seven times and only two *Ligas* and two *Copas del Rey* had been conquered. The 1999-2003 dry spell caused the resignation of Van Gaal and President Joan Gaspart.

The team saw a resurgence with Ronaldinho's signing by newly-elected President Joan Laporta. Laporta also signed Frank Rijkaard as a coach. Endowed with a prodigious technique, Ronaldinho made a point to play beautifully (the Brazilian style "jogo bonito") and with a smile that spread like a virus among the fans. He alone instantaneously lifted the morale of a depressed team and all the supporters. A magical goal against Sevilla – on a late game played at midnight – is specially remembered by the fans, where Ronaldinho received the ball from goalie Valdés in the middle of the field, went through two players like an arrow as he crossed the field diagonally, and kicked a knuckle-ball above the goalie that hit the bar and pierced the net. In the middle of the silent night, the *Camp Nou* roar was registered as a seismic wave from a metereological station 10 km away. The records, as we will see later, show that Rijkaard used an average of 4.5 starting players from the youth academy per game in his five years at FC Barcelona (the highest rate, 4.9, in his first year is notably higher than Van Gaal's average of 3.8 in 2002-2003, his last year at FC Barcelona). Rijkaard will also be remembered as the coach who placed Xavi in his most lethal position, urging him to play 10 metres forward. But Rijkaard's use of the youth academy was inconsistent: in his five-year tenure, the number of *La Masia* debuts per year could swing from 9 to 3 for no apparent reason giving a sense of uncertainty to the whole project (averaging at 5.8 ± 2.8 debuts per year, compared to Guardiola's 5.5 ± 0.6 consistent debut "elevator"). The fans cannot forget that he did not seem to get the potential of some key players: in the 2006 *Champions League* final that Barça won 2-1 (but started losing 0-1) against Arsenal, prioritizing experience over talent: a 22 year-old Iniesta did not play the first half (he came in for Edmilson in the second half), while Xavi (26 yrs, coming back from an injury) and Messi (18 yrs) sat on the bench for the whole game. At that age, Messi was already a better player than Ludovic Giuly and Henrik Larsson, who both played in the final alongside superstars Ronaldinho and Eto'o; upset, Messi did not come out to lift the cup and receive the winner's medal (a decision he now says he regrets). Three years later, Messi, Iniesta and Xavi would be elected Best Three Players of the World.

Ronaldinho is credited for elevating the morale of the club back to *Dream Team* levels. The present FC Barcelona president, Sandro Rosell, who was able to build a personal relationship with Ronaldinho and became a key agent in his signing while he was a Nike executive in Brazil, has said that "Ronaldinho changed the club's wheel from negative to positive. We will never be grateful enough to him". But, unlike the *Dream Team*, this team's glory was brief – during the 2003-2008 period, the team only won the 2006 *Champions League* and the 2005 and 2006 *Ligas*. Afterwards, the team spiraled downwards due to Rijkaard's indulgence (his affair with a young club employee, unhidden from all the players, did not help to earn their esteem) and Ronaldinho's inability to prioritize hard training over wild parties – an attitude that became contagious to other stars. I'm sparing the reader the boring details because this is not a book about the history of the club. Those years are not essential to understand how the club has shaped its youth academy and how the youth academy has, in turn, shaped the club, simply because during those years the youth academy simply kept doing its good work of producing players. *La Masia* – truly an engine that runs independently of imperatives of results, fame, or money – has always acted as a soft mattress for the club to fall at times of crisis.

The rest of this chapter focuses on a simple question: How much of Guardiola's success is attributable to the system (primarily *La Masia*, and also the club by extension) that created him? I will not attempt to try answer this question as a scientist because no control experiment can be done to repeat any of the conditions that existed at the various time points, but we can examine what we know about Guardiola's motives and background in making complex decisions. We will start by stating that, in contrast with Cruyff who came from Holland and revamped *La Masia*, Guardiola was created as a player at *La Masia* (as one of Cruyff's disciples) and, when he came back to the club, he pushed it to unprecedented heights.

A Phoenix is reborn from the ashes

Recall that Johan Cruyff was hired in 1988 by Josep Lluís Núñez, the least likely ally of the Dutch coach, simply by convenience: Núñez needed Cruyff to regain the lost support of the fans. Similarly, Guardiola was brought back to the club against the wishes of many of the directors (including, initially, President Laporta), because Guardiola had been a public supporter of a defeated presidential candidate in the previous elections. But, like Cruyff, Guardiola was a Barça hero, and it was useful to bring him closer to the club when the ship was sinking.

Guardiola had actually been offered the position of director of *La Masia*, but he refused it. It was 2007, he had retired from active soccer about one year earlier, and had traveled around the globe to meet his most respected coaches: Lillo, Bielsa, Menotti. He was itching to coach. "But what team?", he was asked by Barça sports director, *Dream Team* ex-teammate and close friend Txiki Begiristain, thinking that he might be pretending to take the first team. Ronaldinho's team, coached by Frank Rijkaard, had ended the 2006-2007 season without a single title except for Spain's *SuperCopa*, but the president had still faith in Rijkaard's ability to re-lift the team to previous performance heights. But Guardiola had no such pretense. "Any team. Barça B or C would be great", he answered. "They have just been relegated to Third Division for the first time in history." "I don't care. I want to coach", was his answer again and again.

Guardiola did, of course, more than *just* coach Barça B. (First he had to fuse Barça B and Barça C, since both teams could not play in Third Division, picking 23 players out of 50 in only a few weeks, and notifying the families of the discarded players one by one.) He used his time in Third Division to experiment with the latest coaching techniques: videotaping the opponents, analyzing each of their players, preparing a summary for the team, team and diet management, etc. As a result, Barça B was promoted to Second Division. "For me it was easier to innovate with Barça B because I was away from the media lights and we only played every Sunday. So I had a lot of time between games to analyze each game, watch it again and train what had not worked. I could innovate in the training sessions and try different things. To give you an example, if you think about all the scientists that are doing research on new pathologies or new drugs, they need time. Time."

As Rijkaard's indulgence with Ronaldinho's star-filled squad resulted in another fiasco during the 2007-2008 season, the club couldn't help but notice the difference in work ethic between the Barça B and the first team. Begiristain convinced the reluctant board members one by one that Guardiola was the perfect man for the job, and Rijkaard was fired at the end of the 2007-2008 season. Under Guardiola's leadership, two players from that Barça B – Pedro and Sergio Busquets – would leap from Third Division to become World Champions in just two years.

The Pep Team

Exactly twenty years after Cruyff's arrival, in 2008, Pep Guardiola became the coach of FC Barcelona. He recovered Cruyff's playing style using a gentler managerial style and an emphasis on "total pressure" (coordinated pressure by the whole team to recover the ball swiftly), resulting in the most spectacular success in the history of soccer: FC Barcelona won the first sextuplet ever (all the existing competitions) in

2009, a record of 72.46% of victories over 247 games, 14 of 19 disputed titles and 11 victories in 12 finals in the period 2008-2012.

The year 2009, with the conquest of the six titles under the command of coach Josep Guardiola, was the biggest in the history of the club – and in the history of soccer. Never another club has won all the existing six cups in the same year. (Back in 1972, Cruyff's Ajax won all the five existing cups at the time.) We have now seen the enormous benefit of having a coach that was raised by the FC Barcelona youth system (Josep Guardiola, the present coach since 2008). As Gabi Milito (left defender) has said, "he has a lot of knowledge", and, like most children raised in this wonderful school which is *La Masia*, he is eminently a nice guy that treats his players like people, a sensible and sensitive man who likes poetry and cries like a man. Who is going to trust a non-Barça-raised coach from now on? Indeed, when Guardiola resigned from FC Barcelona at the end of the 2012 season, the management immediately announced that the second coach, Tito Vilanova, would now step up as first coach, to preserve the model. At first surprising, it makes total sense: Tito Vilanova knows this team from inside out, is one of its chief architects, was educated at *La Masia*, and played in Barça B with Guardiola. Xavi has said that one of the best games that they have ever played as a team was the Barça-Real Madrid that ended in 2-6, which took place May 2nd 2009. Almost twenty years prior, on May 1st 1989, Cruyff took Guardiola, Tito Vilanova and three other young players (Juan Carlos Unzué, Aureli Altimira and Jordi Roura) from the Barça B to a first-team friendly game. Two things stand out from the historical record: the friendly game also ended 2-6 and all those four players from Barça B would end up becoming part of coaching staff under Guardiola's tenure. Guardiola's success is the best validation of Cruyff's thesis that Barça should implement Ajax's youth school model: the model works even better when the supreme thinker (the coach) has been formed at home, because he has assimilated the system since his childhood. (It always goes back to the children. And Cruyff.)

Dream Team vs. Pep Team

We can extract great lessons from a comparison between Cruyff's *Dream Team* and Guardiola's *Pep Team*. Even Johan Cruyff has conceded that the present FC Barcelona team is better than his legendary *Dream Team*. Guardiola's team has inherited the fast pace, the brilliance and the passion for attack football of Cruyff's *Dream Team*. The circulation in the midfield has achieved pinnacles never seen in Cruyff's years – at the *Dream Team* time, only Guardiola himself as a player and Michael Laudrup had midfield-skills comparable to those of Xavi and Iniesta, so the associations could not have been as rich as in the present day with Busquets, Xavi, Iniesta, Thiago, Fàbregas, and Messi, who stir the ball past defenders with overwhelming superiority and speed. The forward line of the *Dream Team*, on the other hand, with Romario, Stoichkov, and Begiristain, was just as strong (if not more) than that of Pep's team (typically, with Messi, Villa, and Pedro, although it varies widely). It is really the emphasis on the midfield that makes Guardiola's FC Barcelona other-worldly. As Cruyff said, "The barometer in football is the center of the field".

There are two key weaknesses that Cruyff's *Dream Team* had that Guardiola's team did not have. First, Cruyff always neglected the defense. It was obvious: the *Dream Team* defended with three men, with a very slow central defender (Ronald Koeman); even though Koeman had a fast mind and the strongest kick ever seen in *Camp Nou*, these defensive tactics cost the *Dream Team* a lot of goals against. Cruyff really thought that his principle that "While we have the ball, they don't have it" would take care of everything in the end. "We only need to score one more goal than our opponent". The principle works in most cases, but in a few occasions it can fail, for example, on a very rainy day with a pitch full of puddles when the most technical team does not have a big advantage and the inferior team puts 10 players inside the goal area – then a corner kick against can kill you if you have neglected the defense and they have good headers and a strategic trap: one goal, paradoxically, is *also* all you need to lose in soccer. Guardiola, on the other hand, would prepare the corner kick defense with military planning: each player is assigned a specific zone. In Cruyff's *Dream Team*, there were several players that were relieved of pressure duties – Romario and Laudrup were mostly walking around the pitch when FC Barcelona didn't have possession. Guardiola learned this lesson and taught his players to defend all at the same time – "coordinated team pressure": the forwards always force the defenders to boot the ball under pressure (an imprecise pass) and, simultaneously, the midfielders pressure the opponent's midfielders when they try to control the pass (often resulting in a loss of control): the result is that Barça (Pep's team) now recovers the ball in record time. It is truly amazing.

However, another big (if not the biggest) weakness of the *Dream Team* was Cruyff's super-ego. This is rarely mentioned, probably because most sports analysts are too close to Cruyff. He almost always spoke to players from a position of superiority and enjoyed making it obvious to them that he was still a better player than them (for example, by joining in the rondos, an exercise where he did not have a physical handicap). In public, he often spoke arrogantly about matters of opinion. The fans (including me) adored him, accepted his idiosyncrasies as part of the motivational tactics of a genius, and still worship his legacy (including me). Yet his relationship with his players was not a healthy one. Nobody likes to work for an arrogant boss even if this arrogant boss is a genius – everybody, given the choice, prefers to be respected and be treated nicely, but when have we ever heard Cruyff say something nice about someone? His motivational techniques as a coach produced impressive results but were at times insensitive. In Guardiola's debut with the first team in a friendly match when he was just 16 years old, Cruyff's now-famous remark to his performance was: "Today you played slower than my grandma". It has been said that Cruyff's comment stuck with Guardiola forever, helping him excel at compensating his handicap in physical speed with first-touch passes that would pierce through defenses with surgical precision (which was Cruyff's goal). Most people laugh at hearing Cruyff's blunt criticism. The kid, however, went home crying. Was it necessary? Most definitely not. The lack of respect extended to rivals, of course. We have seen how in 1994, at its peak, the *Dream Team* lost a *Champions League* final 4-0 against a weak AC Milan because Cruyff thought that the best way to prepare that game was to convince his players that they had already won the game before playing it – and they went shopping the day before.

Guardiola also changed, by way of example, the overall style of the team. Unlike Cruyff, who over the years has earned a reputation for liking money and, indeed, assigned himself a salary higher than that of any player as a coach, Guardiola earned a relatively modest salary, refused to drive luxury cars, and renewed his coach contract every year to keep the players motivated. He has none of Cruyff's arrogance, he treated his players with respect (he never entered the shower area of the locker room), and has a great emotional intelligence (he cries like a man if he needs to). The concept of "emotional intelligence" was coined in 1990 by psychologists John Mayer (now at the University of New Hampshire) and Peter Salovey (Yale University), but it was not popularized until 1995 by *The New York Times* journalist Daniel Goleman, who wrote a best-seller book on the subject. Now business schools have started to pay attention to emotional intelligence as a form of intelligence that has a bigger impact than I.Q. on success (particularly in adult education), which has great impact in leadership and employee training. It took two or three generations to banish corporal punishment from schools because teachers saw it had counterproductive effects on learning, and we learned to implement instead positive feedback to reinforce good learning attitudes from the youngest ages. Why wouldn't the same philosophy apply to adults? Everyone deserves to be treated with respect – good and bad players alike.

Under Guardiola, every detail seemed dictated by plain common sense. He remembered the unnecessary boredom he had to suffer as a player in hotels waiting for the game, separated from his family for no apparent reason, so he decided that the team would (whenever possible) travel the same day, play and leave; thus the players had much more time to spend with their families. He also got rid of soda machines and established healthy eating habits for all such as drinking multivitamin smoothies after training. Messi used to drink only Coke and eat only steaks, and he also used to get muscular injuries often. Guardiola convinced him that he would get more playing time if he corrected his diet; now Messi enjoys a variety of fish and rarely gets injured. Juanjo Brau, his FC Barcelona physical therapist, also takes special care of him: he follows him even to Argentina's games. (All these changes have become the norm under Tito Vilanova's tenure.)

From Mister detail to cultural icon

Guardiola read the historical mistakes perfectly. He implemented coordinated team pressure almost to perfection level in order to strengthen the defense. He does not like to leave anything to chance, actually. Unlike Cruyff, Guardiola is a very hard worker who was the first to come to work and the last to leave in order to prepare every aspect of the team management, from the strategy all the way down to the diet and the apparel. He hired a small team of close collaborators to assist him in the tactical preparation of the matches using video technology. Torrent and Planchart traveled to record an average of six games for each of the opponents they had to face, including friendly games. Television images do not provide the views they were interested in, so they filmed the games in full panoramic view at high definition to visualize the movements of all the players at once. This material was digitally processed and morphed with TV footage to provide personalized DVDs for each key player (specially defenders) so they were better prepared to face the opponent(s) they would encounter in their zone of the pitch – this forward tends to fake the kick, this other one tends to cut to the outside, etc. With this information, Barça defenders were less likely to be surprised by the opponents' repertoire of tricks. For the *Camp Nou* games, there was a permanently-installed panoramic camera whose images could be replayed from the locker room at half time to correct mistakes. Guardiola carefully picked as assistant coach his long-time friend and fellow ex-player at Barça B, Tito Vilanova, who coached the unstoppable *"cadets"* youth team of Piqué, Fàbregas and Messi. Vilanova was in charge of setting up the strategies for corner kicks and free kicks after studying the opponent. Vilanova, Torrent and Planchart convinced Guardiola that Barça's best defensive strategy for corner kicks was to defend by zone (almost never seen in soccer) rather than individually (the norm). Torrent and Planchart had performed an interesting experiment while coaching a third-division team in order to convince their players of the effectiveness of the zonal defense: at soccer practice, they placed dummies instead of defenders and the attackers verified that even static "players", when strategically-placed, present a significant challenge for scoring. What finally convinced Guardiola, though, is that by switching to zonal defense they would minimize physical contact; typically Barça players do not do well against strong, tall attackers because they have been selected for their quickness and ball handling, not for their physique. Consequently, Barça is careful to not give away corners.

Pep Guardiola is no longer the kid from Santpedor: he has become a cultural icon. His contribution to soccer has been noticed beyond Spain's borders and earned him the covers of prestigious magazines such as *El Gráfico* (Argentina) and *Newsweek* (who misspelled "*Barca*! The best football team ever?" next to a flying Guardiola over the heads of his players). Rob Hughes of The New York Times wrote: "It's the style and not the trophies what defines the success of Guardiola. Even in his farewell he proves once more that he is the style." Even the Wall Street Journal ran an article on Guardiola when he resigned: "What really made Guardiola stand out was the successful implementation of a playing philosophy that bordered on utopia", wrote Gabrielle Marcotti. Craig Foster, the main soccer analyst of Australia, wrote in the Sunday Morning Herald: "Guardiola produced a soccer style widely considered as the most beautiful and captivating that the world has ever witnessed, but he did it in a different way: converting the passing game into a form of art. The pass is the genome of this game and this is Pep's greatest legacy."

The success of the youth academy under Guardiola's tenure is so noticeable that it is being studied even at business schools. *La Masia* has been featured recently by the *Harvard Business Review* and by *The Economist* as an example of strategic long-term planning. The Harvard

Business School sent an expert to *La Masia* to study its methods, since businessmen everywhere are befuddled that these can achieve better results than their favorite method – buying and selling (soccer players), as richer teams like Real Madrid, *ManU* or Manchester City do. Why are businessmen so stupefied? *La Masia* simply reflects the principle that education is a more valuable asset than money. Every parent knows that. Why would the markets know anything about how soccer should be played? The minute Barça blocks the transfer of top players like Messi, Xavi and Iniesta, or players like Cesc Fàbregas and Mascherano take a salary cut to leave their team in order to land onto FC Barcelona and none other, concepts such as free market and competition have no meaning, reflecting the fact that money is not the most valuable asset in this market. It's education. If Harvard Business School cares to look into other youth academies, such as Ajax, they will see that *La Masia*'s methods are very similar and date back to the dawn of soccer. Just as carpenters have passed their trade onto their children for millennia, so Jack Reynolds thought of teaching soccer to kids at an early age about hundred years ago. If you build a solid educational program, such as *La Masia*, the kids will be so good that money alone won't even be able to buy them.

In search of the elusive "team spirit"

The fabric that holds a team together is what we used to call the "team spirit". Every great team needs a team spirit to hold it together. It resides primarily in the hearts of the players, specially those that end up holding the captainship, leading the team inside and outside the field, and giving it all at every game – at Barça, that would be Puyol (perhaps the least gifted player) and Xavi –; however, it is often ignored how much of the team spirit's weight rests on the shoulders of the coach, who devises the procedures to weave it into a solid entity – these can be team-building routines such as throwing parties or watching games together, spending time talking with the players about everyday life problems, saying hello and shaking hands with the clubs' employees to show respect, hugging after scoring, singing anthems together, eating in groups, having barbeques with the players' families, etc. Anything that binds the group together in a positive atmosphere is legitimate and is likely to improve the performance of the team. Because the team spirit is constructed somewhat arbitrarily, it also tends to be fragile: we have already seen how we thought the *Dream Team* was a solid team but it collapsed in a few weeks because of Cruyff's auto-destructive attitudes.

Guardiola has been one of the greatest weavers of team spirit in the history of the club. One of his highest priorities from day one was to eradicate all arrogance from the team down to the smallest residue. His first move as a coach was to remove the "rotten apples" – none other than super-stars such as Ronaldinho and Deco (first year) and Eto'o (second year) which were poisoning the atmosphere of the locker room with their diva attitudes and night-time wild parties. This procedure left him with a team whose core was essentially made of *La Masia* players: the cleansing was perhaps not intended with this purpose initially, but it converged into a pure-bred squad because *La Masia* offered him the values that he was looking for. There was never a branding requirement or belief that *La Masia* offered a better product, in fact the club paid a dear price for Swedish super-star Ibrahimovic thinking they were reinforcing the team, but it did not work out either: Ibra's supernova ego never fit well in that close-knit dressing room of players that have been friends since their teens. Guardiola wanted a team without alpha males, knowing that Messi is not the type – Messi leads by example, not by intimidation. Guardiola had the team meet Fernando Parrado, an ex-rugby player from Uruguay and one of the survivors of the famous 1972 plane crash in the Andes that avoided death by eating human flesh. Parrado was impressed by the human value of the team: "They are sensitive, they are like an amateur team. Guardiola told me that if there is a rotten apple, he takes it out, like Eto'o and Ibrahimovic, who wanted to be stars in a team where nobody feels like a star; and that is spectacular."

Indeed the players are all friends and Barça fans, having grown up together in the club – most of them have been together daily for more than half of their life! –, they barbeque and sometimes vacation together, which results in fewer tensions with the players that are benched.

Friendships are an undeniable cohesive factor in a soccer team: sitting on the bench and sharing stardom with a friend is much more bearable, players are more likely to get covered for mistakes on the field without a grunt (an essential element in coordinated pressure where every team member needs to perform), and practices – the equivalent of everyday work for soccer players – become immense fun. This positive environment is particularly important as a confidence booster to help integrate the young newcomers, who feel as part of a "club-family" surrounded by friends and friendly coaches. Piqué expressed it best: "Since I was a kid, I was a fan; I went to the stadium every week. It was a dream to play for Barcelona. To have so many players spend much of their careers together enhances team unity. It's good for the atmosphere of the dressing room. And there's a lot of confidence. We can help each other as a friend, not only as a teammate. You can see this on the pitch — when we are in trouble we work as a team and we fight to win." Guardiola's idea of providing a cuddling environment for the upcoming youngsters within the first team might prove to become Barça's biggest gold mine for the next years.

Guardiola's team spirit – sustained by a method of managing the team based on good manners and affection – could also crumple like a deck of cards. Gone Guardiola, will his heir (Tito Vilanova) be able to contain the underlying jealousies and occasional tensions? Guardiola was a master at keeping the crises hidden from the public. Unbeknownst to most people, that good boy we know as Messi had a temper fit in the locker room in 2012 after Guardiola announced that his friends Piqué and Cesc would not be in the starting roster against Real Madrid. At first he said he would not play; Xavi and Iniesta were able to change his mind. Guardiola, who did not witness the incident because as a policy he never entered the locker room, personally assured to me that Piqué's and Fàbregas' absences were a purely tactical decision. Barça lost that game 2-1, after two unusual defensive mistakes by Puyol and Adriano. While Real Madrid fought hard to win the first league in many years, the team must have felt the overall lack of karma. The next day, Messi did not attend the training session and the club let the press speculate on flu, but the Argentinian star was simply mad at Guardiola and was throwing a tantrum at home, according to a source close to the club. This type of inappropriate outbursts is unfortunately not uncommon amongst soccer stars. In June 2013, when Guardiola had just started as Bayern Munich coach, I was in Munich for work and Pep graciously invited me for a coffee at the Bayern training grounds. There he explained the key point of the day-to-day of being a coach: "The pre-season is ideal for a coach, because everyone gets to play. The problem comes when the games start and you have to tell this player "you play" and this other one "you don't play", which means "I love you" to this one and "I don't love you" to the other one. In the end, everyone wants to feel loved." Guardiola was exactly right. When the team started spiraling down into its big crisis at the end of the 2013 season, journalists quoted rumors from the dressing room saying that "there were players that couldn't stand Guardiola anymore" and from some directors secretly referring to him as the "Dalai Lama". (Guardiola's silence about his future put the whole club on hold unnecessarily for several months, since it was revealed later that he could have disclosed his contract with Bayern as early as Christmas 2011.)

Note how much of the team spirit rests on the shoulders of the coach: had these conflicts become public at the moment, people would not have got the impression that this was such a close-knit group. But it was: the players behave a bit like a big family and such personal problems tend to die away with time as long as the press does not keep magnifying them. Thanks to Guardiola, these incidents are now troubled waters under the bridge. However, there are limits, and players should get the clear message that one warning is enough. In 2013, after losing the Cup semi-final against Real Madrid, the next day Messi did not appear at practice because "he had a fever", according to the club. Another lie: Messi was throwing another tantrum at home, as Barça's doctor (Dr. Pruna) was able to verify. The only way to stop at once these childish behaviors – that infect other players so easily – is to expose them to the light of day; recall that Messi was by now a 25 year-old with fatherly responsibilities, so he would not bear well the shame. By covering Messi, the club was giving the star a *prima donna* status and was only punching holes in the team spirit that Guardiola painstakingly weaved. Tata Martino seems to have put an end to this nonsense with by imposing a rational regimen of rotations that includes everyone, from Messi to Xavi.

One last example: Xavi has a well-deserved authority in the locker-room and among the technical staff, but he has used it to self-appoint himself as the free-kicker of the team when the ball is too much to the left for Messi. There is only one "little" problem: he is not scoring goals. he is not a free-kick specialist – he does not kick the ball with enough power, so the ball doesn't curve either. He is wasting precious opportunities for the team just to satisfy his vanity. Xavi must have accumulated by now one of the worst free-kicking statistics of *La Liga* ever, and it's time for him to stop embarrassing himself and the immense size of his legend. There are at least four better shooters than him in the roster: Neymar (a world-class free kicker), Cesc Fàbregas (another great free-kick shooter, as Arsenal fans will recall), Adriano, and Alves, so there is plenty to choose. (The same goes for penalty kicks; I believe that Cesc Fàbregas' statistics on penalty kicks far surpass those of Messi, the "official" penalty taker at Barça for some reason.)

The biggest, yet unaddressed problem is that the club has never provided that fabric in the form of proper educational tools for the players. The players are in essence a group of immature teenagers that do not study, get overpaid to play their favorite game, drive Ferraris around, and can have sex with just about any girl they snap their fingers at. Why wouldn't they have their values a little, er, distorted? The club has always delegated the task of finding the magic binding fabric to the coach. Guardiola found that fabric in the affection and respect that the players had for each other and for him. Cruyff, on the other hand, used as fabric his own magnetic personality and the very adoration that players professed for him. In the end, however, when the person that holds the fabric is gone, the team falls apart, as we saw in the crisis that Barça went through at the end of the 2013 season (following a two-month absence of

Tito Vilanova for his cancer treatment). Why? I believe that the fundamental reason is that the soccer players lack the educational tools to be the fabric themselves: if they had studied, and read books and newspapers regularly, they would see how insignificant some of their own problems are, and they would be able to solve them themselves. Keita's disappointment and Messi's fit are just a manifestation of the soccer player's inability to look beyond himself, which comes with education. The players are not to blame – the club is. The club is responsible for the education of the players and, if La Masia produces players that prefer to spend their free time playing the PlayStation rather than going to the theater or a concert – to which they are regularly invited, but almost never attend –, then La Masia has failed in their education and we should not be surprised at the reactions by Keita or Messi. (These are used here only as examples; there are numerous examples for every player, including an account of the Brazilian Ronaldo who was seen having sex with two girls on the sofa of the VIP lounge of the Camp Nou after a game. "What can you expect from a 20-year old full of energy", was President Núñez's forgiving reaction.) In the long term, the only way to strengthen the fabric that holds the team together is by providing the players with a solid education. The day we see a chemist, a carpenter, a mechanical engineer, and a musician on the field, then those players won't whine because their name is not chanted on the field or because their pals are not on the starting roster: when it happens, they will already know why.

It is noteworthy to mention here the human dimension of Eric Abidal (left defender) and Pinto (goalie) and their integration with the team despite being from outside of the youth system and being technically on the weaker side (specially Pinto). Pinto is the second goalie but he is a very good teammate, in the sense that he is always in very good spirits, cheering people up on the bench and in practices. Guardiola, against all opinions (including mine), would field him always in the Cup, the lesser of the three competitions. He did it as a way to promote good personal equilibrium within the team, even though it might have cost Barça two important goals. What is remarkable is the attitude of his teammates after each goal: they picked up the ball and went on, assimilating their part of the blame – it's a team sport. Abidal became sub-champion of the world with France in 2006 one year before signing up for FC Barcelona. In 2011, he was diagnosed with a tumor in his liver. He had surgery and chemotherapy, and after a few months he was back on the pitch in time to play the final of the *Champions League*. In a moving gesture, Puyol, the team captain, gave the bracelet to Abidal right before lifting the trophy so he could be the first to do the honors. In January 2012, a heartbreaking letter from a father to a newspaper revealed that Eric Abidal is, in fact, a very special person. This father explained how he had had to explain to his 15-year old son that he had a brain tumor: "You have in your head what Abidal had in his liver and tomorrow they will take it out". The kid answered: "Dad, I want to have Abidal's shirt and win my *Champion's League*". He was the only one in the whole family that didn't cry. He went into the operating room wearing Abidal's shirt, and the shirt stayed at his bedside for months after. Coincidentally, the father explained in the letter, one week after the surgery he had met Abidal in a store. The father showed him pictures of his son in Abidal's shirt and thanked him for setting such a strong example so that his son could fight on. FC Barcelona players visit sick children in half a dozen hospitals every year at Christmas time, and Abidal arranged to visit that kid's hospital. A nurse made it possible for the kid to spend time with his hero. This time he couldn't help crying in Abidal's long arms, he made some comment about his watch. So Abidal gave it to him, but it's not *just* a watch. It's a *Rolex Daytona* (at least $10,000) with Abidal's name inscribed in the back. Abidal did not want to hear the family's plea to return the watch, because as a cancer patient he knew well how important it is for the kid to feel happy and strong-spirited when he wears Abidal's watch. These are the type of men that Guardiola enjoys working with.

When you consider that Guardiola fired top players like Ronaldinho, Deco, Ibrahimovic, and Eto'o – due to their attitudes –, and decided to keep Pinto and Abidal to form this fantastic squad, it makes you wonder what it takes to create a great team. In an era when many top teams are built on super-star investments (including the *Dream Team*), Guardiola's team might have fielded up to 8 or 9 player-friends that were raised in the youth academy – with the coach and assistant coach (Tito Vilanova – you guessed it: Guardiola's close friend) also from the youth academy. The result is that Guardiola's team irradiated positive team values well beyond their soccer skills, an added social and human value that we never saw (and never asked for) in the *Dream Team*. Xavi, Iniesta and Messi – the shortest players in the squad – represented the triumph of team playing at its smartest, as they drew their unstoppable power against much stronger opponents from their clever associations. When you saw them interact and play, you couldn't help wondering whether their friendship helps them play better in some tantric or telepathic way, even for those of us who don't believe in telepathy. All three – like Guardiola – come from humble families, repudiate ostentatious lifestyles, always respect their opponents (a basic teaching at the FC Barcelona academy), and incarnate the quintessential well-behaved boys that many parents, independently of their soccer star status, would like to see their daughter marry. Xavi, Iniesta and Messi are also first and foremost Barça fans that would rather starve than play for Real Madrid. We did not see this style in the *Dream Team*, which lost two money-hungry players (Milla and Laudrup; three if we count Figo, who left in 2000) to richer-rival Real Madrid.

The whole merit of this change in style is attributable, no doubt, to this intelligent kid from Santpedor, Josep Guardiola, who proved that you can be sensitive, loving and courteous with your players, and still lead them to form one of the most successful soccer teams in history. (Women took notice too, and a poll elevated him into the status of one of the sexiest Spanish men alive.) His managerial motto could have been inspired by the Beatles' song "All you need is love". And that would be one more lovely reason why Barça is more than a club.

Guardiola is very genuine about this aspect of his management style. One of the caretakers at *La Masia*, Carles Folguera, recalls that every time Pep

Guardiola paid *La Masia* a visit, his first question to him always was: "Are the kids happy?" It's all about the children, Cruyff has always insisted. When Messi was awarded his third *Ballon d'Or* (joining soccer giants Michel Platini, Johan Cruyff and Marco Van Basten, the only three players that had won it three times before him – Messi now has four) and Pep Guardiola was awarded best coach of the year, Sir Alex Ferguson, *ManU*'s coach for the last 25 years, reminded the world that Barça's "secret" was that the bulk of its players were friends who had played together since they were children. He recalled that Manchester United also enjoyed one such generation of friends-players, with Scholes, Giggs and Beckham.

Perhaps, Ferguson might have been insinuating, we have underestimated the power of friendships in soccer.

*   *   *

Guardiola is very intelligent and understood that there was another way of being a good leader different from that of Cruyff's – one that would not lead to self-destruction: simply being himself, being nice to his players and staff. There are countless examples. When *Banc de Sabadell* signed a marketing agreement with him that included a set of lectures and interviews, he shared the payment with his staff even though he didn't have to. From his first year, Guardiola refused to accept an Audi (which gives a top-of-the-line model to each team member) unless each member of the technical staff got an Audi as well. Once when they were on the road and the goalkeeping coach's father died, Guardiola took the whole squad on a 500 mile detour on the day before the match to attend the funeral. When the team made it to the *Champions League* final in 2009, he learned that the massage therapist for 33 years at Barça, Àngel Mur, now retired, had not been able to obtain tickets. So Àngel Mur was flown with the team as a personal guest of the coach. The message was loud and clear: if Pep includes you in his inner circle, he will never forget about you. A few minutes before the final, as a motivational tactic, Guardiola cleverly played for the team a montage of the movie *Gladiator* mixed with

94

footage of the entire squad – but he specified to the producers of the movie that he did not want any footage of him, because the movie should be about his players. Prior to Guardiola's tenure, the fines imposed on the squad (e.g. for arriving late at a practice session) always accrued towards a common pot that was then used to pay for team meals. Guardiola saw that this custom was an abuse, since the players were benefitting from their own punishment, and instead made a donation to a biomedical foundation.

The bottom line is that *Guardiola has led by setting an example of behavior*, and the whole team has followed since day one. When Guardiola was going through a rough couple of weeks at the beginning of his tenure – inexplicably, in 2008 the team lost the first game and tied the second one, raising concerns about the new coach –, Iniesta showed up at his office and told him "Coach, we just wanted you to know that we are with you until we die" – then he quietly closed the door in Iniesta's usual discreet manner. Guardiola spent four years collecting the fruits of his innovative management approach. On his last day on the job, Barça beat Espanyol 4-0 at the *Camp Nou*. Messi scored all 4 goals. After his fourth goal, Messi ran to the sideline to hug Guardiola, who whispered in his ear "Thank you for everything" while the whole team joined in the embrace around Messi.

Gone are the days when Dutch coaches with poor use of the language would miscommunicate their thoughts, blatantly insult the players, or stand on shaky moral ground. The coaches have now been raised at *La Masia* and are the bearers of the values of respect that were taught to them. Now we know: the team performs at its peak when the behavior of the coach leads the players by example.

Chapter 7: Creating a "Barça ecosystem"

At FC Barcelona, there is a strong belief that the way we play reflects the identity of the club, so the style of play is an unrenounceable postulate of the club. This paradigm is formulated in simple words (not just television images), so that the youth academy, the management, and the first team can all be enlightened and row in harmony (more or less) in the same direction. For the record, this style is *not* referred to by Barça fans as "tiki-taka". This unfortunate phrase was coined by a Spanish TV commentator during the 2006 World Cup Spain-Tunisia game, when he nonchalantly described what was going on in the field: "We are touching the ball tiki-taka tiki-taka", and the expression stuck, mostly among journalists and foreigners. The expression of "tiki-taka" evokes a playful engagement, as if the goal of possession were to humiliate the opponent. I agree with Del Bosque and Guardiola that the term is disrespectful and should be abandoned in favor of more descriptive terms, such as "possession soccer" or (why not?) "Barça style".

One of the strongest appeals of the Barça style is that it is solidly founded on simple rational principles that can be taught to kids. Perhaps the single most important principle that sustains Barça's style of play is that soccer is a sport that is primarily played with your brain – you use your feet, sure, but these are commanded by the brain, and they are only useful if you are able to quickly look around and interpret your surroundings before passing or kicking the ball. For this reason, the youth academy has focused their selection and training process on raising players that are incredibly fast thinkers. The best examples are perhaps Guardiola and Busquets, two defensive midfielders that were similarly slow, rather slim and weak, but capable of passing the ball at first touch because they were always aware of who was free even before they got the ball. (If they had been athletic and fast, they would have been even better players.) Indeed, the most important corollary of accepting that soccer is primarily played with your brain is that soccer, then, is essentially a passing game – a game where each player amplifies his value by creating frequent and clever associations with his teammates. From this, FC Barcelona has decided that all its teams should play "possession soccer", a soccer style that is characterized by giving preference to not losing the ball (over rushing risky balls).

Contrary to what its critics scream, FC Barcelona does not play possession soccer "to make the opponent fall asleep", even though it might give that impression and the opponents' defensive tactics sometimes result in boring games. Barça has deliberately picked possession soccer as the style of choice for all of its teams because, without the ball, the opponent cannot deploy its tactics. Possession soccer is simply designed to obliterate the tactical planning of the opponent. Keeping the ball is an exercise that requires superior technique, but in return it frees the small, frail FC Barcelona players from having to enter into physical contests with the opponents to fight for each ball. Possession is achieved mostly by circulating the ball in a horizontal direction in the midfield; opponents desperately try to snatch the ball away when they see these tactics being played at them, but Wayne Rooney has pointed out that stealing the ball from Barça midfielders is harder than it might seem: "Xavi waits for one of us to get close to make the pass". As soon as Barça loses possession, every member of the team must cooperate to block the other team's possession, starting from their defense ("total pressure"). Admittedly, possession soccer is the style of the weaklings, a departure from macho soccer – you can tell that Barça players almost wish this were a non-contact sport. Yet the speed and grace with which they avoid unnecessary contact while they fool opponents and keep control of the ball is mesmerizing. The only thing that these goals are lacking is background music.

Many people have noticed that there is something in common in the way Xavi, Iniesta, and Messi, and by extension many of the kids that learn to play at the FC Barcelona academy, are able to pass the ball to each other –

it's as if they are able to organize a dance around the opponents and by some secret sorcery the ball always makes it through to the least-marked player. How do they do it? This ability has been likened to the acquisition of language ability: the sooner you acquire it, the more fluent you become at it, and players that do not acquire it at an early age are never fully fluent at it. Hence the term of a "Barça language". The term has acquired notoriety with Messi's huge difference in performance between FC Barcelona (where he thrives) and Argentina's national team (where he rarely scores): his world-class Argentinian teammates (Barça player Mascherano and Real Madrid players Di Maria and Higuaín, among others), the theory goes, do not speak his "Barça language". We are also reminded of the poor performances of Henry and Ibrahimovic – both fine players –; it has been a long, long time since a non-Barça star shone at the Nou Camp at the level of Xavi, Iniesta and Messi. Is this "Barça language", whatever it is, then, a requirement for success at Barça?

I should first point out that I do not like the term "Barça language" because, as a scientist, I cannot *teach* it. Unlike, say, English, math, or music, you will not find anywhere a description of what it takes to learn this mysterious "Barça language", and that's because it does not really exist. It's sort of a metaphor to describe the superiority of Barça players. The always-commonsensical Guardiola has never referred to it. "All we do is pass the ball as fast as we can, really", said coach Pep Guardiola after winning the FIFA *Club World Cup* final against Brazil's Santos, when he was asked to summarize his "secret" method. It was the second time Guardiola's team won the most prestigious club trophy in the planet in the span of three years (2009 and 2011), and they did not win it by a small margin: they won 4-0, with a ball possession upwards of 75%. The game could be likened to a soccer lecture: "Today FC Barcelona has taught us to play soccer", said Santos' forward and super-star Neymar. But what is this "teaching"? The term "Barça language" is misleading because it implies that FC Barcelona players employ some sort of secret code to communicate with each other in order to impose their superiority. Yet all they do is triangulate, dribble, and shoot. (Ok, head and chest too, but those can be included under one of the above conceptual categories depending on how the ball is handled.) If you have ever played soccer, you will know that soccer is reduced to these three fundamental actions. What makes Barça players other-worldly is the *speed* and *precision* with which they triangulate – and, several times a game, the speed at which Messi (and, to some extent, also Iniesta) dribbles; Barça does not even have very powerful shooters by the standards of, say, the *Premier League* or the *Bundesliga*. For this reason I prefer to speak of a "Barça ecosystem" that elevates the ball circulation speed to levels that make it difficult for the opponents to thrive. The ecosystem concept, on the other hand, is simple to teach – even though it takes many years to master.

This ecosystem started from one concept: the pass, refined to its most precise and swift execution. For all ages, the training sessions emphasize heavily the one-touch pass and the quick vision. The laboratory version of the "Barça ecosystem" – and the most emblematic exercise of the FC Barcelona academy – is the rondo ("piggy in the middle"), although all sorts of tactical and positional exercises (3 vs 3, 3 vs 2, etc.) are also common. If you have attended a FC Barcelona training session, you will know that few things are more spectacular in soccer than watching a rondo executed by Barça players, such is the speed and skill with which they make the ball circulate in all directions. The rondo is a great associative weapon to get out of pressure situations, at which Barça players excel. The final against Santos was in essence a repeat of the 2009 game against Real Madrid, which FC Barcelona won by 5-0. In that 5-0, Guardiola used an old tactical trick (the "false center forward") that decimated the Real Madrid defense (and many others to come): Messi would fall back into the midfield to associate with midfielders Xavi and Iniesta. (The fans now fervently call this trio the "Holy Trinity".) The false center forward (in this case, Messi)'s shift always presents the opposing defense with a tough choice: either the central defender goes up to the midfield to follow Messi (leaving a hole in the defense – a gift for the other forwards as well as for Messi, who is faster) or he does not follow him (leaving the midfielders in the midst of a rondo where they have numerical inferiority against the Holy Trinity – a dire prospect too).

"All" it takes is to train a generation of players with the same exercises (e.g. the famous rondos) and playing style consistently during their whole youth – which means that the whole club must comply with this philosophy. Barça recognizes the imperative of playing in a well-defined, time-stable style because all the youth teams are constantly looking at the first team and are trained to play in the same style. We have seen how this concept, pioneered by Jack Reynolds at Ajax, was introduced at FC Barcelona by his pupil, Rinus Michels. But FC Barcelona's play style did not stay constant as the coaches changed before Cruyff's arrival as a coach in 1988, much to the frustration of the youth academy coaches, so there was not a strong connection between the first team and the youth academy prior to 1988. Without a method to guide the formation of the young, only the exceptionally talented made it to the first team in the period between 1972, the year that marks the youth academy's birth, and 1988. That year, when Johan Cruyff signed to coach the first team, represents the biggest inflexion in the history of the club. In the period 1972-1988 (16 years), only two major players (Carrasco and Calderé) had made it to the first team from the youth academy; by comparison, in the 16 years after 1988 (1988-2004), 56 players from the youth academy debuted with the first team (32 in the 8 years that Cruyff was the coach, 1988-1996).

Johan Cruyff had a very clear idea of how to run a soccer club and how to make it the best club in the world. He was cunningly smart, and since day one he obtained from reluctant President Josep Lluís Núñez great powers to restructure a team that was in disarray. In exchange, he promised to deliver attacking football so that people would have fun at the stadium, and to do it while at the same time bringing up Barça kids to the first team. The promise was delivered, and the team played with such Michael Jordan-like speed and precision that we called it the *Dream Team*.

Johan Cruyff transformed the club from the ground. For the first time in many years, the team practiced attacking football and possession, playing at first touch, and mindless running was substituted by clever positioning and anticipation. "One must not suffer while playing soccer; if you are suffering, things cannot turn out well", once said Charlie Rexach, Cruyff's assistant coach during the *Dream Team* era and Cruyff's teammate at Barça during the 1970s. Most important, young midfielders from the youth academy (Milla, Guardiola) who had been taught these concepts for many years were put in charge of the *Dream Team*. The children. Cruyff knew, from his experience in Ajax, that the capital of a great club is not the foreign players, with big egos and adaptation problems. The long-term capital is in the youth academy. Cruyff, who runs a foundation for disabled children, firmly believes in the use of sport as an educational tool that promotes coordination (physical education) and respect (psychological education). "Nothing seems more important than children," he has said. Cruyff knew that if one gets to train children according to the same mold of a style of play (in this case, the style of Total Football), then the method will produce – like a sausage machine – a string of skilled players that have the system embedded in their memory: Van Basten, Bergkamp, Kluivert, ... So in his first week as coach of Barça, Cruyff went to watch the "*juvenils*" play a game under Rexach's command. Just before the break, Cruyff came down to the bench to ask who was the skinny fellow playing as right midfielder. "Guardiola – he is good." In reply, Cruyff ordered him to try in the center midfield. In the second half, Guardiola came out as defensive midfielder (or "pivot", a term borrowed from basketball) and adjusted well to his new demarcation, as anticipated by Cruyff. He lacked maturity, but luckily Cruyff found in the youth team another young player with similar characteristics, Luis Milla, to play as "pivot" in the first team. Guardiola was not called for a league match until 1990 against Cádiz, but from the 1991-1992 season on he was a starter (when Milla, in a conflict with Cruyff for the renewal of his contract, decided to join Real Madrid). The first pigeons were starting to fly.

As it turns out, Cruyff did more than deliver that promise: he created a team that played with a recognizable style. The fans, the players, the youth coaches, even other teams' fans thought it was so irresistibly attractive that a consensus was created in the club to never abandon it. It didn't happen in one day, because it required *educating the fans*. It was a huge undertaking. Not every fan is equally educated; we also have illiterate fans, and violent fans that throw objects at the opponents – these needed the most convincing, because this type of fan is the fan that typically wants to win at all cost. At the beginning you could hear some disapproval in the *Camp Nou* – such as when Bakero would triangulate back in the middle of a counter-attack. But we gradually fell in love with it: now everyone and their grandma at the stadium understands that corner kicks are executed in short (with exceptions!), if needed even back to the goalie, in order to safeguard possession. Possession has become a mystical candy that all Barça fans like to savor slowly. Sure, it does not guarantee the victory in itself (what system does?), but it does decrease the odds of scoring for the other opponent and, statistically, over ninety minutes, it translates into more chances for the owner of the ball. Sometimes (rarely, if your players are this good), it can result in a loss. Possession is a weapon only appropriate for patient hunter-gatherers. That is essentially what the FC Barcelona style has proven: that patience bears juicy fruits – the fans, even the violent, illiterate fans understand that now. And, of course, there is room for improvement. But the club, after educating this huge mass of fans that hold voting rights, does not want to hear of changing the model. "We are not here to argue about the soccer concept. We are here to develop it", has said Andoni Zubizarreta, Barça's Director of Football.

The biggest strength of *La Masia* is, without a doubt, its constancy: the club has been able to rely on its performance for over three decades. This constancy is an asset that has allowed for further development of the original model, refining the educational planning and the long-term sports programs. Without constancy there would not have been solid stuff to build dreams on. It was not built intentionally according to this plan, but now that it is built, the club is sitting on it. *La Masia* has become the structural foundation of FC Barcelona, the uterine organ from which all the club's progeny and also its brain mass are engendered, and now this burgeoning nest cannot be removed from under it without demolishing the whole club.

The postulates of FC Barcelona's style

All the FC Barcelona teams throughout its youth and professional divisions play in the same play style to preserve a unique flow of learning and teaching methodology. This methodology and style, which we have to recognize that inherits many values from the principles of the best Ajax school of the 70s, rests on three simple postulates:

1) **Position**: The function of a player on the field and within the team depends on their position on the field, therefore it is essential that players memorize the functions associated with a given position in the team. All teams shall play with the same formation as the first team, i.e. 4-3-3 (which can be easily mutated into a more attacking 3-4-3). Usually the 4 defenders play in line. The 3 midfielders play in line, and should not hesitate to rotate and exchange positions in order to facilitate triangulations with defenders (during build-up) and with forwards (during circulation, see below). The two outside forwards should play as close to the line as possible to enlarge the field and adapt their positions towards the center when the defenders make attacking runs along the side. This 4-3-3 formation should not be regarded as static, on the contrary: players should continuously shift positions so as to seek numerical superiority in any given sub-section of the pitch and create situations of 2-on-1, 3-on-2, 4-on-3, etc. whereby a small rondo is established to jump from one imaginary line of the field to the next. One of the main pillars of Barça's present supremacy is undoubtedly that Xavi, Iniesta, Messi, Busquets, Thiago, Pedro, etc. learned to help each other find that numerical superiority since a very early age.

2) **Possession**: The number one priority of the team, aside from scoring, is to be in possession of the ball, because as Johan Cruyff put it simply,

"when we have the ball they do not have it". Accepting this simple postulate has five important consequences: **A**) The three midfielders or "brain-players" must excel at distributing the ball fast, passing it with precision, and interpreting the tempo of the game (accelerating or slowing the attacks, as appropriate). No doubt that the present high FC Barcelona moment is due to the coincidence in time of two of the best brain players ever, Xavi and Iniesta, who grew up together and have an almost telepathic coordination on the pitch. Preference is given to short or mid-range, quick passes: "Playing simple and easy is the most beautiful way of playing soccer. Why send a 40-meter pass if 20 meters are enough?", has said Cruyff. Johan Cruyff imprinted into *La Masia* and FC Barcelona a deep sense of what is it that allows a team to take the control of a game: "The barometer in football is the center of the field". **B**) The build-up must go through the midfielders, i.e. the goalkeeper and the defenders must not boot the ball as is done in traditional English football (unless no alternative is possible, or they see a clear chance), since high balls are typically lost 50% of the times. **C**) Also, to improve possession it is crucial to add the goalie to this equation, adding one element of triangulation when the defenders are pressured. The ideal FC Barcelona goalie is a goalie that can pass the ball well with his feet and that can act as the last defender, coming out of his area quickly to intercept a pass if needed. Cruyff always encouraged his goalies to come out of the goal area with a simple reassurance: "The great fear of goalkeepers that they will be beaten by a ball lobbed over their head is not based in reality". **D**) Corner kicks should be kicked short (unless a very good header and a powerful kicker are present in the team, the chances for a successful goal by header from a corner are extremely rare, and taking a long-kick corner only produces a 50% chance of *losing* the ball). **E**) **Circulation soccer**: In the 1980s, the Ajax coaching school developed a theory dubbed "circulation football", inspired in handball tactics, that has proven very fruitful for them and for FC Barcelona. According to this theory, when a forward of team A is surrounded by two defenders of team B, someone else in team A is alone and it should be possible to quickly find him simply by methodical passing. What the circulation football theory states is that the ball circulates faster than the players can run, so if the forward passes it quickly to a teammate, and this one to the next, and so on, the circulation method is likely to find the least-marked man – either the player who is alone or the skilled player who can easily dribble a single opponent. "It's the ball that must run, not the players", said Johan Cruyff to summarize circulation theory. Another advantage of circulation football is that it continuously displaces the defenders out of their position, tiring them out and creating potential distractions in the marks of the forwards who run between the defenders. In general, circulation football should only be played by highly skilled midfielders that do not miss any of their passes and that are in good fitness (since it requires a lot of running to escape the marks). An excellent exercise for the practice of one-touch circulation is the *rondo* ("piggy in the middle", imported from Ajax into *La Masia* by Rinus Michels in 1973), which should be practiced at all ages. Circulation football has also its critics, since it can result in very long, sterile possessions. Even Cruyff has offered a bit of his commonsensical wisdom to speed up the game: "We should not speak of a pass unless it is used to get past an opponent – I'm tired of so much playing back!"

3) **Coordinated pressure**. The goal of this old defensive tactic, dubbed "Total Pressure" in Rinus Michels' writings, is to optimize the physical resources of the team by recovering the ball as close to the enemy goal as possible and avoid the unnecessary running that one sees, for example, in counter-attack tactics (where 60 or 70-meter runs are not uncommon). Total Pressure requires the focus of the whole team such that pressure can be exerted in a coordinated way: the forwards put pressure on the opponent's defenders so that they have to boot the ball in panic or pass it in a hurry, and their midfielders or forwards (who are also being closely marked) do not receive a ball in good enough conditions to control it, so possession is quickly regained. However, for this exercise to be effective, everyone in the team needs to be close to their mark (so it requires good physical fitness). Only teams with superb technique and that can think

extremely fast in small spaces can escape this type of pressure; even Barça players often succumb to it if correctly pressured.

Other smaller-group tactics also deserve consideration, for example the renowned "Third Man", a triangulation tactic consisting of looking for a pass to a teammate via a third teammate that is in a different line, which always confuses the opponent and usually frees the mark of the passer. Another example is the "pass to the busy forward" by the midfielder, a pretense move that the forward understands as a code to further attract players to him and clear space for the midfielder – so he immediately returns the ball to the midfielder.

Logical simplicity

There is something to be said about the fact that the tactical edifice of Total Football is built on a simple set of geometrical notions and the fact that the methodology of Total Football is so amenable to teaching it to kids. This means that kids can get taught the complicated tactics of the first team using very simple geometrical diagrams. This connection does not exist, for example, in other soccer styles, such as the "jogo bonito" (Brazilian soccer) or the English soccer styles that are equally respectable – how do you teach them to kids? Other soccer styles do not have such a well-formulated, simple-to-teach methodology as Total Football, so the FC Barcelona kids have a few years of advantage in tactical training on their particular soccer style with respect to Brazilian or English teams. (I am sure that their first teams, too, employ sophisticated tactics, but note that the question here is whether these sophisticated tactics can be taught *to the kids* in their respective youth teams, if they care to follow the sacred principle that the young should play like the first team.) The first team and the youth team coaches are coordinated so that the "ecosystems" that the kids find during the long period of their formation (which can extend to ten years of their life) are a clonal copy of the ecosystem that they will find in the first team. While it is difficult to measure whether this advantage has a direct effect in improving foot technique, it does contribute to widen the base of players that understands the same "Barça language" from a very early age. This point is crucial: the more players understand the "Barça language", the higher the selective pressure will be for the players to improve and the players that will finally make it to the first team will be better over the years (the ones that have adapted better to the "Barça ecosystem", as measured by the youth training coaches).

Darwin would have marveled at the cross-pollination of soccer concepts between Ajax and FC Barcelona. The ideas of "circulation football " and "total possession football" appear already in a book by Rinus Michels ("Teambuilding"), as well as the idea that the youth should play in the style of the first team. And the "Third Man", to which Xavi and Iniesta refer constantly in their interviews, has been one of the favorite tactical figures in the Ajax classrooms for over a decade. (It is not certain that these ideas are attributable to Michels, neither does he claim their invention, and they are also found in other *ManUals* of the soccer trainer, such as the essential "Coaching Soccer" by Bert van Lingen, used by the Netherlands Football Association.) Nobody has managed to bring the training techniques of football players and coaches to an almost scientific level like the Dutch do. Holland is a very small country with just 16 million people, which puts them at a clear disadvantage compared to, for example, the 200 million Brazilians. Even then, Holland has been for decades a leading power in football – thanks no doubt to its thousands of football schools that have agreed on using the same exact methods.

Why 4-3-3?

All the FC Barcelona teams throughout its youth and professional divisions play using the same tactical formation as the first team, i.e. 4-3-3 or one of its variants. There are three main reasons for this choice:

1) **The three forwards pressure the defenders**: In goal kicks, the pressure prevents their goalie from playing short balls with their defenders, forcing him to take long goal kicks – this represents automatically recovering about 50% of the goal kicks, assuming the ball tends to fall in equally-guarded zones. When the ball is in the possession of their

defenders, the pressure of the three forwards also forces the defenders to take risks and make long passes, which increases the chances of recovery (as long as everyone is alert to the pressure!).

2) **The three midfielders offer three exit triangles** to the four defenders (in 4-3-3) rather than four rectangles (in 4-4-2). While it seems counterintuitive that three triangles is better than four rectangles, we have learned over the years that *a*) from the midfielder's perspective, the two options to pass back (the base of the triangle) are always there, as they would be in 4-4-2; and *b*) from the defender's perspective, it does not help to have an extra midfielder because the rectangles are easy to spot and easy to defend by the opponent.

3) **The three forwards and the three midfielders in attack formation can envelop the opponent while seeing all each other**, which facilitates combinatorial play. Note that this is harder to achieve with a line of attack where four midfielders attack side by side (at least one of them is probably going to lose perspective of one of his teammates' position). If the other team insists on mounting a wall of 6 or 7 defenders, the back defenders should not be shy and make penetrations as soon as they see a hole in their defense (always keeping a count of manpower!). For the midfielders, it is important to see forwards in front of them, and seeing them in motion: the trajectory of the forward in his field of view is what indicates to the midfielder where he has to send the ball. Did I forget to add that it is more fun to play with more forwards?

The secret screening tool
All youth football coaches in the world agree on one thing: for children under 10 to 12 years, the best coach is the street. On the street the soil conditions are not optimal (develops good ball control), game situations and adversaries vary each day (develops flexible tactics), and competition is fierce (develops both physical speed and awareness). Barça youth coaches have observed a geographical pattern: the children who come to Barça with better footwork technique are the Africans; the coaches attribute it to hundreds of hours kicking the ball in fields that are full of

pits. The Western child starts with a handicap, hence the football teaching methods (developed by the Dutch) that optimize performance with a few hours of training per week are now more important than ever. The number of hours that a child plays soccer every days seems to be a most important factor, likely because the neuromuscular system needs to build and reinforce its connections at an early age for optimum performance. Coach Laureano Ruiz invites soccer stars or retired footballers to his soccer camp and asks them how many hours they used to spend practicing; Kubala: "6 to 8 hours"; Cruyff: "5 or 6"; Laudrup: "5 hours"; Messi: "Every hour of the day".

The youth football coaches insist that constant renewal is necessary to select the best at the end of the road, because it is impossible to predict how the youngsters will develop, both physically and psychologically. It is true that Andrés Iniesta was already very good at a young age, but in the videos where we see him dribbling other kids he doesn't do the marvelous *croquettes* (a move that consists of rolling the ball from foot to foot around the opponent) that he does now; he learned them later, in the Barça school, watching Michael Laudrup, as Iniesta himself has explained. Many children, upon reaching puberty, do not develop the positive attitudes and the discipline that one must have to be in First Division, especially when they receive their first contract and enjoy a bit of financial independence (which for them is too much money). Others, when they grow, develop the mother's biotype (with wider hips and slower than their peers). The coaches of youth football at Barça still remember that one of the best children footballers who passed through the house was neither Iniesta nor Xavi or Messi but Antoni Pinilla, but he never reached the elite. Then there are the injuries. Barça's brilliant forward Juan Carlos Rojo, who at 19 was chosen second-best player in the U-20 1979 World Cup in Japan (the same year that Maradona was chosen best player), and who a few months later would have a devastating knee injury that ended his career, comes to mind. And finally, there might be some inherent noise in the various selection processes: a famous example, mentioned previously, is that of the great youth coach Albert Benaiges who failed to pick Sergio Busquets among other young kids (but he was picked at a later occasion, which emphasizes the need for selection and re-selection).

I pointed out in the preface of the book that both Zidane and Maradona had recently said, out of sheer ignorance, that FC Barcelona was "lucky" to have accumulated players like Messi, Xavi and Iniesta in one same team. Of course, any club is fortunate to have Messi by definition, as he is the best player in the world. But the point is one of accumulation of good players, which is what makes a good team. We have seen Messi play poorly with Argentina, a team filled with stars, because he is not surrounded by midfielders that can triangulate fast in the same "Barça language" as him. What Zidane and Maradona were insinuating is that FC Barcelona would not be where it is if Xavi and/or Iniesta had not been first discovered by the scouters and later raised at the youth academy. Any FC Barcelona fan is insulted by this insinuation. First, there are many reasons to believe that they would not have been achieved their full potential if they had been raised in another academy – Messi has not reached Barça's level of performance with Argentina's national team, outside of the FC Barcelona's "ecosystem" where the surrounding players do not play his "FC Barcelona language". Second, Zidane and Maradona forget that the scouts' jobs would have been futile if the families of Messi and Iniesta had not been attracted by the reputation of FC Barcelona's youth academy. It took decades to build that reputation, and they were courted repeatedly by other clubs, but they decided for FC Barcelona for a reason, not by chance. Last but not least, Iniesta and Xavi have been chosen the second and third best FIFA World players of 2010, but if they had not been brought up through the youth academy, another world-class player would have taken their place. How do we know that? Was there an excess of quality players waiting in line, and perhaps left the club because they did not see how they could possibly have a place in the team? Yes! That's exactly what happened and keeps on happening. At the time, Cesc Fàbregas left for Arsenal for the simple reason that he was under the impression that he would not have a place in the team (he was a 15 year old who didn't get good advice at the time). Other excellent young players that have recently left (with a buy-back option) to seek more playing time are Mikel Arteta (Everton, now at Arsenal), Bojan Krkic (Roma), Miquel Àngel Toral (Arsenal), and Oriol Romeu (Chelsea), but they might well come back. The youth academy is always planning the replacements *more than ten years in advance*. There is no luck in that.

Yet this is the same selection system that operates in all the clubs elsewhere in the world: the kids are screened according to their technique and the worst has to leave when a better one arrives. If it were only for this selection system, the club would not have a school that produces creative midfielders by the dozen. What is the magic mechanism that ensures that players of similar profile come out of the school, in this case, Milla, Guardiola, Iván de la Peña, Iniesta, Xavi, Cesc Fàbregas, Arteta, Busquets, Thiago Alcántara, ad infinitum? Any FC Barcelona fan knows this list of these 10 players in this exact order – the order in which Darwin's pigeons were born. Why don't Real Madrid and Manchester United, to cite two elite clubs that compete with FC Barcelona in Spain and in Europe and which also invest heavily in their soccer schools, manage to produce the same continuum of excellence? And, more important, are we on track to achieve a similar string of goalies (in line with Victor Valdés), defenders (following Puyol and the upcoming Marc Bartra) and forwards (following Messi and Pedro)? Everything seems to indicate that this will be the case.

The magical mechanism was implemented by Cruyff, although Michels had already brought the idea from Ajax many years before him, and capitalized on Ruiz's and Tort's talent to build a solid youth base – Cruyff only had to pick the fruits when he arrived in 1988, but the mechanism needed continuity. So he ordered that all the youth teams play in the same style as the first team – just as Reynolds had started doing at Ajax seventy years earlier. This is the magical mechanism that ensures FC Barcelona's supremacy to this day, just as it had ensured Ajax supremacy in the 70s. It is a very simple principle, as most of Cruyff's principles. Children are screened based on their quality, of course, but also – here's the difference with Real Madrid and *ManU*'s youth academies – based on how well they fit the style of play of the first team. The principle is simple but not so easy to apply. It took a genius like Cruyff to realize that the skinny, slow fellow playing on the side named Guardiola should play center, running the show as he would for the rest of his career – not even a great coach like Rexach had seen that. Importantly, FC Barcelona recognizes that winning competitions is not the primary objective of the youth academy. "The most important is to create and train players for the first team," admits José Ramón Alexanco, ex-captain of Cruyff's *Dream Team* and director of the FC Barcelona academy from 2005-2010. The youth teams, he says, operate "with a reference to the model of the first team," which "requires that the youth teams adapt" (when there are changes in the first team). "They are prepared to assimilate the changes and it is good to know how to play in different ways."

The FC Barcelona youth coaches strive to find in each player the best "individual tactics" (his repertoire of moves, touches and plays). The slender type (Guardiola, Busquets) uses the first touch, usually to the benefit of the team. The short guys (Milla, Xavi) have developed quick turns to escape from taller players. And the lucky ones endowed with a fast start (Iniesta, De la Peña) get rid of the opponent simply with a couple of strides. The youth coaches have honed to perfection their ability to identify which individual tactics are best suited for the first team style. The process has been perfected to such an extreme that most stars, when they come to FC Barcelona, have a much harder time adapting to its quick-passing style than the players raised in the youth teams: even fine players like Ibrahimovic and Henry sound like heavy trumpets amidst an orchestra of finely tuned Stradivarius. The analogy with music is relevant: seeing their overall poor performance in the short time that these and other great stars have been in the first team, it's almost as if Total Football needs to be taught from childhood. (The reverse argument is most likely true: Barça-raised players would not do well in teams that do not play possession-style soccer.)

This additional youth-team screening criterion based on a first-team proposed style is what has characterized the great successes of the Ajax and Barça schools. Their success cannot be understood without dissecting the most essential of Cruyff's thought: its utter simplicity. "If we have the ball, they cannot score". "It is better to lose with your vision than with someone else's vision". "Every disadvantage has its advantage". These statements are so irrefutable precisely because they are so overwhelmingly commonsensical. Herein lies Cruyff's great dialectic power: there exist no counter-arguments to his logic. "Everyone plays soccer well if you give him five meters of space". He also has a great sense of humor. "If I wanted you to understand it, I would have explained it better". This simple language must be very appealing to children players. "Football is simple but the hardest thing is to play simple football". It could not be otherwise than what is surely the most powerful team-playing football of all time is based on a concept that needs to be understood even by children: You must play like the grown-ups.

In summary, Cruyff was one of the greatest players that ever existed and the neural center of Total Football, which is still the tactical essence of Barça's style of play. Even the Spanish national team would not have won the 2010 World Cup without the contribution of FC Barcelona's school, both in quantity of players and in its characteristically Barça-like style, inherited from the postulates that Johan Cruyff set in stone in the club more than two decades ago. The modern game is based largely on tactical and educational concepts derived from both Cruyff and his pupils, as the pupils of his pupils are already perched among the stars. Inasmuch we cannot understand modern biology without Darwin's contribution, because he taught us to consider where we come from and how we relate to other species, we cannot understand modern football without Cruyff's contribution, because his style amplified the importance of coordinated team playing. Johan Cruyff is the Charles Darwin of modern football.

From Guardiola to Busquets: the first touch and the positional intelligence

If there is one position in which the FC Barcelona youth academy concentrate the most screening efforts, that is the "4" – the "pivot" or defensive midfielder. It was Johan Cruyff who defined its importance and picked, from all the players that were available in the Barça B, first Milla, then Guardiola: players whose foremost skill was to make quick decisions – they were so aware of their surroundings that they knew who to pass the ball to even before receiving the ball, so they could often pass the ball at first touch. In the present Barça, the "4" is Sergio Busquets (although he wears number 16), another player with an uncharacteristic, rather unathletic complexion. Despite his rickety physique, Busquets is one of the pillars of FC Barcelona, without whom Xavi, Iniesta, and Messi would not be able to triangulate back; without him, the defense would not be able to transition to the forwards with the same clarity and speed. It is no surprise, then, that coaches consider his role so vital that he accumulates more minutes than any other midfielder – including Xavi, Iniesta, or Cesc Fàbregas.

The "4" is a player that is selected for his privileged brain, not his physique. Milla was small, so he developed a clever "quick turn" technique to get rid of markers (very similar to Xavi). Guardiola and Busquets are rather tall, so their only chance was/is to be positionally intelligent and to try to be a few steps away from an opponent. I always say that if you want to learn how to play soccer, watch how Busquets moves during a game. Very few things give me more pleasure than the positional intelligence that he displays in the midfield – sometimes I replay portions of games and I just watch him instead of the ball. Constantly looking over his shoulder, he mostly walks, a few steps at a time; yet he intervenes in practically every Barça play, connecting the different lines with great precision and unsurpassable speed. He always manages to be alone in the center of the field, surely the most important part of the pitch through which all the action goes. How does he do that? Very simple – rather than watching the ball all the time, he is mostly watching the other players so that he can step away from them: a couple of steps usually give him enough space for what he needs to do. By the time he gets the ball (when the opponents look at him and start running toward him), he is already aware of where his teammates are and he deflects the ball at first touch. Busquets, like Guardiola as a player, has learned to play quick because his body is sluggish – both players are the perfect example of Cruyff's insistence that soccer is first and foremost a sport that is played with your brain. "If I were a player I would like to be like Busquets", has said Vicente Del Bosque, Spain's national coach.

Corollary: if you want your team to start playing like FC Barcelona, you better find a "4" that can pass with great accuracy at first touch.

The importance of numbers

As opposed to most other youth academies, at FC Barcelona the kids do not wear names on their jerseys – not even on games. The reason is that the number on their back designates their position on the field, which can change from game to game. (Obviously this designation is arbitrary in that it is communicated to the referee by the coach for every game, so the coach is also free to decide if any given player should shift positions within a game.) This policy is not simply a way to avoid quarrels and jealousies for the most popular numbers, although the policy does have that positive side effect. The policy is actually a key educational precept of the club, one that has been shown to be crucial to the success of the youth academy: this way kids learn from an early age to associate a role with a position on the field ("today you play as 6"), which always has a mirror-reference in the first team (e.g. 6 = Xavi, etc.). At the earliest ages, the *pre-benjamins* (7 yrs), *benjamins* (8-9 yrs) and *alevins* (10-11 yrs) do not play 11 vs 11 – they play "Football-7" (6 plus goalie, small fields and small goals). Barça teams typically play in a 3-2-1 formation, with "1" = goalie, "2" = right defender, "3" = left defender, "4" = pivot or defensive midfielder, "6" = right midfielder, "8" = left midfielder, and "9" or "10" = forward. (Other numbers can also be used for the subs.) At later ages (on

FIFA-sized fields, 11 vs 11), the numbers mirror exactly the positions of the first team.

The making of the *Holy Trinity*

Any book on FC Barcelona's youth academy must have a short section dedicated to Xavi, Iniesta, and Messi, whose emblematic association – known by the fans as the *"Holy Trinity"* – has produced the best soccer in the last few years of FC Barcelona. Messi, Iniesta, and Xavi shared the 2010 *Ballon d'Or* podium as top, second, and third best players, respectively – the first and only time that the podium was taken entirely by players from the same youth academy. This high honor bestowed upon *La Masia* was prominently featured by the international press. Messi would repeat 1st place in 2011 and 2012; Xavi would repeat 3rd place in 2011 and Iniesta would take 3rd place in 2012.

Xavi Hernández (b. 1980) is short and is not fast, but has a precise, soft touch. His master move is the so-called "magic turn", a fast, low-point-of-gravity spin while protecting the ball, such that an opponent that challenges him is forced to go around him taking the longer, slower circumference. He is the chess player of the three. Like a grand master, he can visualize what will happen ahead in complex situations involving a lot of players, and he has a unique gift that only a few chosen have in soccer: a control over the tempo of the game – he knows when it is time to accelerate and when it is time to slow down. Xavi is like a spider that weaves the invisible web through which the rest of the team can stay connected: when he is not there, the team suffers in performance and in style. He has won 7 *Ligas*, 2 *Copas*, 3 *Champions Leagues*, and 2 *FIFA Cup World Cups*, among 21 trophies with Barça; add to those five trophies with *La Roja* (including 2 *EuroCups* and the World Cup) and a long list of individual prizes. He has an encyclopedic knowledge of all existing teams – he knows by heart all the squads, including ones that are as inconsequential to Barça as Japan's national team. The club is already planning a transition for Xavi, now past his prime, as the coach of the first team in the near future. There will be no substitute for Xavi: rather, the team will need to adapt to a slightly different style when a new master chess player (Iniesta, Fàbregas, Sergi Roberto) takes his leadership role.

Four years younger than Xavi, Andrés Iniesta (b. 1984) has quicker feet and always uses the inertia of his opponents to his advantage – he does it effortlessly and with graceful coordination, as if he were engaging the adversary in an elvish dance. His style is a re-mix of Cruyff's and Michael Laudrup's. His start is so swift – if not the world's fastest, for sure the most elegant – that the first defender becomes irrelevant to Iniesta. His family chose to bring him to *La Masia* instead of Real Madrid's youth academy. The coaches of *La Masia* taught him to take advantage of his speed to avoid contact, given his frail physical condition: as a result, he has developed an acute sense of awareness of the opponents that surround him at all times. Like Xavi, he can dampen a high drop ball on his toes in front of a defender ten times out of ten. Xavi has explained that once he went to watch a game of the youth academy with Guardiola when they were both in the first team. "I will be replaced by you, but you will be replaced by that one", Guardiola said pointing to Iniesta. Later, when Guardiola became their coach, he shattered his own omen by conceiving a joint role for *both* of them on the field – which marks the beginning of the genesis of the *Holy Trinity*. Iniesta has won 6 *Ligas*, 2 *Copas*, 3 *Champions Leagues*, and 2 *FIFA Cup World Cups*, among 20 trophies with Barça; he has also won 5 trophies with *La Roja* (including 2 *EuroCup*s and the World Cup) and countless individual prizes. With fewer leadership ambitions than Xavi, he has the biggest heart in the team. His deceased friend and modest player from city rival Espanyol, Dani Jarque, is now better remembered everywhere because Iniesta hand-scribbled the most famous obituary in the history of soccer ("Dani Jarque With Us Forever") and showed it to more than one billion TV viewers in the 2010 World Cup Final as he took off his shirt to celebrate his victory goal: the message was written in his undershirt. "For me, the most moving connotation of the World Cup goal was that I was able to dedicate it to Dani Jarque, so that the goal will be remembered not only by me, but it will also stay for him, forever", Iniesta has said. He is fond of recalling the occasion when, at a bar, an old lady confused him for a waiter (he jokingly admits he looks like one): "Waiter, a Coca-Cola please!" – so he ordered a Coke and served her the Coke just to amuse himself. He has wisely invested large sums of money in an excellent (now profitable) winery in his native small town of Fuentealbilla for the purpose of giving employment to large amounts of people. Even if he were not able to play soccer, Iniesta is the type of person many people would be fortunate to have as their best friend.

Lionel Messi (b. 1987) is the best player that has ever come out of the FC Barcelona youth academy and arguably one of the best soccer stars of all times. Messi was not born in Barcelona or Spain – he was brought there at age 13, in year 2000, from Rosario, Argentina. His precocious soccer talent had earned him fame in Rosario since a very early age, and soon his phenomenal speed and dribbling abilities attracted the attention of the FC Barcelona scouters.

There was one problem, though. Messi was small, down to a medical condition. He had growth-hormone deficiency. This genetic disease is now perfectly curable by injection of recombinant growth hormone, but the treatment is too expensive for a poor working family like the Messis. When the Messis were told that their little boy had this rare disease, they were devastated: since Argentina's medical system does not cover this condition, it would be the end of their son's soccer dreams. One day, a FC Barcelona scouter saw Messi and immediately proposed that the club could take care of the medical treatment if Messi was accepted in the youth academy – would they come to Barcelona for a full evaluation? The whole family flew out. The day he was being evaluated, it became immediately clear to Charly Rexach that this kid would go far, very far, and issued a fast contract on a restaurant napkin in order to convince Messi's father not to return to Argentina.

And the rest is history, a glorious one. Messi entered the youth academy in the same team as Cesc Fàbregas and Gerard Piqué, and won almost every competition on the ascent to the first team. There was one year when Leo's improvement was so stratospheric that he had to be promoted to a higher team *twice* during the same year. Outside the pitch, his explosive stardom remains hidden behind a gentle smile, good-boy manners, and unadorned talk about the game that he loves like a kid. "I don't know what would have become of me without football. I play in the same way as when I was a little boy. I go out there and I have fun, nothing more. If I could, I would play a match every day", he has said. He smiles mischievously when he admits to playing online (under an alias) to the *PlayStation* – always as a Barça player – against kids who would never suspect they are playing against the real Messi. Most journalists have given up trying to interview him: with Messi, they have now learned, the stuff that is worth writing about happens when he has the ball at his feet. He is known to cry like a little boy after a big loss. Guardiola understood perfectly that playing every minute was a vital necessity for Messi and advised Argentinian coach Alejandro Sabella: "You don't need to talk much to him, just protect him and listen to the very things he says. And don't take him off, not even for an ovation". He handles his stardom with patience and sense of humor, as when he recalls with a kind smile the time when he was denied a table at a restaurant on the phone. ("I'm Lionel Messi" – "We realize that, we are full".) According to Guardiola, "Messi does not compete to appear in magazines, attract girls or appear in advertisements, but to win the match, the title, the personal challenge. He competes against the rival, against Cristiano Ronaldo, against Madrid, against Mourinho. Rain or shine, whether they foul him or not, basically he competes against himself to show that he is the best. He is not interested in the rest of it. Our obligation is to give the ball to the boy in the best conditions. The rest is a case of sitting down to watch how it turns out". His technique does not know limits; once, as he was being chased by a player, Messi captured on his left foot a 40-meter-drop ball ... and continued juggling the ball without dropping it while running! The *Camp Nou* erupted in applause and started chanting his name as if he had scored a beautiful goal. He has won 6 *Ligas*, 2 *Copas*, 3 *Champions Leagues*, and 2 *FIFA Club World Cups*, among other trophies. He is the first soccer player to have won 4 *Ballons d'Or*, the only player to have scored 5 goals in a *Champions League* match, and he holds the record of most goals scored in a year (91), European record for most goals in a season (73), Spanish record for most goals in *La Liga* (50), and youngest player (at 25) to reach 200 goals in *La Liga*, among other records. After his recent 200th official game with Barça, Messi had won 174 games (87%), tied 20 (10%), and lost only 6 (3%); during those games he scored 322 goals (an average of 1.61 goals per game – he scored his 300th goal on Feb 16th 2013), in four occasions he scored a "poker", 18 "hat tricks", and in 68 occasions he scored twice. Most of us might not live long enough to see the player that will beat his records. Cesare Prandelli, Italy's national coach, has poetically described the effect that Messi's presence causes on his rivals and on the fans: "Messi can be likened to the mermaids' song, he exerts such a fascination with his game". He's a living legend, the jewel of *La Masia*'s crown.

A quick comparison comes to mind when it comes to soccer geniuses, because the last soccer genius that ever existed, Ronaldinho, also passed through FC Barcelona, but was not raised at FC Barcelona's youth academy. When Ronaldinho was 13, his club, the FC Grêmio, beat another club 23-0. Ronaldinho scored all 23 goals, possibly one of the highest individual scores in the history of soccer (at one goal every less than four minutes). As impressive as the record might be, it also speaks for the differences between the Brazilian youth system and the FC Barcelona youth academy: Messi certainly had many games where he could have scored very large numbers of goals, but the coaches would have never allowed him to stay on the field and score all the goals by himself – they would give other players a turn, or make him play in other positions, etc. What lesson did Ronaldinho's teammates learn the day of the 23-0? Nothing – that he was a superstar, that's all. His coaches could have used his talent to try to activate a larger group of players, motivate them to grow faster as players alongside him – but they wasted the opportunity. Brazilian soccer is more fundamentally a *jogo bonito* than it is a team sport.

On the positive side, there is the example of Pedro, a player who is clearly neither as technically gifted nor as amazingly fast as Messi but who can understand the "Barça language" just as well as Messi. Arrigo Sacchi, the great soccer coach of AC Milan in the 1980s, once said of Pedro that "he would not be able to play in most great teams", but he failed to recognize that this hardly matters to the FC Barcelona coaches: Pedro reads the moves of the midfielders and fellow forwards with lightning speed and runs to open spaces with great tactical clarity, offering his trajectory to his teammates as a stellar signature for a future, silent pass. He might not be the forward over whom the defenders lose sleep, but once he is on the field, he knows how to wreak havoc using his runs to make the defenders go crazy. All these tactical moves Pedro learned them at the youth academy.

Barça coaches now know that they can coach kids to imitate Busquets and Xavi, but they cannot coach kids to play like Messi – Messi is physiologically and genetically unique. He does the things he does simply because his neuromuscular system works much faster than the rest of most players: he has a natural advantage. Does this mean that Barça was "lucky" to find him? Any team that has Messi is fortunate by definition, but simplifying the whole Messi scouting operation and training (as explained above) as a matter of "luck" would be unfair to the FC Barcelona youth program who worked hard to attract and polish this gem. As with the Iniestas, the Messis knew very well that they were not taking their boy to just another club. They didn't take Lionel to Real Madrid, or Manchester United, because in the year 2000 these other youth academies had nothing to offer to him. It was not luck that Messi and Iniesta came to Barça: rather, it must be understood that Barça had become already a worldwide-reaching attractive magnet for young talent by year 1996, when Iniesta landed at *La Masia*. Their parents *chose La Masia* knowing that they were leaving their boys in the hands of the best youth academy in the world.

Those that say that FC Barcelona is "lucky" to have Xavi, Messi and Iniesta in the same team (and why not add Busquets, Cesc Fàbregas,

Thiago Alcántara, and the long list of kids that are following their path?), should instead wonder why their team failed to attract Messi, Iniesta, and the great line of talented youth players that keep on knocking at the door of *La Masia* from all the corners of the world (including Ben Lederman from the U.S.A.!). The only "luck" that FC Barcelona has is that, despite the methodological evidence of its high success, most other clubs do not want to run a similar model of youth academy. We certainly find none in the *Major League Soccer*, as I will analyze later. Go figure.

Tactical vulnerability

It should be stressed that, with the full support of the fans, Barça has sometimes played a dear price for this style of play that has such an obvious, automatic implementation with kids: FC Barcelona's tactics are predictable, even transparent – every team knows how Barça will play. Unlike FC Barcelona, its opponents can afford to play with flexible formations and tactics because their first teams are not being used as a teaching tool for hundreds of kids. The opponents come out to the pitch ready to surprise Barça with rigid defenses, creative counter-attacks, choking pressures, rotations, a pitch in poor conditions (tall or dry grass), or combinations thereof, and try to get as much juice as they can out of every ball into the box: that's where rebounds make it into the net or an involuntary handball might be called by the referee. Unlike in most sports, the best team not always wins because there is a lot of noise in soccer. (Noise could be cancelled with the use of technology, such as taking advantage of the more than a dozen viewpoints offered by the TV cameras, instant replays, 3D projection algorithms to reveal offsides positions, wearable chips, and balls containing sensors; soccer will stay noisy until the day we all play on artificial turfs with electronic referees, a money-saving scenario for the clubs that FIFA, a body known for its corruption scandals, has refused to embrace on the basis that controversy generates media attention and, thus, revenue for FIFA.)

My personal opinion is that the Cruyff heritage of playing with open-book tactics is a bit *too* vulnerable to counter-tactics. So far, Barça's tactics have been implemented with a Cruyffian, quasi-religious rigidity, and to improve in tactical flexibility it would not hurt to add to the squad a center forward with the "Van Basten profile" – such as Colombian Radamel Falcao or Polish Robert Lewandowski, both with feet as quick as Iniesta's but with a header as strong as Puyol's. A team should never embrace the postulates of possession soccer style like the dogmas of a religion – there is nothing in these postulates that prohibits the use of a tall center forward, the sending of high balls into the box to save the day, or playing counter-attack when you are winning (specially if the opponent has a lethal counter-attack). Rather, the postulates should be embraced like scientific postulates: those that allow to build an evolving system upon them. I'm sure that, in time, Barça's style will evolve and settle to a new, optimum system with less vulnerabilities. (Some say that Barça has tried to bring stars with "Falcao profile", such as Ibrahimovic, but the attempts have failed because Messi has vetoed every player that plays in the center-forward lane; even Villa or Alexis have to play on the side, where they are less efficient. If it is true that Messi has such powers in the club, then it shows what a big mistake it was to let Messi go through *La Masia* without finishing high school.)

Barça has accepted, almost arrogantly, that this tactical transparency is its Achilles' heel and has decided to live with it with a sense of inevitability. "We don't know how to play in any other way and sometimes we pay a high price for it", Messi has said. The whole club is now scripted on a model that extracts talent continuously from a nest, but the nest needs to be exposed to the sun and the elements in order to be fertile. The model will not be changed. But FC Barcelona might not fully realize that it actually has a second Achilles' heel. Barça kids are trained to focus on using their brains to amplify their technique and thus the resulting "Barça style" is a very cerebral soccer (comparatively speaking). As the brain has its funny ways, mental strength can become psychological illness in a matter of days if, for example, the team goes through a period of depression. We have seen this already when coach Tito Vilanova had to be treated for cancer in a New York hospital and the team suffered a couple of bad losses in 2013 – suddenly they seemed like they had lost all their speed, their energy, their old karma, and some Madrid journalists wishfully spoke of the "end of a cycle". Nonsense – how could a group of players have all of a sudden forgotten how to play soccer? They were simply depressed, and they needed psychological help. "The coach is very important in a million details. We feel Tito's absence", Messi surmised. (The week after, with extra motivation, they beat AC Milan 4-0 in a *Champions League* game, one of the best performances that the fans remember about this team; the starting roster was the same exact one that beat *ManU* 3-1 in the *Champions League* final in 2011, except for Jordi Alba instead of Abidal.) Busquets explained it vividly: "When we don't play at 100 percent, anyone can beat us".

The 2013 crisis: forecasting the death of possession soccer?

Towards the end of the 2013 season, however, Barça presented obvious signs of weakness, excessive "Messi-dependence" in its attacks, and was eliminated from the *Champions League* by Bayern Munich by a sum total of 7-0 in two semifinals. Non-Barça fans all over the world, in particular many Germans and Real Madrid fans, understandably celebrated and rushed to the conclusion that FC Barcelona's "cycle" was over. Although Messi was injured in both games, two of the goals in the first game were illegal, and a goal in the second game was an own goal, Bayern was clearly superior. So it is time for some introspection.

Before starting the critique of FC Barcelona's state of affairs I'm always reminded of Guardiola's cautionary words right after the team had won one of its titles: "There will come a time when we will be criticized too. It's easy to defend a winning style – what is hard is to defend it when you are not winning". Barça didn't just loose 7-0 against Bayern suddenly. In the 2013 season, the team only won one of its 12 matches against top rivals (Real Madrid or *Champions League* teams), most of them with Messi in his best form. Most analyses blamed the defense because Barça received many goals in those games, but few seemed to remember that *the whole team*, under Guardiola, defended like clockwork; the defense was rarely even bothered. It was not until after a new coach had arrived that Xavi spoke up: "Total pressure is a set of automatisms that degrade with time and that unfortunately, in Tito's absence, we were not able to train its tactics very well". (The revelation must have sounded like an accusation of incompetence in the ears of Jordi Roura, Tito Vilanova's substitute.)

I fear the 2013 crisis might not have been due to a simple relaxation in the pressure – although it will certainly help revving it up. The team had other problems, such as the "Messi-dependence", that could be the symptom of a larger wound. Again, it's helpful to consider the team as an ecosystem of players interacting with each other; the ecosystem was thriving under Guardiola but it got some sort of mysterious weakness under Tito Vilanova. Journalist Ramon Besa has made a very poignant analysis of the delicate balance of possession soccer: "That Barça's football becomes venerable or abhorrent is a matter of one meter and one second". But who was to blame? Who was the most irreplaceable piece in the midfield, the player through whom every ball was distributed, who would slow down the whole machine significantly if he became just a tiny bit slower?

The answer comes as clear in my mind as it is heavy on my heart: Xavi. Our beloved Xavi (who turned 33 in January 2013), the brain and chief architect of this Barça, now has aged past the reasonable prime time for his position and has lost his youth speed that allowed him to execute his "magic turn". Xavi is the first to feel this loss of speed, so he retreats to less consequential positions away from the goal area – and the opponents let him play there for as long as he wants because in that position, even conserving his youth touch, he is not a threat. Most opponents now wait for Barça in two parallel formations of 5 men each, the first line about 15-20 meters from the midfield and the second one on the box; as soon as someone (e.g. Messi) dares to dribble in between, both lines close on the player like a mechanical grip, leaving no space for shooting or for passing. Xavi's limitations are most obvious against opponents with fit, young midfielders that can put intense pressure on him and don't give him time to use his best weapon: his brain. Let's recall that Xavi truly blossomed under Rijkaard, who told him to step up ten more meters so he could hurt the rivals. Thus we see that the "Messi-dependence" is in fact the spectral image of the "Xavi-dependence": as the circulation through Xavi has gradually slowed down or become inconsequential, the team has unconsciously opted for short-circuiting the options to Messi, who as his teammates well know can take on a surreal number of opponents. The Messi-dependence did not arise from coaches' instructions to "play more through Messi" but from the combination of all the players' instincts to bypass a rusty cogwheel, a diseased element in their ecosystem. In fact, the only reason the 2013 performance dip is a crisis is because the player to be replaced is as monumental as Xavi, and it will take a while to re-adapt all the cogs and wheels. It is not "Xavi's fault" – if that's all you got from this paragraph, you did not understand my point. My point is that the team is suffering from its own dependence on Xavi's greatness, which is decaying.

In June 2013, national coach Del Bosque nonchalantly mentioned in an interview that Xavi had called him to let him know that he would not participate in the 2014 World Cup, but that Del Bosque had changed his mind. ("Are you depressed or what? How can you miss a World Cup in Brazil?" were Del Bosque's words.) The press didn't follow up, but to me those words sounded as if Xavi had pressed the red alarm button for help. We can't ask soccer players to drop their job and favorite entertainment from one day to another. Xavi was not depressed, he was just very aware of his physical abilities coming to an end and he was letting the world know. We cannot blame him if the coaches are not listening. The truth is that the coaches prefer to adapt their style of play than to lose a player like Xavi. (In another occasion, Del Bosque's assistant Toni Grande leaked to the press that Xavi pays attention to every little detail, like the height of the grass, and even offers unwanted tactical advice over where he should play when he does not like the role he is assigned; I'm sure the corrections make sense, as humiliating as it might be for the coaches: at the time of Grande's leak, the national team had been playing with mostly Barça players, two Real Madrid defenders and Valencia forward Soldado.) A few days later, Spain lost the final of the Confederations Cup 3-0 against Brazil in Maracaná Stadium; Xavi lost the ball several times, specially when he penetrated into the danger zone close to the goal area. While Xavi's technique will remain intact for many years and his brain will not be slowing down any time soon, his body will. I had a chance to debate this point with Pep Guardiola when I met with him in Munich in July 2013. To my surprise, he thought that Xavi could still last "if the coaches reserve him for the big games", as if Xavi's problem were a question of endurance. Xavi is not losing more balls in the second halves of games, where he might be tired: this is a question of *speed*. Biology does not forgive: his muscle fibers are now slower than a few years ago and they will continue to become slower, even though he still has plenty of magic in his boots. If he is not fit to play for the national team, why would he be for Barça?

To add injury to insult, the only person that was capable of finding the solution to this dilemma, Tito Vilanova, became ill with throat cancer and decided to seek treatment in New York. Replacing Xavi is not a one-day operation – it's a whole process that needs to be planned carefully and executed gradually. Nobody can blame Tito Vilanova for not prioritizing Xavi's replacement at a time when he was fighting for his life, specially seeing how spectacularly the team performed in auto-pilot in *La Liga* for a few months (they broke a *La Liga* first-round point record). What is more debatable is whether the club should put the future of the team at risk just to offer the noble image of a club that has higher goals than winning. (Disclaimer: I'm a big fan of Tito, but I personally think that as soon as it was announced that he had cancer, a replacement coach should have been hired until Tito was able to return.) In any case, the club made the decision to sacrifice a few titles to keep Tito (it could have been worse – they won *La Liga* with 100 points, which is impressive!), and decided to move on.

In July 2013, Tito told Rosell in a dramatic midnight meeting at the *Camp Nou* offices that his tumor had grown back. The next day it was announced that Tito had to resign from his coaching job to seek treatment. Rosell's plan of letting a cancer-stricken coach manage the team had been medically unreasonable, but to his credit, Rosell acted quickly to mend his errors and grasped the chance to steer the club with his leadership. Fortunately for FC Barcelona, Rosell (who has an excellent knowledge of the Latin American soccer sphere from his days at Nike) was able to identify literally overnight a new coach that was unknown to the fans but is in excellent sync with the club's philosophy and who was available (the Argentinian Gerardo "Tata" Martino). He is also in good sync with many of the players, starting with Messi who is delighted because Martino was the coach of Newell's Old Boys, where Messi started as a boy. Although Martino is an admirer of Guardiola's system (which he has implemented in all his teams) and of *La Masia* (he is fond of using the youth academies of the clubs where he has been employed), he arrives at a demanding club where most fans thought that we would never need to hire outside coaches. To be from outside the club will be Martino's challenge (he will need to get acquainted with the system) and advantage (he will be able to think outside of the box). As Martino demands high physical intensity in all his teams, Xavi's age will soon become self-evident. Martino should be able to heal this wound with excellent material from the youth academy (Cesc, Sergi Roberto, Sergi Samper, etc.), so I'm not too worried in the long term about this problem. Rather than lengthening the life of a decaying Xavi, Martino should start planning Xavi's retirement (he would be an excellent coach assistant) and replace his lighthouse role in the famous Busquets-Xavi-Iniesta triangle with Cesc Fàbregas or another player as soon as possible because the replacement will require critical readjustments. Fàbregas, a footballer that is distinguished by his eloquence and depth of analysis, has warned: "Whenever someone asks me about Xavi, I always say the same thing: the same way that there will never be another Leo [Messi], there will never be another Xavi. We can keep scouting in the youth academies, but when Xavi retires, FC Barcelona will play a different game".

The bad cocktail of Xavi's age and Tito's illness was not the only cause of the 2013 crisis. The team's training schedule was relaxed under Tito Vilanova; as a result, physical endurance – a crucial component of total pressure – suffered. The advanced age (30) of Dani Alves, a crucial defender in the Messi axis of attack, might have been a factor, too: he was the player *in the whole team* who lost most balls during the season – a liability in a defender who joins the attack as often as he pleases and is occasionally yelled at by his teammates for not returning to his position. The fact that most of the players have won the *Liga* five times and the *Champions League* twice, some even three times already, might have toned down their level of motivation and opened leaks in the previous ultra-coordinated system of total pressure and possession soccer established by Guardiola. Perhaps paternity duties were a factor (Cesc, Pedro, Piqué, Messi, and Valdés all had children within one year): no *Champions League* trophy is more important than a child. Three crucial defenders (Puyol, Mascherano and Abidal) were out injured for most of the season. And for the two most important games of the year (the *Champions League* semifinals against Bayern Munich), Messi was injured.

Perhaps, for the fans, the saddest consequence of leaving the boat without a captain is that it did not all end well – despite the fact that the team did win the league with 100 points, an all-time record. An irreparable mistake was made, an unforgivable oversight that cost FC Barcelona one of the jewels of the crown of *La Masia*: Thiago Alcántara, who in the eyes of many fans was destined to be Xavi's heir, not in style but in his ability to command the Barça centerfield. In 2011, Thiago Alcántara's agent (who happens to be Pere Guardiola, Pep's brother), to protect the player, insisted on including an unprecedented clause: Thiago's buyout clause of €90 M would default to €18 M if the player didn't play at least 30 min in 60% of the games. The president didn't like the clause and should have never accepted it, but he was reassured that he would play those minutes. The technical staff – overwhelmed by Tito's illness – didn't follow up. In 2013, Thiago played exactly 60% of the games but the coaches failed to compute that he had not played the required amount in 14 of his 36 games. (To complicate the calculation, he had been injured for a total of 18 games; he played in 50% of the games when he was fit – but that was not enough for him.) Two weeks after Pep Guardiola started coaching Bayern Munich, Thiago Alcántara signed for the Bavarian club for €25 M. It is now clear that the club underestimated this kid's ambitions. In June 2011, Thiago had said: "I would lie if I said that my dream is to succeed at Barça. My dream is to succeed in football. I want to be a player that people remember forever." While Thiago has never reached the level of "chess-player" anticipation that characterizes Xavi's game, Thiago has qualities that Xavi never had: enough speed to dribble past opponents, strong shot, a good free-kick – much superior to that of Xavi, who kept on taking the shots based on seniority –, and the ability to whip a surprise pass with the outside of his foot "à la Ivan de la Peña". Pep Guardiola has been criticized for taking advantage of insider's information (through his brother), and Pere Guardiola for devising a clause that, in the end, has damaged the interests of the club, but these criticisms forget that Pere Guardiola only did his job – and he did it very well –: to guard the best interests of his client. The blame is clearly on the president and the sports director (Zubizarreta) who put the whole club in jeopardy during Tito's illness. More efforts could have been made to keep Thiago and reassure him that he was essential; in the absence of these efforts, it might not have been very productive to keep Thiago unhappy at FC Barcelona, and Pep Guardiola will continue to mentor him. Yet, giving away one of the brightest young gems of the European continent for €25 M to one of your top *Champions League* rivals seems to me not just an oversight but utter incompetence.

Most of the analysis in this 2013 crisis has been limited to looking at FC Barcelona's shortcomings (weak defense, Tito's cancer, Messi's injury, etc.), as if the rivals were not part of it. I disagree completely – Barça's wounds can and will be patched away, but in my opinion a bigger menace is coming from outside of the club. If we look at the big teams that have beaten Barça of late or have done well in the advanced stages of the *Champions League* (Real Madrid, Bayern, Milan, Dortmund, and

ManU), they all have one thing in common: they are all very comfortable giving the possession away to Barça and deploying counter-attacks. They simply mount an impenetrable wall of ten defenders. Referring to these last critical twenty meters, Tata Martino has recognized that lately Barça "struggles to find passes" – but of course: there is no physical space for a pass. Against Barça's supreme Cruyffian postulate that "while we have the ball, they don't have it", which has guided the implementation of possession soccer at all levels in the club, Borussia Dortmund's coach Jürgen Klopp brilliantly argues that he prefers not to have the ball so that his players can put very intense pressure on the good players and the ball ends up being handled only by the worse players, causing these weak players to make mistakes and creating an opportunity for a deadly counter-attack with Borussia's fast, tall runners. Simeone coaches his pupils at Atlético de Madrid with the same philosophy and impressive results. There is very little positional defensive tactics one can build against speed and height: in a well-directed counterattack or a well-executed corner kick, the witty positional skills of small FC Barcelona players – those same skills that became the wonder of the world in the last five years – seem utterly useless. Dortmund targeted Pepe and Coentrao and, the next day, Bayern followed the same tactic giving space to young, inexperienced defender Bartra. It's as if, by a cruel Darwinist process, Barça's style (and, in general, possession soccer) had engendered its own antibodies.

Unfortunately for FC Barcelona, this mutation happened right at a moment when Tito Vilanova fell sick with cancer and when Xavi and Puyol are aging, so the team as a whole is less able to react accordingly. A crisis is coming if the Barça coaches insist on explaining the performance dip simply as a consequence of being overloaded with games and plagued with injuries – a circumstance that happens every year around these dates, so if anything it is the result of poor planning. The crisis is clearly deeper and will require some serious brainstorming by the best minds at *La Masia* (or perhaps an outsider like Martino), who would need to get involved in formulating more flexible tactics to surprise the rivals.

But how? The first experiments by Tata Martino in the 2013-2014 season have raised murmurs of disapproval at the *Camp Nou* because the style of play at times has degenerated into mindless bootings by defenders Mascherano and Piqué. The team produced the highest average goal differential in history in the first six games, but the new long-passing tactics resulted in more imprecise passes and a bypassing of the midfield, the brainpower of the FC Barcelona style. "It's good to have other options", have said Messi and most other players without sounding too convinced. Piqué voiced a similar opinion: "With Pep and then Tito, we occasionally tended to exaggerate our possession style of play to the point where we were slaves of our own philosophy. Tata has the same football philosophy but also has other alternatives and that is a very positive thing in my opinion. You have to keep improving and developing or you will become predictable". Piqué hit the right point: there is nothing wrong with possession soccer; they just need to find a way to make its tactical execution *unpredictable* to the opponent beyond using Messi (who is always unpredictable). Every FC Barcelona fan knows that the solution, however, is not indiscriminate booting.

The solution will come, as always, not from the coaches but from the players. Total Football was invented primarily by the brain and boots of Johan Cruyff and his Ajax teammates, not by Rinus Michels: if Rinus Michels had not existed, Total Football would have existed all the same, but if Johan Cruyff had not existed, soccer would not be the same today. Cruyff would remind us that the possession soccer style is not a mere aesthetical whim to please the spectators – as the Brazilian *jogo bonito* is –: the style is the framework of thought that dictates why you do things the way you do them. Long-ball play ends up favoring the strong, tall players that will intercept the high balls whereas short, fast passes on the ground favor Barça's quick-footed small midfielders. Mascherano might need to be reminded that this is why *La Masia* teaches the kids to play on the ground, selecting the kids that are best at doing it. Argentinian coach César Luis Menotti (who led Argentina to win the World Cup in 1978 and coached Barça in 1983-1984), a footballer that is distinguished by his eloquence, recently was asked about Barça's predictability conundrum: "I hate it when people debate about predictability. As if talent were predictable. I think it's foolish to try to alter a work of art. One must not invent what has already been invented. For me, for example, Paco de Lucía is predictable, and because he is predictable I go to his recitals. We are talking about innovation and creativity." As Xavi's flame dies off, this innovation will come from the minds of creative midfielders like Cesc or Sergi Roberto – choreographed by Iniesta and Busquets –; also, strong center forwards such as Dongou can give Barça header options at corner-kicks or when the opponents mount a double-wall defense ("the bus"). What is clear is that the fan is not going to be convinced with simple words – Guardiola's team played better, and Tata Martino agrees: "There are a lot of things to improve". He has also reassured the fans that he will not change the system and he is here to recover what this team did best. "I don't want a Barça modeled by Tata Martino, I was already in love with Barça's concepts before coming, so I don't have to innovate", he has said. "What happened [during the 2013 crisis] is that some of the concepts were forgotten or were not implemented anymore." After all, soccer is not a terribly complex science. Since it all boils down to the players, I'm confident that *La Masia* will soon help produce another team that will marvel the world again.

I agree with Tito Vilanova – an eminently reasonable person – that the quality of the team offers a lot of room for hope, and I'm not alone in believing that. Just five days after the Bayern fiasco, in May 2013, I attended the tryouts for a local Seattle soccer club, and I saw that the "Barça fever", more than 5,000 miles away from Barcelona, is still running high. I was able to obtain accurate statistics from the club's photographic cards of each player: out of a sample of 121 nine-year-old boys, 15 kids (12%) wore Seattle Sounders shirts, 14 kids (11%) wore Barça shirts (11 of whom were "Messi"), 5 kids (4%) wore *ManU* shirts, and 3 kids (2.5%) wore Real Madrid shirts. Despite the "7-0", none of these young Barça fans want to see a "change of cycle".

A bright future

We have been talking about replacing Xavi with Iniesta or Cesc in the face of the "2013 crisis". For those of us who have followed the youth academy closely, we have no reason to worry that this crisis could end up in a "change of cycle" because so many excellent players are coming up through the youth teams. I'm certain that FC Barcelona will still be at the top of *La Liga* and the *Champions League* for many years to come. What follows is a list of the best players (by order of age) that, in all likelihood, you will soon see arriving to the first team, along with their characteristics. This is not secret information or information that the club tries to hide in any way, on the contrary. The list was obtained by compiling published sources from the two most authoritative journalists on *La Masia* (Martí Perarnau from newspaper *Sport* and Oriol Domènech from *Mundo Deportivo*, see References) and by consulting with coaches at the youth academy (see Acknowledgments). Some of these players have already played with the first team; anybody can evaluate any of these players (even the youngest ones) by watching them on YouTube.

Martín Montoya (born 1991)
Position: Right defender. *Height*: 175 cm.
Characteristics: Very fast and strong, has played already for Barça B for many years and has recently been promoted to the first team. He is due to replace Alves soon.

Javier Espinosa (born 1992)
Position: Attacking midfielder. *Height*: 174 cm.
Characteristics: The first time you watch Javier Espinosa play you wish there were a soccer prize for elegance just so you could recognize the beauty of his game. Many fans have placed a lot of hopes in this graceful player whose style reminds Iniesta and Cruyff. He carries the ball with exquisite control and has a unique ability to see that deadly "last pass" to the unmarked man. Unfortunately for him, elegance is a rather superfluous attribute in soccer and he will have to improve in his aggressivity with and without the ball before he reaches the *Camp Nou*.

Sergi Roberto (born 1992)

Position: Center midfielder. *Height*: 177 cm.

Characteristics: The closest to Xavi that has produced *La Masia* in a long time, but with longer legs and with a powerful physique. He is now starting to get minutes with the first team. His positional skills are already impeccable. If he starts making assists like Xavi did in his youth, he will be his natural replacement in the long term.

Rafa Alcántara "Rafinha" (born 1993)

Position: Midfielder and 'false 9'. *Height*: 175 cm.

Characteristics: Thiago Alcántara's younger brother, better known as "Rafinha", he entered *La Masia* at 13 years old. When everyone talked about Thiago, his dad, the Brazilian midfielder Mazinho who won the 1994 World Cup, warned: "Rafa is better than Thiago, he works harder and defends better". He has exquisite technique, great speed and punch. With double nationality until 18 years old, he had the option like his brother to play either for Spain or for Brazil; Thiago chose Spain and Rafinha chose Brazil.

Sergio Ayala (born 1993)

Position: Central defender. *Height*: 182 cm.

Characteristics: This powerful and promising central defender has a great skill for dividing the rival defenses when he pushes up, imitating his idols Gerard Piqué and Paolo Maldini. Left-footed, he has excellent positioning skills and rarely makes mistakes. He has to improve in aggressivity and in his long-passing skills. He is a good student (he studies Science of Sport and Physical Activity).

David Babunski (born 1994)

Position: Midfielder. *Height*: 177 cm.

Characteristics: David Babunski was born in Skopje, Macedonia. His father is a Macedonian ex-footballer. The FC Barcelona scouters called him after he played a great Spanish Championship with the Catalonia U-12 team. He is an intelligent and elegant midfielder, with a deadly finishing pass, and on the field he cooperates very well with midfielder Sergi Samper.

David Babunski is already being considered for the future Macedonian National team. He has a younger brother, Dorian Babunski, who plays for the Real Madrid youth academy.

Pol Calvet (born 1994)
Position: Right/Left midfielder. *Height*: 180 cm.
Characteristics: Calvet, together with Gerard Deulofeu, is one of the most talented players of the "1994 generation" and is tactically flawless. He usually plays on the wing but sometimes he has played as center-mid and forward as well, showing that he can be a versatile player. To reach a professional level, he needs to improve his shooting skills, increase his level of intensity, and be more aggressive without the ball. He studies Business Administration and Management at the prestigious *Institut Químic de Sarrià*.

Gerard Deulofeu (born 1994)
Position: Forward. *Height*: 180 cm.
Characteristics: Deulofeu is considered by many to be the present jewel of the youth academy. At one point his fame grew so fast that the coaches feared the boy had been spoiled forever. He is certainly a very talented, incredibly fast forward; his unpredictable stops and starts make his penetrations deadly. "He only had eyes for Ronaldinho" [when he was 9 years old], says his father, yet his style of play is more reminiscent of Cristiano Ronaldo – very direct. In my opinion, his passing skills and associative intelligence need to improve a notch to become an elite Barça player.

Joseph Fabrice Ondoa (born 1995)
Position: Goalkeeper. *Height*: still developing.
Characteristics: Since Víctor Valdés announced (rather capriciously, the fans felt) that he would not renew his contract with FC Barcelona, all the eyes to substitute him for the 2014-2015 season turned to Cameroonian goalie Ondoa, who will be 20 years old in 2015. He came to Barça through the *Samuel Eto'o Foundation* (as did Jean Marie Dongou and Frank

Bagnack, who play together in the same team) and has been called to the Cameroon National Team already.

Frank Bagnack (born 1995)
Position: Central defender. *Height*: still developing.
Characteristics: Bagnack (together with, of course, Ondoa) is the only defender to have come to Barça through the *Samuel Eto'o Foundation*; the rest are talented center-midfielders (Enguene, Kaptoum), wingers (Ebwelle, Moussima) or center-forwards (Dongou, Alexis). Although he tends to use excessive force that he will have to learn to control, he carries the ball with his head high, he has the technique of a midfielder or a forward, and he chooses the best pass with great composure. Tata Martino has already given him some minutes in the 2013-2014 season.

Àlex Grimaldo (born 1995)
Position: Left defender. *Height*: still developing.
Characteristics: Àlex Grimaldo was only 15 years, 10 months and 20 days old when he debuted with FC Barcelona. Only two other players have debuted at a younger age: Paulino Alcántara (15 years, 4 months and 18 days) and Haruna Babangida (15 years, 9 months and 11 days). Even Leo Messi and Bojan Krkic, the earliest debutantes in recent history, started later than Àlex Grimaldo. He is called to be the heir of Jordi Alba. His best qualities are his dribble and his bullet-speed, which he uses to reach the end line and center the ball with precision, even though he still has some shortcomings in defense that he compensates with his quickness. The *Camp Nou* is eagerly waiting for him.

Sergi Samper (born 1995)
Position: Center midfielder. *Height*: still developing.
Characteristics: A lot of hopes have been placed on this kid, for various reasons. He is the center-mid of one of the best generations produced of late by the youth academy (the "1995 generation"), and as we know *La Masia* pays a special attention to the center-mids because they will be called one day to take on the key roles of Guardiola, Xavi, or Iniesta. In addition, if Sergi Samper makes it to the first team – and everything

indicates that he will very soon –, he will be the first FC Barcelona player ever to have never won any other shirt other than Barça's: he started at the *FCBEscola* as a child. He has been nicknamed "the Pirlo of the youth academy". He has an exquisite touch, great composure, good positioning and a privileged vision for the game, although he obviously still needs to mature physically. He was wise to reject a handsome offer from Arsenal that would have snatched him away from Barça for many years like Cesc Fàbregas.

Jean Marie Dongou (born 1995)

Position: Center forward. *Height*: still developing.
Characteristics: This shy Cameroonian that speaks Catalan and is so infatuated with soccer that he spends his nights at *La Masia* watching soccer games is the stellar pupil of the *Eto'o Foundation*. He made the debut with the first team at 15 years of age. He might well be the "strong 9" that Barça has been seeking for a while to expand the team's repertoire of game strategies: he has an explosive physique that allows him to win the ball in tight spaces, good technique, better definition, and tactical intelligence.

Xavier Quintillà ("Quinti") (born 1996)

Position: Left or Central defender. *Height*: still developing.
Characteristics: Quinti is a very technical and strategic left-footed defender and also a charming group leader whose destiny is the *Camp Nou*, if it were not for his short height (a big handicap in his position). He is technically very good, is endowed with the ability to play at first touch, and his intelligence allows him to anticipate the movements of the opponents. His best asset is to be multi-skilled, although he needs to improve his ball circulation speed when he plays as organizer, be more aggressive when he plays as central defender, and generate more danger when he plays as lateral defender.

Wilfried Jaures Kaptoum (born 1996)

Position: Center midfielder. *Height*: still developing.

Characteristics: *La Masia* has many African-origin players playing in various positions, but Kaptoum is the only one that has been chosen to play as a center-mid, the position that is watched with the strictest scrutiny at FC Barcelona. He is technically very good, he has great composure and controls the rhythm of the game, although he will sometimes abuse of unnecessarily long ball circulations and his own "magic turn" (which he has copied perfectly from Xavi). He will need to improve his intensity in defense and to pass the ball faster.

Adama Traoré (1996)
Position: Right winger. *Height*: still developing.
Characteristics: This kid may count as African (his parents are from Mali) or as genuinely Catalan (he was born in Barcelona, right next to *Camp Nou*), or both, depending on who you ask. Adama works hard and is very self-disciplined. He is a very fast forward who plays very open and uses his speed to leave his opponents behind with incredible ease and he crosses the ball well, although he tends to get into the play only when he gets the ball.

Lionel Enguene (born 1996)
Position: Right/Left midfielder. *Height*: still developing.
Characteristics: This right-footed Cameroonian kid is one of the best of the crop that have come out of the Eto'o Foundation. He is responsible and very competitive and he also knows how to work hard on the field. Enguene has an exquisite technique, using both the inside and the outside of his foot, he is good at short and long passes, at dribbling, and at shooting with both feet. Tactically speaking he looks like a veteran: he can pause, he can keep the ball, and he likes to join the attack with his powerful physique; he scores with ease too.

Ferran Sarsanedas (born 1997)
Position: Left midfielder. *Height*: still developing.
Characteristics: Perhaps because of his shy character, this player has not been on the media as much as some of his teammates but with his talent and intelligence he is just as likely to reach the *Camp Nou* as they are. He

spends lengthy hours watching soccer games, yet he is a great student. His style of play is similar to that of Sergi Roberto, always playing simple. He is always well positioned, can play at first touch, has a privileged vision, and brings danger to the penalty area. His attitude on the field is spotless but he needs to improve one notch in aggressivity with and without the ball.

Seung-Ho Paik (born 1997)

Position: Right midfielder. *Height*: still developing.

Characteristics: Known in his South Korea as the Korean Messi, Seung-Ho Paik was "discovered" by Albert Puig (then coach of the Infantil B) while participating in a soccer tournament in Barcelona in November 2009. Puig quickly alerted the club, because Real Madrid was also trying to recruit him, but the kid loved what *La Masia* had to offer when he was invited for a screening in the Spring of 2010. Fortunately his father was a university professor of physical therapy in Seoul, and was able to ask for a temporary job transfer and move to Barcelona. Although he used to play forward, the coaches are now playing him as a right midfielder and sometimes as a left midfielder. He still conserves his forward-like change of pace and his scoring ease. He has effortlessly assimilated DNA Barça concepts such as the ability to play easy, not to lose the ball, and the association with his teammates, always with his head high. His biggest challenge is physical (he is very small), but he uses his speed to his advantage to fight for every ball against much stronger rivals.

Ayoub (born 1998)

Position: Midfielder/Forward. *Height*: still developing.

Characteristics: Ayoub Abiu Oulam was born in Casablanca, Morocco but his parents sent him to live with his older brothers Latif and Mustafa in Barcelona, where they work. At age 9, Latif enrolled him in the *FCBEscola*, where he quickly progressed and caught the attention of *La Masia* coaches. Thanks to his great talent and privileged physique, Ayoub has been skipping teams. He is very versatile and can play in various different positions. He has the talent to combine in midfield and the shot to finish up front. He is a big fan of Xavi and Iniesta and he watches every one of their games.

Carles Aleñá (born 1998)
Position: Left midfielder/Center midfielder. *Height*: still developing.
Characteristics: The son of a footballer, Carles Aleñá is affectionately known as "the Maradona of the youth academy" because both his frizzy black hair and his precise left foot remind of Argentinian footballer Diego Armando Maradona. He is a mature, extroverted kid who is very sociable with foreigners, so he is always chosen as team captain. He forms a great and unusually "twin" tandem with teammate Dani Morer, who not only looks like Carles but also plays like him, is from the same small town, and was born just one month later (!). Although he still lacks intensity in defense, he has great technique, a privileged vision, and knows how to bring danger to the opponents' goal.

Seung Woo Lee (born 1998)
Position: Forward. *Height*: still developing.
Characteristics: This Korean-born exceptional young right-footed forward is the closest to Messi in style, speed, technique, awareness, and intelligence that *La Masia* is brewing right now. The fantastic speed and ease with which he slaloms through defenders is breathtaking – only a handful professionals reach that level of control, and he is just a teenager. One of these players that will bring nights of magic to the *Camp Nou*.

Dani Morer (born 1998)
Position: Right midfielder. *Height*: still developing.
Characteristics: Maybe the "twin brothers" Dani Morer and Carles Aleñá are meant to lighten up the *Camp Nou* one day. Like Aleñà, Morer has talent and creativity in his feet, speed – which he uses wisely to reach the end line and create danger –, and a great vision for the pass. He has a strong work ethic and he is humble and discreet.

Alex Collado (born 1999)
Position: Right/Left/Center midfielder. *Height*: still developing.

Characteristics: It is still too early to guess what will become of this kid, although he has started very well. His anticipation skill is excellent and plays the ball with great intelligence. He is left-footed but he can dribble, carry and pass the ball well with his right foot too. Technically brilliant and with great ability in the one-versus-one, still lacking aggressivity as is typical at his age, some say he is an "Iniesta or Silva in the making".

Oriol Busquets (1999)

Position: Center midfielder. *Height*: still developing.

Characteristics: Oriol Busquets is known in the *Ciutat Esportiva* as the "next-decade Busquets" because of his last name (unrelated to Sergio Busquets) and his position on the field (Oriol also plays as a center midfielder), although he scores many goals unlike Sergio and his style is very different from Sergio. Oriol is a total midfielder: he is very talented for creating plays, he is a powerful runner, and he is a precise shooter. He is introverted, yet more mature than the kids his age and a bright student that often gets A+ in almost every subject. As he lives in Sant Feliu de Guíxols (more than 100 km and 75 min by car), he is one of those kids that goes back and forth from Barcelona every day in a taxi paid by Barça. His father, Jordi Busquets, was also a footballer trained at *La Masia* (where he coincided with Tito Vilanova and others), and so was his brother Pol (a goalkeeper), although neither of them made it to the first team. It looks like Oriol has the best chances in the family to fulfill the dream of playing at the *Camp Nou*.

Ben Lederman (born 2000)

Position: Left midfielder. *Height*: still developing.

Characteristics: This boy from Los Angeles has made history by becoming the first American to have worn the FC Barcelona shirt. His parents, Danny and Tammy, are so invested in his future that they decided to move to Barcelona, which made it easy for Ben. He is an excellent left-footed midfielder, with accurate technique and good vision for the last pass; he rarely loses a ball. In any other team he would be a star – indeed, at 12 years old he was called to the sub-14 USA National Team! –, but here he will have to compete with the best of the best.

Takefusa Kubo (born 2001)

Position: Forward. *Height*: still developing.

Characteristics: Nicknamed "Take", at his young age he is already a celebrity in his country, where he is known as "the Messi of Japan" because of his unbelievable dribbling abilities. Take is an intelligent player that combines easily with others and scores with ease. He has adapted very well to Barcelona, where his parents have moved with him. He already speaks Spanish and it appears that he also has superior ping-pong abilities, for which he becomes the center of attention during the evenings at *La Masia*.

*   *   *

There is not enough space here to describe all the kids that will become excellent players – the kind we will see playing all over Spain and Europe –, even if they do not make it to the *Camp Nou*. No other youth academy in the world is capable of concentrating so much talent in such a small space-time. The list goes on and on. In the same generation as Take is Guillermo Amor (born 2001), son of the first *La Masia* graduate by the same name, member of the *Dream Team*, and now director of *La Masia*. (If you are concerned about nepotism, my Barça friend coaches assure me that little Guille is one of the best in the team.) A year younger is midfielder Kais Ruiz (born 2002), a player of exquisite touch who at 11 years of age can already do *elasticas* like a professional Brazilian. Even younger is another outstanding generation (born 2003), with defender Xavi Pleguezuelo (who is able to curl corner kicks into the goal at 10 years old!) and the quick-footed midfielder Marc Pelaz.

When Barça was eliminated from the 2013 *Champions League* semifinals by Bayern Munich by a total of 7-0 in two games, many friends asked me what was going on with the team. Was the team that had been the wonder of the world for about five years, now gone? I thought for a moment of these young players at *La Masia*, and I told my friends not to worry. The team had a bit of a setback because it had an unfair disadvantage for a while: cancer, nonetheless. Never mind that Messi will be retiring in five, seven years or so. The future is looking brighter than ever for FC Barcelona.

Chapter 8: The galactic waste

By now, the reader must be wondering why the other major clubs do not copy the highly successful Barça youth academy model, which Barça largely copied from Ajax's – isn't it enough evidence that it has worked twice in history?

Actually, both Manchester United and Real Madrid, arch-rivals of FC Barcelona outside and inside of Spain, respectively, also invest dearly in their own youth academies (and so do many other clubs, of course). Why don't they produce the same results as FC Barcelona's one? Here I will tell you briefly about the history of their youth academies, which have had their share of glorious moments. I have picked these two clubs because they are respectively chosen by the press as the second- and third-ranked rivals in the world (who is second and who is third depends on which press is reporting); I have picked *only those two* because there is not space here to produce a report of the global state of affairs of youth academies. However, they will serve to illustrate the extremes: FC Barcelona has without a doubt the best youth academy in the world, and Real Madrid and *ManU* presently ignore theirs (but do have very active and historically prolific programs). Many mid-ranked clubs are doing great efforts to follow in the footsteps of FC Barcelona's example, and in fact are rushing to hire the coaches of Barça's youth academy to re-structure their clubs – such is the case of Liverpool (who recently signed up Barça youth coaches Pep Segura and Rodolfo Borrell to run their youth academy), Roma (who signed up Luis Enrique, the Barça player from 1996-2004 and former coach of Barça B from 2008-2011, to run its first team), or Dubai team's Al Wasl (who signed up Albert Benaiges, the legendary Barça youth coach, to direct their youth academy). Whether the methods of Total Football and the "Barça language" are translatable to other soccer styles (or can be successful in other leagues) is a very interesting question that will be answered in the following years and which might be implemented with variable success depending on the skill of the coach.

The Manchester United youth academy

At one point, *ManU* did have arguably one of the most productive youth academies in the world, fueling its first team with the energy of a volcano. That team was called the "Busby Babes" after its coach Matt Busby and to denote the tenderest average age ever seen in a champion team: 22. The team won an FA Cup (1948) and a league (1952). This is the only team that might have stopped Di Stéfano's Real Madrid in the late 1950s; in 1957 they lost to Real Madrid in the final of the *European Cup*, but they beat Anderlecth 10-0 in the semifinal. In 1958, the team was tragically decimated by a plane crash in Munich that killed 23 of the 44 passengers, including 8 *ManU* players (among them midfielder Duncan Edwards, the biggest rising star). Matt Busby and Bobby Charlton were spared. Busby rebuilt the team with youth players and, despite the tragedy, the team made it to the FA Cup final – starting the legend of the *"Red Devils"*. Bobby Charlton, Scottish phenomenon scorer Denis Law ("The King"), and a new youth player of fantastic ability called George Best (in Pelé's words, "the best player in the world", who self-taught the art to dribble with a tennis ball through the streets) formed the so-called "United Trinity" (*ManU* is the only team that can boast to have fielded a team with three "European Footballers of the Year"). The impetus of that legendary youth academy might have helped the genesis of one last stellar youth team with Ryan Giggs, Paul Scholes, David Beckham, Gary Neville, Keith Gillespie, and Robbie Savage (all future internationals), which won the FA Youth Cup in 1992. That talent spike, however, did not find continuity in the first team – the 2012 star-filled team, for example, was full of foreigners and most of their main English players of recent times (which usually played in the English national team) were formed at other youth academies: Rio Ferdinand and Michael Carrick (West Ham United), Michael Owen (Liverpool), Wayne Rooney (Everton), Chris Smalling (Maidstone United), Ashley Young (Watford), Nick Powell

(Crewe Alexandra), and Phil Jones (Blackburn Rovers). In the 2012 first-team *ManU* squad, there were 40 players, of which 12 were English and one (Giggs) was Welsh. Of these 13, only 6 players (including Giggs), were from *ManU*'s youth academy, but Giggs (at 38 years old) and Scholes (37) were dying stars and didn't play all games. In total, only two of the 13 were starters. In the 2013 squad, only three field players (Jonny Evans, Danny Welbeck, and Tom Cleverley), and the two substitute goalies Ben Amos and Sam Johnstone, are from the youth academy.

What happened to all the great young players that would come out of this fantastic youth academy? Where are they going now? Obviously they cannot play at *ManU* and after a long training they get sold to another club. What is the reason for this waste of talent? I do not have access to *ManU*'s internal screening files, but I refuse to accept that the number of good players that emerge from the youth academy has suddenly been reduced so much. A more likely explanation is that the present management finds that buying talent is a safer bet than raising it. This new mode of thinking has coincided with the arrival of businessmen to the top management and the influx of "easy" money from peripheral markets (TV, construction, advertisement) that has distorted the soccer market. The money is no longer mostly coming from the fans, so the fans are not in charge of the decision-making. (Note that this does not happen at FC Barcelona, where the club is still owned by its fans.) In fact, many clubs are in serious debt because they are operated as part of larger companies, and for this reason the UEFA has established since 2009 financial "fair play rules", under which clubs cannot repeatedly spend more than their generated revenues and are obligated to balance their budgets (including meeting transfer and player payment commitments). As of March 2013, eight clubs have been sanctioned already (among them Málaga).

Between 2003 and 2005, *ManU*'s public shares began to be acquired by Malcolm Glazer, a Florida businessman (born in New York in 1928) who is the owner of First Allied Corporation, a holding company that deals in food processing, marine supplies, health care, and real estate, among others. By the end of 2005, the Glazer family owned 100% of *ManU*'s shares, which they had bought at high prices by borrowing most of the money, provided by three New York hedge funds. In 2006, he appointed two of his four sons and his daughter to the *ManU* board. Presently *ManU* (i.e. the Glazer family) is worth £660 M, but as a result of the borrowing, interest payments amount to £62 million a year. As the Manchester United Supporters Trust protested, "It is difficult to see how these sums can be reached without significant increases in ticket prices, which, as we always suspected, means the fans will effectively be paying for someone to borrow money to own their club".

Nothing good can come of this. These businessmen are preying upon soccer simply because it is a thriving market sector, but they do not know its agents and its forces. To invest in wineries, you are expected to have knowledge of how wines are produced and to distinguish a good from a bad wine. How can an ailing old man that lives in Florida and has never played professional soccer begin to understand the century-old passions that brew in the *Theatre of Dreams* – a most poetic nickname that Bobby Charlton devised for *Old Trafford*, *ManU*'s stadium –? I strongly suspect that Malcolm Glazer does not know the difference between good soccer and bad soccer: he just cares about *ManU* as a brand, which is plenty of profitable. The expectation that he can delegate the management to some other expert is one that has been shown to have a bleak future, as any business school student will tell you. The abundance of money – borrowed or real – from *ManU* and Real Madrid should be used to improve the way soccer talent is raised at *ManU* and Real Madrid, not to *only* buy soccer talent raised elsewhere.

Unfortunately, among the large clubs, *ManU*'s strategy has become not the exception but the rule. For the English teams, a great source of young players is, paradoxically, FC Barcelona's youth academy (and many others), benefitting from an international legal loophole: British law allows British clubs to sign a player into a contract as soon as they turn 16. The practice is prohibited by law in Spain (the legal age is 18, as it is considered that at 16 they do not have the capacity to decide on millionaire contracts that tie them to a club for many years), so British clubs snatch them for bargain prices. For comparison, a 16 year-old *cadet* earns a €12,000/yr stipend at *La Masia* (increased by €3,000 every year until they can sign their first professional contract). Excellent creative midfielders ended up in the *Premier League* by this route, attracted by the money and by promises that they will not have to sit on the bench as they would if they stayed at FC Barcelona (a clever calculation, by all means): Cesc Fàbregas and Jan Toral (Arsenal), Mikel Arteta (Everton, now at Arsenal), Oriol Romeu (Chelsea), etc. The year 2013, for example, was a normal one, and three 16-year-old *cadets* were snatched away by Chelsea (Josima Quintero), Arsenal (Julio Pleguezuelo), and Liverpool (Sergi Canós). The problem is not that they leave the club – FC Barcelona is used to that –, but rather that the British clubs lure the young players into long contracts: they all regret it later, which is exactly the type of situation that the Spanish law (a law to protect minors, after all) is meant to avoid. As with all loopholes, it is unlikely to last. Already, this problem has been mitigated of late by the publicity of the case of Cesc Fàbregas, who had difficulties returning to his home club after a great few seasons at Arsenal: FC Barcelona uses the case with all the youth to show them that, if they choose to sign for an English club, they might never be able to return to the club of their dreams – it works effectively.

The Real Madrid youth academy

In many ways, the history of Real Madrid follows a parallel path to that of Manchester United (except for the tragedy). Real Madrid has also had an effervescent youth academy in the past. The youth academy – dubbed *La Fábrica* by its fans ("The Factory") – was started by president Santiago Bernabéu, who appointed ex-player Luis Molowny as its first director. Molowny had played with Real Madrid for 11 years and, in his last two years, had won two *European Cups* with the Di Stéfano team that would win three more. Miguel Muñoz, who had been European Champion as a player those same two years in that team full of foreign stars, became first-team coach and decided to build a team entirely with Spanish players (dubbed "*Los Yé-yés*"). Between 1960 and 1972, they won *La Liga* 9 times (5 of them in a row), the Copas del Rey twice (the 1962 title was a "double"), and the 1966 European Cup. In the 1980s, five players came out of the Real Madrid youth academy almost at the same time: Emilio Butragueño (a.k.a. "El Buitre" or "Vulture", born 1963), Míchel (b. 1963), Manolo Sanchís (b. 1965), Martín Vázquez (b. 1965), and Miguel Pardeza (b. 1965). Starting 1985-1986, the Quinta del Buitre (translated as "the cohort of the Vulture") and the rest of the teammates won 5 Ligas in a row, along with a Copa in 1988-1989 (a "double"), and two consecutive UEFA Cups (1985 and 1986). They did not win any European Cup. More recent graduates of the Real Madrid youth academy include Raúl, Guti, Íker Casillas, Álvaro Arbeloa, Esteban Granero, and José María Callejón. Other notable players that have come out of the youth academy but went to other clubs include Luis García, Juan Mata, Borja Valero, Álvaro Negredo, Roberto Soldado, Dani Parejo, Juanfran Torres, and Javi García. In its present day, the Real Madrid youth academy consists of 303 players distributed amongst 14 teams (from the 8-year-old benjamines to the Castilla, the Real Madrid-equivalent of Barça B that plays in 2nd Division). In all the youth soccer divisions, Real Madrid and FC Barcelona are fierce rivals at all ages. Other clubs are often contenders as well, which speaks for the quality of the youth coaching in Spain in general. The biggest difference is that FC Barcelona's first team makes use of its best youth players – and the others most often don't – because it has educated them to play in the Barça style.

In the present times, Real Madrid is similar to ManU in how its first team closes the doors to its own youth academy. Real Madrid's 2012 official squad of 24 players had 8 Spanish players, of which 4 were from the youth academy, and only two (Casillas and Arbeloa) were usual starters. By only buying, ManU and Real Madrid are clipping the wings of the pigeons in their lofts. Wasting money is one thing – money can be recovered. In fact, I have soccer friends who do not feel strongly about youth academies: all they care about is watching good soccer – so for them Real Madrid's model is just as moral as any other one. But what if everyone adopted this model – who would raise young players? As youth coach Laureano Ruiz would put it: "Can a tree live without its roots?" I will leave this dilemma up to you. (Below I offer additional, economical reasons to argue that, in fact, it is an unhealthy model that can damage the whole economy when it goes out of control.) In my opinion, wasting soccer talent is as unforgivable as converting a forest into a parking lot: sure it raises money, but it is forever. As a Barça fan, I can only rejoice in the incompetence of the upper management of *ManU* and Real Madrid who prefer the easy, rich-and-dumb route to success of buying at the cost of blocking access to their youth players – this incompetence will help prolong Barça's dominance. However, as a global football fan, it saddens me to know that there are in the youth academies of *ManU* and Real Madrid countless kids with great abilities who are aspiring to become great players – we'll never see them. (This is, of course, an exaggeration to help make a point: Real Madrid youth coaches would not miss a Messi or an Iniesta type of kid, with superior dribbling skills, but the issue at stake is one of targeted player development. Their system would more likely fail to detect and develop players like Xavi, Busquets, or Pedro that are strong specifically in the Barça style of play.)

The Real Madrid youth academy has great scouts and coaches and their teams usually compete in the finals of most youth tournaments. The problem is not there – it's in the connection with the first team: the link that Cruyff engraved forever in the club's genome when he arrived at FC Barcelona as a coach in 1988. If the style changes every two or three years, then the youth teams cannot use it as a didactic example. Real Madrid's Santiago Bernabéu stadium does not remember a team that defines a style since the wonderful *Quinta del Buitre* generation – but unfortunately the *Quinta del Buitre* dissolved away, because its rise (now we know) was due to proximity of birthdays, not to a change in coaching methods at the youth academy. Later, the "Galactic" players (including three *Ballons d'Or* – Zidane, Figo, and Ronaldo, a FIFA World Player – Fabio Cannavaro –, plus Beckham) indeed reached Galactic levels – in that period, Zidane regaled us with moves of such grace that the videos are often accompanied with music on *YouTube* –, but without any replacement from the youth academy, all retired or left for greener pastures and the Galaxy died off.

Being ultra-rich helps to build a great team *in the short term*, but maintaining a Galaxy *in the long term* requires an unsustainably large investment. Even if you are the richest club in the world, *money might not even be enough* to attract the best star because stars don't change teams based only on the wealth that is offered to them (e.g. Messi, Iniesta and Xavi would never leave Barça for richer clubs). "Playing once with Messi is for me a bigger dream than playing a whole season with Cristiano Ronaldo", said the Brazilian star Neymar before signing for Barça in May 2013. The titles that a super-star is likely to win in the new team must also be a crucial decision factor. A super-star usually has individual sponsorships many times higher than the salary offered by the club anyways. Over a long period of time, it is in fact very difficult to maintain a level of investment like the one displayed by Real Madrid and Manchester United: soccer alone, with all its TV and advertisement revenues, cannot generate it. German teams such as Bayern Munich have been more creative at attractive sponsorships from powerful firms (car manufacturers and banks), but the Spanish and the British economy are not as healthy. Indeed, the major titles that we can attribute to the *Galácticos* (from 2001 until now) are the 2002 *Champions League,* the 2002 *FIFA Club World Cup* (previously called *Intercontinental Cup*), 5 *Ligas,* and two *Copas* – at a cost of €1,153 M invested in 64 new signings, not including the 11 coaches. Much of the fiasco is attributable to Florentino Pérez, who has presided for 10 of these years, spent €860 million in new signings, fired 8 coaches, and obtained only 6 major titles – the 2002 *Champions League,* 3 *Ligas,* one *Copa,* and the 2002 *FIFA Club World Cup* – and 4 minor ones – 3 Spanish *Supercopas* and one *European SuperCup* (these are one- or two-game trophies between the winners of other competitions): the price tag is €86 M/title; the statistic is very generous because, in fact, six of these 10 titles (more than half, including the *Champions League,* two *Ligas,* a *Supercopa,* a *European SuperCup* and a *FIFA Club World Cup*) were won by one same coach (Del Bosque). In the same period 2001-2013, competing with about half the total spending (counting the cost of *La Masia*, which provides the majority of Barça's constant supply of "signings") and using only 6 coaches (three of them from *La Masia*), FC Barcelona has conquered 3 *Champions Leagues* (2006, 2009 & 2011), two *FIFA Club World Cups* (2009 & 2011), 6 *Ligas*, and two *Copas*. Florentino Pérez – who never had any soccer training – has failed to grasp that, in soccer, contrary to construction, money does not guarantee you the quality of your finished product: soccer is a sport where the team's power is derived not simply by multiplying the power of its pieces but also by the strength and creativity of the associations that the players are able to produce with each other. These associations, *La Masia* has concluded, are best trained *together* during early adolescence, when the neuromuscular system is still developing. Guti, the only creative midfielder (a magnificent one!) that came through the ranks of the Real Madrid youth academy, was miserably wasted on the bench by all the coaches of the various Galaxies. Here again, as in *ManU*'s case, we see that the answer of why these academies do not produce the same results as the FC Barcelona youth academy lies in a lack of coordination between the first team and the youth team. The problem is that the top management is businessmen that can only make decisions based on an obsessive financial principle: Is the investment worth it? When Arrigo Sacchi was the sports director of Real Madrid (for just one year, in 2005), he recommended signing up Milan's midfielder Andrea Pirlo, then 26 years old. Pirlo is one of the best midfielders that have come out of Italy in the last decades, a sort of Italian Guardiola in many ways. In 2011, already at 32 years old and past his prime, Milan made the mistake of not renewing his contract, so Juve signed him up for free – and won the 2012 *scudetto*. Back in 2005, Real Madrid badly needed a creative midfielder, but Florentino Pérez's was betrayed by his businessman-like approach to soccer: he replied to Sacchi that he was not interested because "Pirlo will not win a *Ballon d'Or*".

Soccer style and ethical values have not guided decisions at Real Madrid for a long time. I can recognize the pattern because I have seen it before:

FC Barcelona also went through a long, similar presidency marked with stellar signings (Maradona, Schuster) by a construction magnate (Josep Lluís Núñez). At the time Barça fans were fooled into the notion that money could buy this sport: the club was always in mood swing until Johan Cruyff brought back to the club the familiar clarity of Dutch soccer teachings and said "We will all row in this direction" – and everyone followed enthusiastically: at the time, all the other directions looked grim while his direction pointed to long-term soccer education.

Financing soccer with revenues from other businesses

As was the case in FC Barcelona thirty years ago, the top management of most rich clubs such as Real Madrid, *ManU*, Paris St.-Germain, Chelsea, etc. is presently dominated by businessmen, used to solving problems by writing big checks. Since for them time is money, they do not have the patience to build a strong youth academy and wait 10-20 years to collect its fruits, like Barça did. Where is the money coming from? Many years ago, rather naïvely, legendary FC Barcelona midfielder Josep Samitier expressed his doubts that soccer could ever become a business: "If soccer were a good business, the banks would have owned it for a long time already". As a case example that has heavily influenced the way FC Barcelona and *La Masia* are managed, because of the competitive proximity, we will start by taking a close look at Real Madrid. Most of the money has not even come from soccer or its TV contracts, as you might innocently have thought. In Spain, many clubs – including Real Madrid – used the booming real estate industry to finance their soccer operations, but most of them – not Real Madrid – saw their investments evaporate when the financial crisis hit Spain.

Before being president of Real Madrid, Florentino Pérez started as a politician. In 1979, him and his buddy José María Álvarez del Manzano coincided as Madrid city council members for the now defunct centrist-party UCD. During Spain's real-estate boom in the 1980s, Florentino found his calling and left politics to make a fortune in the construction business. Álvarez del Manzano (who also invests in construction, along with his wife) would transfer to the right-wing party *Partido Popular*, PP, and would become mayor of Madrid for the PP, from 1991-2003. In 2000 Florentino Pérez was elected president of Real Madrid. In 2001, Real Madrid had accumulated a debt of €270 M and Florentino convinced his old friend Álvarez del Manzano to approve the re-zoning of a Real Madrid-owned green zone as buildable land, now called *Ciudad Deportiva*. The sale of these lands reported for Real Madrid €480 M – enough to pay off its debt and to buy Figo, Zidane, Ronaldo, Beckham (in the Galactic era), Kaká, Cristiano Ronaldo (the Second Galaxy), and construct a new complex on the outskirts of Madrid. Four skyscrapers, between 230 and 250 meters high, were erected in one of the densest areas of Madrid: fuck the neighbors, in the purest Franco style. Florentino Pérez is not the type of man that would have done this operation to rescue Real Madrid with his savings. Part of the deal consisted of giving his company (ACS Dragados) the building contract for two of the skyscrapers, so Pérez made a lot of money with it. Real Madrid is just the tip of the iceberg, one node in a vast network of corruption: the contractors for the other two skyscrapers, Acyr and OHL, were so close to PP that their presidents have been indicted in a recent case of illegal donations to the party. Summarizing: Real Madrid's glory is not even self-sustainable because it cannot exist without these occasional shady deals.

A big problem in clubs that are owned by a single shareholder is that the fate of the club is often in the hands of one person's whim. We have already seen the state of affairs at *ManU*, a powerful club in terms of results. In Spain, Málaga C.F. was purchased in 2006 by Lorenzo Sanz, an ex-Real Madrid goalkeeper turned successful construction businessman who has been arrested twice for fraud. Málaga has been for many years the equivalent of construction heaven, with plenty of corrupt politicians who would issue permits in previously protected lands. Lorenzo Sanz appointed his own son, Fernando Sanz, as president of the club; under Fernando's management the club went into financial troubles, which prompted father Sanz to sell the club in 2010 to Sheikh Abdullah Al Thani from a well-known Qatari family. Under the Sheikh the club has done well for a while, after investing heavily in new players – then in 2012 the Sheikh decided out of the blue that the club was not financially sound and sold its two biggest stars (Cazorla and Rondón) to compensate the debt. Everyone is confused as to what the Sheikh wants.

Several other soccer clubs have fallen prey of single shareholders. Soccer is now a delectable market in the eyes of many voracious investors, whether they know anything about soccer or not. Paris Saint-Germain, the top French club, is owned (like Málaga C.F.) by a Qatar prince. We have already seen that Manchester United is owned by a Florida-based food industrialist. Since 2003, Chelsea is owned by Russian billionaire Roman Abramovich. Manchester City is owned by an Abu Dhabi investment group. FC Anzhi (from Dagestan, but plays in the Russian Premier League) is owned by billionaire Suleyman Kerimov. Saint Petersburg's Zenit main shareholder is Gazprom, the largest Russian company that holds the state-owned monopoly for extraction of natural gas. The wealth of any of these investors dwarfs Florentino Pérez's bank account.

The injection of money from one area (real estate, construction, energy, etc.) into another (soccer) of the economy raises many issues that warrant the intervention of citizens and politicians. FIFA will not intervene because it ultimately benefits from this cash injection, but it is a dangerous proposition, especially when the money comes from an economic area that, in Spain, is politically corrupt and financially unstable. Even when the money comes from healthier financial sectors, such as television or food (e.g. ManU, Paris St.-Germain, Manchester City), it is not clear that those sectors can always support such high levels of outgoing cash flow: it is the workers of those sectors who are creating extra riches and effectively subsidizing soccer. Such subsidies seem fine while the extra riches last, but what if they disappear? Shouldn't the parent company be forced to reduce its investment in soccer before contemplating any layoffs?

Similarly, if Real Madrid's model is to build its glittering teams by selling their green areas to companies, Real Madrid is getting rich by artificially modifying pre-existing social contracts. Is it fair to the people of Madrid who were counting on the placid views of the previous land when they purchased their property? Is that fair to other teams who do not have access to such contracts and political influences? When FC Barcelona tried to play a comparable trick in the outskirts of Barcelona, I was similarly outraged and was ashamed at the indignity of Laporta, the president who unsuccessfully presented the deal to the Barcelona city council. (Laporta further disgraced himself when he was forced to reveal that he had stealthily used his influence as president of Barça to bring millions of euros to his private law firm from Azerbaijan; similarly, president Sandro Rosell has been formally accused by a Brazil judge for having pocketed large sums of money in illegal transactions concerning Brazilian National team games.) These episodes remind us that no club is immune to corruption – transparency in the governance is the key.

Soccer clubs should abandon the obsolete and costly "model of success" borrowed from the banking and telecommunications industry (based on huge cash injections) and adopt instead the grass-roots educational model proposed by Ajax a long time ago and successfully implemented by Barça, Bayern and several other German clubs. (I am a fierce opponent of the sponsorship contract with Qatar Foundation because Qatar is a non-democratic country that allows flogging and stoning as punishments and we cannot be sure of the origin of the money.) I share my admiration of *La Quinta del Buitre* and Zidane with many Real Madrid fans who would like to see an end to Pérez's behavior. It is shocking that the city of Madrid does not scream at Florentino Pérez that he is a crook when he walks around the streets pretending he is a finance guru. It is up to the people of Madrid and the Real Madrid fans: in the end, they will have the team – and the city – that they deserve.

The critical reader will wonder whether all this rant against Real Madrid is not misplaced in a book about FC Barcelona's youth academy. After all, many will argue, quite rightly, that Barça has also historically spent large sums in record signings to bring the top stars of the moment (Kubala, Cruyff, Maradona). Even the *Dream Team*, which propelled the rise of *La Masia* to a modern youth academy, cost a fortune to build ("the money must be on the field, not in the bank", successfully argued Cruyff to President Núñez) – and to maintain: Cruyff gave himself the highest salary. Not even the strongest supporters of youth academies like me will defend that teams like Barça (that invest heavily in their youth academy) should refrain from hiring the best external players (e.g. Neymar): otherwise the team would be out-competed very soon; also, external players can add a competitive incentive for the youth academy players. What is unprecedented about Florentino Pérez's finances is the *origin* of the money, which required the intervention of corrupt politicians to generate it. (This story is too reminiscent of Franco's intervention in Di Stéfano's signing, which produced enormous benefits for Real Madrid.). Nevertheless, there are a few positive readings about Real Madrid's money-driven strategies and treacheries. In the same way that works of fiction such as Orwell's *1984* and the movie *Blade Runner* are a warning of a future that we would not want for our children, Real Madrid is the ideal negative role model that constantly reminds old Barça fans (who lived the Núñez era) of the path that should never be taken again. We could film a new comical episode of *Star Wars* where *Darth Pérez* uses *Dark Money* to try to rule the Galaxy of Soccer. A three-word, untranslatable Spanish phrase has been coined to describe this ongoing battle: "*cantera contra cartera*" (youth academy versus wallet). "Without the youth academy we would not be able to compete against Real Madrid, who can spend €100 M in Bale", has said Gerard Piqué. Florentino Pérez and the Real Madrid directors and coaches, upset at losing the "cantera contra cartera" war, sometimes resort to propaganda and repeat unsupported statements such as "Real Madrid is the greatest club in the world" or "Cristiano is the best player in the world" simply to satisfy Cristiano's pathetic vanity, but fans around the world know better. As the collective memory of the fans only registers the great players but forgets the names of presidents and everyone else around them, many years from now people will remember that the time when Real Madrid was most aggressive with its expenditures in player signings, it was also, by a calculated reaction, the time when *La Masia* attained the highest productivity ever seen in the history of any soccer youth academy.

Chapter 9: The measure of success

Why don't all clubs invest in a youth academy?

If a soccer club is very rich, a simple logic seems to dictate that the shortest path to success is to simply sign up a group of great stars and a great coach. That has been, indeed, the path taken by many wealthy clubs in the past. Following the same thinking process, many small clubs have centered their efforts on looking for investors willing to invest towards the future success of a team that will bring them, the clubs argue, financial benefit if they become successful. These investors typically inject large amounts of cash into the soccer club from other businesses (e.g., the entertainment or the construction industries) in exchange for a share of the future profits if the team does well.

Considering that there is only room for one at the very top in every country, the history of the success of FC Barcelona's youth academy in competition with Real Madrid (undoubtedly one of the richest clubs in the world) shows you that the "rich club" strategy is, in fact, a losing proposition in the long term when it competes with a productive youth academy. We can establish meaningful comparisons by producing a measure of "cost per title" over long periods of time. As an example, in the period of 2003 till the end of the 2012 season, Real Madrid spent €894M to buy 57 players and sold 80 players for a total €316M, representing a net deficit of €577M. In that period, Real Madrid only earned 7 titles – coming at a cost of €82M/title. In that same period, FC Barcelona bought 45 players for €579M, sold 79 for €238M, and earned 19 titles, resulting in a cost of €18M/title – more than 4.5 times smaller than Real Madrid's investment. If we had taken slightly different periods, e.g. from 2001-2013, the Real Madrid titles would have increased to 11, but the investments would have had to include Zidane, Figo, Ronaldo, Beckham, Isco, Illarramendi, and Bale. If we only count the last 10 years,

Real Madrid has spent €1100M compared to FC Barcelona's a bit over €600M. During the 2013-2014 season, 17 of Barça's 25 first-team players – 68%, an all-time club record – had come up through the youth academy (although three, Piqué, Fàbregas and Jordi Alba had to be re-purchased), and 7 were regular starters. Real Madrid, on the other hand, had only 5 (Casillas, Jesús, Nacho, Jesé, and Morata) and fans everywhere are still shocked that none of them (not even Casillas!) are regular starters.

There are, of course, examples of rich clubs that have managed to secure titles with this strategy, but so far the strongest youth academies in Europe are getting the best return for their investment in almost all the countries. Thus the "rich club strategy" is clearly unsustainable in the face of competition from a prolific youth academy. Holland is a country that is weaved by youth academies so its culture forbids it to not use its youth. As we will see below, in England and France (where the ultra-rich clubs owned by foreign investors have thrived) the youth academies have decayed lately. In Germany and Italy, on the other hand, many clubs have taken notice and are following Barça's example.

I do not want to leave the reader with the impression that Real Madrid is an incompetent club and FC Barcelona does everything right – nothing farther from the truth! Also, there are many factors that dictate the success of a club other than their youth academy. In fact, with a bit of data fudging (which us scientists love to do), we will get to an interesting conclusion. For example, since year 2000 (until July 2013), Real Madrid bought 72 players for €1,186M (~ €16.5M/player). Over the same period, FC Barcelona bought 62 players for €838M (~ €13.5M/player). The numbers are somewhat similar, in any case much larger (sadly) than any other club in *La Liga*. Even more similar is *where* they are buying those players from: Barça and Real Madrid spent 73% and 76% of the money on foreign players, respectively. This means that the two richest clubs in Spain together have spent €1,523M abroad and only €502M nationally. That's €1,021M that might never come back. Spain's economy will not be able to sustain this financial bleeding for much longer. Who is to blame? The disparity in riches – and performance – in *La Liga* has a very clear origin: the TV rights. With the exception of Villarreal's 2nd place in 2007-2008, it's been nine years since a team other than Barça or Real Madrid won La Liga, or ended second. In 2013, Real Madrid had a budget of €517M, of which €140M (27%) came from TV rights. Barça's budget was slightly lower at €470M, but received the same TV rights (€140M, 30% of budget) as Real Madrid. The club with the lowest budget was Rayo Vallecano (€18M), which received €16.7M (93%) in TV rights. In other words, Barça and Real Madrid receive about 8.4 times more in TV rights than the least-paid team. In contrast, in the Bundesliga the best-paid team is Bayern Munich (€35M), and the least-paid team is Cologne (€14M) – a difference of a factor of 2.5. In England, 70% of the amount generated by the TV rights is distributed in equal parts, which guarantees that each team receives at least €45M/year. (Manchester United generates much more than this because it has a huge penetration into the Asian market.) In Italy, this percentage is 40%. None of these leagues except for La Liga is so polarized at the top, with two teams winning so predictably. Therefore, the first step towards having a healthy league with clubs that can each sustain their own competitive youth academy would be to implement an equitable distribution of the TV rights. The present system implemented by La Liga is blatantly unfair and does not encourage clubs to maintain good youth academies because it destroys what soccer is all about: competition.

The "secret" methods of the FC Barcelona youth academy

Can the Barça style of play and coaching methods be taught outside of its school, and most important, can they be extended to the youngest kids? I get asked this question over and over by friends and coaches. First of all, FC Barcelona does not restrict access to its youth academy, so the coaching methods are not really secret. In fact, FC Barcelona publicly teaches its methodology in a set of courses (now available through the FCBEscola) to prospective coaches so that the philosophy and methods are properly understood and widely disseminated. Albert Puig, then coach of the alevins and now coordinator of youth soccer, had no problems sharing his coaching notes and practice exercises with me when I asked.

Truth be told, the exercises do not differ much from those of other clubs and youth academies whose coaches are aware of the latest methods. I was able to make an even closer comparison when I volunteered as a coach for an FC Barcelona camp in Bellevue (Seattle) in August 2012. To my surprise, I noticed that I had seen almost every exercise already in my son's club, whose coach does not know anybody at the Barça youth academy but is a big fan of its coaching methods. It turns out that his source of information about Barça methodology had been from a very successful U.S. soccer coaching organization that (unbeknownst to my son's coach) was not connected to FC Barcelona but runs soccer camps under the labels of "Barcelona USA" and "total football" (they cannot use "FC Barcelona" because they do not have an agreement with Barça). This organization has perfectly competent coaches, and in fact one of its graduates is none other than Ben Lederman, who is now at FC Barcelona's youth academy. This is the best proof that the Barça methods can, in fact, be copied. There are very few secrets in soccer because, as legendary Scottish football manager and former player Gordon Strachan reminds us, "soccer is a very simple game. It's the players that make it complicated".

The biggest difference between FC Barcelona's youth academy and any other youth academy in the world is its intimate connection with the first team – that concept pioneered by Ajax coach Jack Reynolds in the early 1900's (the only truly genius idea that soccer coaching has seen – the rest is common sense) and that Cruyff brought to Barça: have the children play with the same style as the first team, throughout all the categories of the youth academy. But that is hardly a secret either – it's simply a club policy that requires a lot of work and a lot of planning, very careful planning at all levels. (It has taken FC Barcelona 30 years to build the "planning team" too: the coaches are now better prepared and coordinated than many years ago.) At FC Barcelona, the strength of this connection has been analyzed, scrutinized from every possible angle, and has been elevated to the status of a club postulate that will never be abandoned. There is no other secret: play like the grown-ups.

It should be stressed that Tito Vilanova, educated through the ranks of *La Masia* and first-team head coach since Guardiola resigned, has insisted that the above is not exact. "The first team also learns from the youth academy", he says. "There were times when the first team did not play 4-3-3 formation, but the youth academy kept playing it". This view emphasizes the central role that the youth academy has had in preserving the style of play. After Cruyff was ousted, there were some directors at FC Barcelona that pushed for a change in style and even brought coaches that either opposed Cruyff's style of play (Robson) or did not really know how to implement it (Serra Ferrer, Van Gaal). At one point, right before hiring Guardiola in 2008, the management was so confused about what direction to take that they even considered the option of hiring Mourinho, a coach that represents the antipodes of Cruyff's soccer style. But the inertia of the youth academy, set in motion by decades of Total Football teachings, made it virtually impossible to change the model, as preserved by a team of dozens of educators. Thus the youth academy has become the trustee for the style of play: in difficult times, while the first team recovers from its upheavals, the style of play is incubated here, in the warmth of the primeval nest, where the original molds are kept, so that more young players can be developed away from the noise of the media. In prosperous times, when the first team is in symbiosis with the youth academy – as in the present era – the results are so spectacular that they are featured on the covers of *Time, Newsweek* and *The New York Times*.

The United States challenge

Unlike in the U.S. where youth soccer education is dominated until ages ~8-10 by the "soccer dad" type of coach, in Spain and in the majority of Europe, the question of how to teach soccer to children is largely irrelevant to most people: youth soccer education is taken care by professional educators in clubs (such as FC Barcelona, who have a vested interested in discovering talent) from ages around 7-8 and beyond, as we have seen in the preceding chapters. Before that age, soccer is usually played in elementary school teams until the best kids are detected and attracted by the clubs' scouters. As noted earlier, as soon as a kid enters a major club in Europe, all (or most of) the training expenses are covered, because these clubs are usually the same clubs that have teams in the professional divisions and get revenues from television and advertisements, so for them the cost of running a kids' team is the equivalent of peanuts. Playing soccer has always been virtually free to a working family in Europe.

In the United States, the situation is diametrically opposite. Money does not flow into professional soccer as in Europe but there is actually a large population of kids that play soccer. It is now the sport with most registered youth players in the U.S. According to the United States Soccer Federation, the number of youth soccer players has doubled, to more than 4 million, since 1990 – whereas Little League, the competing baseball youth system that covers kids 4-18 years old, declined from 2.5 million in 1996 to 2 million in 2010. The geographical distribution of youth soccer is far from uniform. A 2010 study showed that the state that contributes the most to the *Major League Soccer* (MLS) is California (58 youth players that year, mostly from the Los Angeles and San Diego area), followed by Texas (17), Florida (15), and Illinois (13). Just about half of the kids under 8 or 10 who play sports in the United States play soccer at some time during the year, alternating between baseball, basketball and/or (American) football. (Sports diversity is encouraged, and in many circles to specialize a kid in one sport is even frowned upon with religious zeal.) One of the quarters of the season, these kids will enroll in a soccer team of their school. The popularity of soccer as a recreational sport in the United States has increased enormously – hence the figure of the "soccer mom" and the "soccer dad" who take care of the team. In that sense, soccer is probably more popular in the United States than even in Spain, where only a small fraction of the kids plays sports, and then only a small fraction of these plays soccer in a team (although they might play quite regularly at recess). In 2002, statistician Scott Berry published in the journal *Chance* an interesting study that showed that the rate at which Olympic records have been broken in the last century is correlated with population growth patterns. Athletes find it three times harder to compete for a podium spot now compared to the 1920s, when the world's population was 1/3 of what it is now. This correlation suggests that the increase in competition is driving improvements in athletes' performance and in coaching methods through population pressure. Applying this reasoning to U.S. soccer demographics (the population of Spain is 6.7 times smaller than that of the United States), one would expect that a bit of scouting in the United States would bring up a few Xavis, Iniestas and/or Messis in no time. What is wrong in the U.S. soccer education?

There are two things that are wrong. First of all, American kids, on average, have not traditionally *watched* much soccer, they only *played* it. Playing it mostly trains the feet's neuromuscular connections, and that's good, but watching the professionals is essential to learn what the best option in any given game situation is. My son (who has been raised in Seattle but watches Barça games on TV with me), when he was seven he already knew that on the midfield he was supposed to open the ball to the wing, and when he got stuck up front he would make an unusual pass back to ensure possession – he learned that from Xavi and Iniesta, watching FC Barcelona game after game after game. This is the *usual* way of learning soccer tactics for most European kids. However, most American kids are behind in this aspect of soccer education – they have played more soccer than they have watched it, while in Europe (especially in Spain and Italy, where soccer is a quasi-religion) the tendency is reversed: they have watched more soccer than they have played it. As a result, a Spanish kid that plays regularly at recess and watches FC Barcelona or Real Madrid games all the time is probably a smarter soccer player (if less technically able) than the equivalent American soccer kid that plays in his elementary school team two months a year but does not watch any soccer games on TV. The fact that American kids do not grow up watching soccer contributes to explain why they don't learn the proper soccer concepts – "Position, Possession, Pressure" –, which makes them non-competitive when they reach professional age. Most importantly, kids learn by emulation: How would a kid that has never seen Michael Jordan be able to know the limits of basketball? The same question applies to soccer and the star of the moment, be it Maradona, Ronaldinho, or Messi. Fortunately, this state of affairs is likely to change very rapidly with the advent of satellite TV, which brings high-quality matches to every house and every sports bar. The youngest generation of American kids is now, for the first time, watching Messi, Cristiano Ronaldo and the rest of the pack.

But there is something else that, in my opinion, is much more fundamentally disturbing about U.S. soccer education than not watching soccer. The biggest problem is that the MLS does not invest in soccer education at an early-enough age. MLS clubs' youth academies compete in the U.S. Soccer Development Academy (USSDA) league (the top tier for youth soccer in the U.S.). As of 2013, the USSDA lists 80 Development Academies, but it only covers U-17/U-18 down to U-13/U-14 – so most MLS clubs do not have an incentive to run U-10 programs because they would not compete in the USSDA. Of these 80 clubs, as of 2013 only 17 are MLS clubs, and only a handful of these offer subsidized academies for U-10 programs. Chicago Fire was the first MLS club to offer a (fully subsidized) U-10 (pre)Academy since 2012. FC Dallas has the largest program in the nation, with 1,800 boys and girls from 6-7 year-olds until U-19's. For American parents contemplating their kid's options to become a professional soccer player, considering that there are more than 4 million registered kids in youth soccer in America, the bottleneck is very steep and the selection process must be noisy, missing much of the talent on the way. The scenario is very grim.

When American kids reach age 10 or so, the organization of youth soccer changes and becomes very dedicated – it's called "Select Soccer", because from that point on the clubs hold tryouts for selecting the players into their various teams. The kids now train two or three times a week, play one game a week on average, all year long, and often have to travel inter-state distances to play tournaments. They typically don't have much time for other sports. Select Soccer is played under the auspices of either schools or "clubs", although these clubs do not typically play in the MLS. As a result, their only source of revenue is from the bottom – the players and their families. This is the biggest tragedy of American soccer. Select Soccer is expensive: at least $2,000 per player to cover the necessary expenses of coach, fields, attire, etc.; with travel, for teams that make it often to out-of-state tournaments, it is not rare to see a family hit $5,000 bills. For this reason, while soccer has a huge social penetration at earlier ages in the United States, Select Soccer has an elitist stigma – a lot of young athletes from under-privileged families opt early on for cheaper sports (baseball, basketball, and football) that are covered by clubs' subsidies. Even though the United States had 307 million people as of 2011, its effective soccer-active population by age 10 is much smaller than that of a small European country such as Holland (which has 17 million people, or 18 times smaller than the U.S. population). The MLS clubs have conveniently adapted to this situation by "cherry-picking" from the talent produced by Select Soccer clubs at an advanced age (typically around U-15 or U-16, when kids can enter one of the subsidized Development Academies). As a result, the MLS clubs do not control the educational process in the critical years from 7-14 and this process is not tied in with the style of play of the first team, as occurs at FC Barcelona or Ajax. Furthermore, the MLS clubs' "cherry-picking" strategy is only an illusion: it only scans a very small fraction of the population – the wealthy that can afford the high fees. I believe the United States will never be a soccer power horse until the majority of MLS clubs take the burden of soccer education off the shoulders of the poor and start subsidized youth academies from at least age 10.

It has been argued that the Ajax/FC Barcelona (free, club-subsidized) youth academy model cannot be implemented in the U.S. because soccer in the U.S. is not the "king sport". I don't see a cause-effect relationship. While it is true that soccer has to compete with American football, basketball and baseball for TV revenues – unlike in Europe –, it is not clear that the dire situation of youth soccer in the U.S. should be blamed entirely on the competition from other sports. The percentage of kids that play soccer in the U.S. is much larger than, say, in Spain (where soccer is definitely "king"), and soccer is clearly growing as a professional sport, so the landscape of TV revenues is bound to change very fast. In any case, the competition won't go away, so a model must be found that allows for soccer to coexist with the other sports. People (i.e., all the youth soccer associations in the U.S.) that adhere to the line of thinking that the European, free youth academy model (sponsored by a professional-league club) is not possible in the U.S. have been trying for many years the Select-Soccer-based system and have become accustomed to a self-congratulatory feedback mechanism. Everyone pats each other in the back at the end of each season because the objectives are all too easily reached.

However, if you care to be critical, you will see that the present model is not working: How many American players can you name that are good enough to play in a top European first division team? One, perhaps two? You would think that a country with a larger population than Brazil and with more kids who play soccer than in Spain, but a country that cannot retain them because soccer does not have a proper outlet for them, should – by sheer statistics – have at least a dozen top players in each of the five top European leagues. But that's clearly not the case. Therefore, there is something that is obstructing the American youth soccer pipeline.

It can't be the quality of the coaching: I have seen the coaches in Seattle youth academies and they are just as good as anywhere else. I can see the problem right away: it's the connection between the scouting and the MLS clubs. In the U.S., MLS clubs are disconnected from Select Soccer clubs (the ones that do the scouting and early development). After the players are more than half-developed, the MLS clubs recruit the best players into their Development Academies, and each MLS club adopts a different style of play that completely disconnected with the Select Soccer clubs that developed those players. Recall FC Barcelona's centralized scouting strategy, whereby all scouts have unified criteria for selection of players according to how well they match the style of the first team: that strategy is a central pillar of the success of Barça's youth academy because players learn within the same methodological framework throughout their lives. In the U.S., many Select Soccer clubs have seen the benefits of using possession soccer as an educational tool for kids but the fruits do not end up producing the promised juice because the MLS clubs are still directed by coaches who do not believe in possession soccer. The MLS desperately needs one success story of a Barça-style team to unclog its pipeline.

Given this state of affairs, it is surprising that the MLS clubs do not have lower-division teams to gain a presence in local Select Soccer divisions. For example, in Seattle, the local soccer team, the Sounders, doesn't have an active team in any of the Select Soccer divisions, and their Development Academy program starts at U15 or U16. How are they supposed to scout the best local kids? They end up capturing them through contacts with the local clubs (the best are always easy to detect), but this disconnect between Select Soccer and the professional teams misses a whole section of the social stratum (those that can't afford Select Soccer) and, most important, does not guarantee that the kids will be brought up playing with the same style as the professional team. There is no thread connecting the children and the professionals.

It has also been pointed out that American elite youth soccer puts too much emphasis on games (where the ratio of ball to player is at most 1:18, in 9v9 format) and not enough on training (where the ratio of ball to player is typically 1:1). Sports journalist Tom Turner underwent a study of elite youth female soccer players and concluded that with an average game duration of 80 minutes, a maximum roster of 18, and with the ball out of play an average of 33% of the time, each player would experience only 1.5 min of active play in contact with the ball – less than 3 hours per year! However, this is not the major ailment American soccer suffers from. The real problem is that 4 million kids converge towards a pipeline of just 17 MLS Development Academies with very rudimentary scouting methods. There are plenty of excellent kids – even with only 1.5 min of ball-contact time – (I have seen many of them!), but the MLS doesn't have instruments to systematically find them before they go onto other sports or activities.

I realize that not everyone is a fan of running a youth academy to promote the MLS. Recently, an American soccer friend asked me: "Why should I care about youth academies? All I care about is to watch good soccer". My answer to him is that the two are, in the long term, inextricably tied. We all want to watch good soccer, but a model based on only buying talent is not a sustainable model because the stars are too expensive for the amount of revenue that the sport generates – so you might as well get into the business of creating the stars and use them in your team. In Spain, many clubs used investments in real estate to finance their soccer operations – resulting in huge debts (a "soccer bubble") when the financial crisis arrived. Some people have been reluctant to start subsidized youth programs at the club level with the argument that the club would deplete the region of the best players in every category. This argument reflects a complete lack of knowledge of youth soccer: Barça kids do not win all the time either, as there is much more to youth soccer than simple scouting (scouting is often imperfect and dynamic – the other teams end up having plenty of good players, players evolve, etc.). Another argument against starting youth programs has been the low budget in which most MLS teams have to operate. Yet the cost of signing and maintaining, say, Fredrik Ljungberg (a great Swedish midfielder in his youth, but well past his prime at 32 years old when he landed in Seattle), would have paid for the development of hundreds of young players (not to speak of the coaches salaries, which contribute to the local economy). Ljungberg only scored two (!) goals during his two-year tenure at the Sounders. Adrian Hanauer, general manager and part owner of the Sounders (who made his fortune with pizzas and a framing business, among others), is still skeptical about investing in youth development: "We're spending roughly $1 million on youth development. In order to do it really, really right we probably need to spend $3 million a year on youth development. The pure economic argument is, are we developing $3 million of assets every year? My gut tells me no today." The problem is that Hanauer sees everything through the lens of a businessman used to making very short-term projections, and youth development is a "business" whose basic material takes 10 years to mature and whose art takes 20 years to master. The Sounders board (made up of a Hollywood guru and a Microsoft billionaire, among others, with no soccer experience) made their cost and risk projections when they decided to hire limping stars rather than build a youth soccer education program. I would not even hesitate: I have seen children that will be better than Ljungberg in a few years – and I'm sure there is plenty more outside of the Seattle area that I haven't even seen. All the Sounders would need is patience, and ask around to find the best kids. Without a solid and systematic connection between the children and the professional U.S. teams, the success story of kids such as Ben Lederman will be a statistical fluke.

In the end, I firmly believe – because I've seen the magical process unfold at Barça once before – that it will all come down to how the fans respond to the new generation of homegrown players that are coming up through the ranks of the MLS youth system. The Sounders do have a Development Academy (i.e. U15 and up), which has already produced one player for the first team (DeAndre Yedlin), and his goals and enthusiastic runs receive louder cheers than comparable efforts of those of his teammates. Why? Because he is a local! Everyone knows that he feels the colors of the club and he is not in this just for the money, so the fans connect and identify with him in a way that they can't with the other stars. This phenomenon is as old as soccer – fans have always loved the kids raised at their own club, be it at Liverpool, Manchester United, FC Barcelona, Real Madrid, or the Sounders. I'm sure this extra appreciation by the fans must have a money value in terms of sponsorships and shirts sold. So the lesson for Hanauer and other skeptics is clear: soccer fans, here, there and everywhere, adore strong and healthy youth academies. The alternative is to let the MLS be reduced to a marketing competition where the big teams are owned by large investors and the fans have to suffer how Microsoft or a Qatari prince play against Apple and Google.

The more players from *La Masia*, the better?

On Nov 25, 2012, FC Barcelona played against Levante with a starting line-up of 10 players from the youth academy. It was not the first time that Barça played with 10 players raised at *La Masia*. But in the 13th minute, the Brazilian defender Alves got injured and was substituted by Montoya, a youth academy player recently promoted to the first team. Aside from him and Leo Messi, the rest were European Champions with the Spanish National team (*EuroCup* 2010). From that minute on, FC Barcelona played with 11 players from the youth academy for the first time in modern history (counting official games). They beat Levante 0-4, making a record-winning series that left Real Madrid 11 points behind in only 13 league games. Remarkably, the next day's headline in most newspapers was not that distance with Real Madrid but the fact that, at last, the *Camp Nou* had seen a full squad from *La Masia*. There is, indeed, a perception floating in the stadium's air that, the more players from the youth academy, the better.

This perception is a fairly recent phenomenon at FC Barcelona, so it can be studied quantitatively. It was Johan Cruyff who systematically started bringing up young players from the youth academy in 1988. In the graph below we see the number of debuts of youth academy players per year. Johan Cruyff (with a 4.0 average) was actually the least consistent of all the coaches: one year he did not debut any player, and in his last year he debuted 10 (some of them not worth of the first team). Rijkaard had the highest average (5.8) but is ranked second in inconsistency, as one year there were 9 debuts but the next year only 3. Van Gaal had the lowest average (3.5) but was fairly consistent and, to his credit, he did debut some of the biggest stars of the present Barça (Xavi, Puyol, Valdés). *La Masia*, after all, does not produce players at a constant rate; if one thing cannot be blamed on Van Gaal, is to have overlooked the talent in the youth academy. "I would like to win the *European Cup* with eleven Catalan players", Van Gaal said once. Guardiola has debuted one of the largest average number of players (5.5) and also with the largest consistency: every year he debuted either 5 or 6 players.

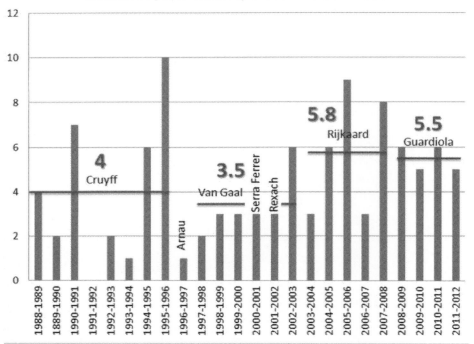

Number of youth academy debuts in the first team

This graph depicts the number of players from La Masia that debuted with the first team on any given year. The red bar represents the average for each coach's period. Note that Van Gaal's tenure (3.5 debuts/year in average) had two periods (1997-2000 and 2002-2003). The lowest and the highest number of debuts occurred both under Cruyff (0 in 1991-1992 and 10 in 1995-1996, respectively), the highest average occurred (5.8 debuts/year) under Rijkaard, and the most stable average (5.5 debuts/year) occurred under Guardiola.

The average number of youth academy players that play with the first team has been increasing in the last ten years, as shown in the following graph. (The data has been obtained from *"BarçaEternal"*, a book that compiles all the statistics by FC Barcelona since its foundation.) Rexach hit the lowest point in April 2002 against Athletic Bilbao, when he fielded a starting squad with no players from *La Masia* (although by the end of the game there were three). At the other end of the spectrum, Guardiola used a starting squad with seven players from *La Masia* to beat Manchester United 0-2 in the 2009 *Champions League* Final. Such statistics are an object of pride among Barça fans, who have become accustomed to treasure the youth academy as the source of its best players.

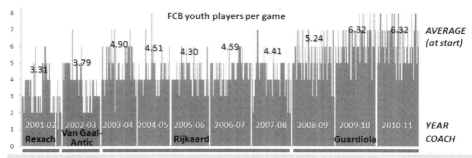

The blue spikes in this graph depict the number of youth players at the start of each game on any given season (years shown in white). The average number of starting youth players for that season is shown in black. The corresponding coach for each group of years is shown at the bottom of the graph. The graph clearly indicates that there is a trend to increase the number of youth players in the starting roster (usually the most important players), implying that the quality of the players from La Masia is increasing (at least in the opinion of the coaches).

Is that so? Did I just spoke from the heart? Many excellent – some would say legendary – players from outside its youth system have passed through FC Barcelona in the last ten years: Ronaldinho, Eto'o, Henry, Deco, Ibrahimovic – to name a few. Yet if you ask an average Barça fan, none of these is esteemed as highly as the jewels of the crown: Xavi, Iniesta, of course Messi, but also Busquets and Thiago Alcántara. These are *untouchables*. But we did sell Ronaldinho, Eto'o, and the lot.

I'll be the devil's advocate for a minute and I'll try to be fair to these stars that were sacked by questioning some coaches' policy of giving priority to the youth academy players. It could be that they were given priority simply because the coaches (Rexach, Guardiola, Vilanova) were from the youth academy themselves and have some bias for working with players raised at *La Masia*, or sympathized with the concept because they came from Ajax (Van Gaal, Rijkaard). If that were true, it would be very simple to prove. The *BarçaEternal* book lists all the games, squads, and goals for every game played by FC Barcelona since its existence (up until 2011). We can count, say for the last ten years (which encompasses 568 official competition games), the number of youth academy players that were fielded in the starting squad, and see if that had any influence in the average number of goals in favor or in the goal differential. I'm sure that the stars are waiting to hear that the number of youth academy players on the field had little or no effect on the team's performance.

2001-2011

Correlation between the average goals in favor scored by Barça in the period 2001-2011 (blue line), the average goal differential in the same period (green line), and the number of players from the youth academy in the starting roster (red bars). Note that it is presently impossible to evaluate the action of "hidden variables" such as the performance of a given coach because the statistics do not include enough games. However, if this correlation stays true for a few more years, one should be able to conclude that "until now, the more youth academy players, the better".

Amazingly enough, the graph above seems to show that FC Barcelona has benefited from having higher numbers of youth academy players in the starting squad – both in terms of goals in favor and in terms of goal differential. The difference between fielding two or fielding eight players from the youth academy can be summarized as a two-fold increase in the average goal-scoring capacity and a seven-fold increase in the average goal-differential capacity over the 2001-2011 period.

This graph must be interpreted with caution. First of all, it could be that the team simply performed better in the times when it played with more youth players *for other reasons* – for example, because they played with a certain coach (for example, Guardiola). Unfortunately, there are not enough statistics (yet) to confirm or refute this point, but time will say as future coaches keep on adding to the statistic. Also, this graph should not be interpreted as a principle against players raised outside of *La Masia*; it does not mean either that *La Masia* players are naturally better than players from outside. It only means that the youth academy, *together with the first team coaches*, have done *until now* a very good job at selecting the best players. Remember that statistics do not give us predictive power: it would be foolish to use the graph as a selection criterion for the future because the graph only tells us about the past. This graph simply supports the idea that soccer is a team sport requiring a high level of training, and since FC Barcelona benefits from training its teams from a very early age, higher numbers of players from the youth academy are more likely to result in successful associative interactions (i.e. passes, goals, assists, etc.) involving a large number of team members.

The strongest youth academies

Here is a simple question that is difficult to answer: Which clubs have the strongest youth academies? First of all, how can we measure (or define) the "strength"? As a scientist, I believe that the measure should be obvious in the form of an objective graph and numbers. We cannot trust the coaches to evaluate their own academy because their job is on the spot. And most journalists are not prepared to perform a scientific study.

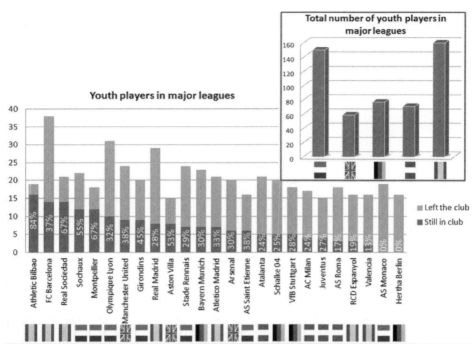

This graph, elaborated at the end of 2012, depicts the clubs with the highest numbers of players originating from their own youth academy; the percentages over the total that are still in active top European leagues (but have left the club) are shown in white. Athletic Bilbao is first, with 16 (84%) of its players being homegrown. Both FC Barcelona and Real Sociedad are second, with 14 players (37% and 67% of the total, respectively). Note that the next three, and the 8th place, are French youth academies. Real Madrid is in 9th place with 8 homegrown players still in the club (28% of the total). If we had ordered this list by the total contribution to any league, the first three clubs would have been FC Barcelona (38 players), Olympique de Lyon (31), and Real Madrid (29). As we can see, both FC Barcelona and Real Madrid have a highly productive youth academy, but compared to FC Barcelona, Real Madrid sells a larger portion of its youth talent to other clubs, uses less of its youth players for its first team, and places less players in top professional leagues. The inset offers a surprising revelation: Spain is almost tied with France in number of youth academy players playing in top leagues, which speaks highly about the ongoing efforts to promote French youth soccer.

Since 2007, every year the Swiss *CIES Football Observatory* provides detailed demographic and statistic studies on all the professional players in the so-called "top 5" leagues (Spain, England, Italy, France, and Germany), including the average age, weight, youth training, etc. (Note: This "top 5" designation is purely based on TV rankings; below I will show you that it is a big mistake not to include Holland in any youth academy study.) From those studies one can extract very interesting data, as summarized in the graph above that plots the number of youth players (defined by CIES as trained in the club between 15 and 21 years of age) produced by each club. The players that are still in the club and the players that have already left the club are plotted separately.

FC Barcelona is, not surprisingly, the club that produced the most players (38), of which 14 (37%) are still in the club as of 2013: Messi, Valdés, Bartra, Montoya, Iniesta, Dos Santos, Pedro, Busquets, Puyol, Xavi, Muniesa, Thiago, Cuenca, and Tello. The remaining 24 players (only players in the top 5 leagues are counted) play mostly in Spain (Nano, Sergio García, Verdú, Baena, Botía, Marc Valiente, Fontàs, Giovanni dos Santos, Trashorras, Víctor Rodríguez); four English teams have players from *La Masia*: Chelsea (Oriol Romeu), Arsenal (Mikel Arteta), Liverpool (Pepe Reina), and Wigan (Jordi Gómez); one plays in Italy (Bojan Krkic for Milan) and one in France (Thiago Motta for Paris St.-Germain).

If we order the list by the number of players that are still in the club (as shown in the graph), FC Barcelona is not even the first (Athletic Bilbao has 16). Does this mean that Athletic Bilbao has a "stronger" youth academy than Barça? No, because few of Athletic Bilbao players make it to the Spain's national team, and the presence of youth academy players is not dictated by the excellence of their youth academy but by cultural pressure: their fans and directors traditionally favor Basque players, even at the expense of player quality (it's their choice and their style).

Ordering the list by the total number of youth players playing in a major league, the next five clubs after Barça are Olympique Lyon (31/32%), Real Madrid (29/28%), Stade Rennais (24/29%), Manchester United (24/38%), and Bayern Munich (23/30%). It is surprising how many French clubs are at the top of the list, given that it has been a while since a French club has won a major title in Europe. French clubs occupy 6 of the 15 top spots. Does this mean something good or bad for French soccer? The cumulative number of youth players is shown in the insert. France appears to almost tie with Spain – the triple champions of two *EuroCups* and a World Cup – so one might be inclined to conclude that France is doing the right things. Is it? One problem with these statistics is that they confer the same weight to Xavi, Iniesta and Busquets than the worse youth player in any other team. In other words, the problem with the insert is that it only takes into account quantities of players, disregarding their quality. Although the main graph did confirm what everyone knew (that FC Barcelona has the best youth academy in the world), how meaningful is Olympique Lyon's 2nd place, Real Madrid 3rd place, and so on?

The proof that this definition of "strength" is not very meaningful is that not all the studies show the same ranking. A recent study undertaken by the *Scuola Allenatori di Coverciano*, a center for soccer-related studies, counted the number of players from each youth academy that make it to first division and arrived at the shocking conclusion that the most productive youth academies in Europe are (by this order) FC Barcelona, Real Madrid, Ajax, Osasuna, Bayer Leverkusen, and Atalanta. Now, where are the players produced by the Osasuna youth academy, does anyone remember their names? Only two of them made it to the Spanish national team in the last 30 years. Similarly, only four times a player raised by the Bayer Leverkusen youth academy has been called to the German national team in the last 30 years. Atalanta's youth academy has had 9 calls to the national team (in the last 30 years), but AC Milan (34), Roma (23), Inter (21), Parma (15) and Torino (15) are ahead of Atalanta in Italy alone.

Can we come up with a more meaningful ranking that takes into account the quality of the players? The best way to look at this problem is to look for an outcome of the youth academies that is periodically evaluated by someone who is not related to any of the clubs. I found that a good measurement of the quality or strength of a youth academy is the number of players it contributes to the national team within a given period (so the strength can change depending on what period is evaluated, but as long as we agree on the evaluation period, the numbers are consistent). Note that a club has no power whatsoever to alter or modify this number (unlike the number of players that make it to first division, which could be increased artificially by, say, reducing the players' price): the composition of the national football team is decided every two years (for every World Cup and for every *EuroCup*) by a professional (the national coach) who is not affiliated with any club and is independently appointed to select players from each club for playing for the national team. (Usually the national team coach appointment lasts more than just two years, especially when results are good, but the coach does not always call the same players to the national team.)

Using Wikipedia, it is now possible to find the squads for every competition as well as the youth academy of origin for every player in the roster. For some reason, the biographical data entered into Wikipedia is consistently better for Spanish, English and German players (for whom the youth club is almost always listed or explained in the biography) than for Dutch and Italian players (for whom the youth club is less often listed, specially for Italian players); when the youth academy could not be known, the credit went to the first club (typically at 17-18 years of age) where the player played professionally, because usually the first club is the one that has the biggest impact in the soccer education of the player. In England the pre-professional formation period is often referred to as an "apprenticeship". In Italy it is not uncommon for players to change clubs up to ten times in their career (staying in clubs for only a couple of years at a time) and to start in second- or even third-division teams. In the case where the player had been in more than one youth academy, I gave credit to the last one prior to him becoming a professional player, around the critical formation period of ~16-17 years old, because (in the absence of additional information) that youth academy was more likely to have had the biggest impact in the player. Over the 30 years considered, the

National Teams had the opportunity to compete in 8 World Cups and 8 *EuroCups*, although they did not always qualify and that affects the total number of contributions by all the youth academies: Spain missed one *EuroCup* (335 contributions in 30 years), Holland missed 3 World Cups and a *EuroCup* (269 contributions), England missed 2 *EuroCups* and one World Cup (291), Italy missed two *EuroCups* (314), and France missed one *EuroCup* and 2 World Cups (290); Germany is the only country that didn't missed any competition (358 contributions). In the years when a national team did not qualify for either the World Cup or the *EuroCup*, the competition is shown in parentheses in the graph and the line is simply interpolated between the adjacent data points. (In the case of Holland, which did not qualify for the first three competitions of the graph, to make the graph more realistic I used numbers obtained from the squads that participated in the qualifying rounds of WC'82 and Euro'84, but interpolated WC'84; similarly for France, which did not qualify for Euro'88, WC'90 and WC'94, I interpolated Euro'88 and WC'94 but I used the squad that participated in the qualifying rounds of WC'90.) When a national team did not qualify in any given year, the contribution of all the youth academies for that year was set equal to zero (for fairness, since the graph depicts a process of competition between youth academies). Undoubtedly these decisions add noise to the measurements; however, as we see below, the noise is small, because the total number of players per country is large (around 300), which produces very striking conclusions.

Below are six graphs (corresponding to the six top soccer European countries: Spain, Holland, Germany, England, Italy, and France) that show the number of players contributed to the national team by the different youth academies encompassing the last 30 years, i.e., during the period 1982-2012. As a figure of merit, and also for clarity, only youth academies that contributed 3 or more players at any given year during the 30-year period are shown in the graphs. The number of youth academies that satisfy this criterion (which leaves out a few good academies that will be cited later) is, overall, similarly small for all six countries: 8 in England and France, 7 in Spain, 6 in Italy, and 5 in

Germany and Holland. It should be noted that the time-course graphs depict the competition of players for a finite number of slots (22 prior to 2002 and 23 from 2002 on), so as one academy rises it is naturally at the expense of the others – i.e. the measure of the "strength" of an academy is only relative.

The inset pie graphs depict the percentages of the total number of players contributed by each youth academy over the 30-year period. The pie graphs show all the youth academies that contributed more than 2 players at any given year during that period (i.e., the largest pie piece in all the pie graphs corresponds to the sum of all the youth academies that only contributed a single player in all years where they contributed one player).

We can extract the following conclusions:

A) There is no evidence of a direct correlation between the strength of a youth academy (measured as the number of players it places on the national team) and the ability of its first team to win either the league or the cup. There is simply not enough data because FC Barcelona's and Bayern's ascending trends are too recent, and the various "supremacy peaks" of other youth academies have been too short or not high enough above the fluctuations of the other youth academies.

B) Over the 30-year period, Ajax has been by far the most prolific youth academy in the continent, having contributed almost 90 players (the same player on two different years is counted as two), an impressive one third (32%) of Holland's National Team. That contribution is constant if we only count the last 20 years (34%) or the last 10 years (33%). Of note, at Euro'96, the Ajax youth academy contributed 10 players (almost half of the squad of 22) to the Dutch national team, the largest contribution ever by any of the youth academies studied here. Ajax is the only youth academy that has never contributed less players than its contemporary youth academies (i.e. its graph always looks "above" the others for 30 years), for all the countries studied. In Holland, 7 clubs contributed 2 players (or more) at least one year during the 1982-2012 period considered; these 7 clubs contributed 56% of the 269 youth players to the National Team (44% of the contributions were from "weak" youth academies that contributed only one player or less at any given year). The 5 youth academies that had contributed 3 players (or more) in at least one same year during the 30-year period (shown in the time graph), overall accumulated 43.9% of the contributions.

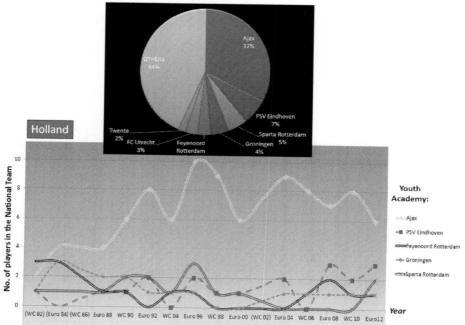

The graph depicts the number of players contributed by each youth academy to the Dutch National Team over the last 30 years in the two major international competitions (World Cup and EuroCup). The years that appear in parentheses indicate that the Dutch National Team did not qualify those years; the number of players was either obtained from qualifying games or extrapolated between previous and following years. The pie graph (inset) depicts the cumulative number of players (shown as a percentage of the total) contributed by each Dutch youth academy. For clarity, the graph only shows Dutch youth academies that contributed at least 3 players at some point in the last 30 years; the pie graph includes all the Dutch youth academies that contributed 2 or more players at some point in the last 30 years.

C) Spain's time graph reveals more fluctuations than Holland's graph: there is clearly more competition. We notice that Real Madrid's youth academy contributed a peak in the period between World Cup '86 and World Cup '90, due to the generation of *La Quinta del Buitre*. However, in 1990 those seven Real Madrid players were all between 24 and 29 years of age (24, 25, 25, 26, 28, 29, and 29, to be precise). In other words, there had been a coincidence of birthdays. As the players aged, since the youth academy was not properly fueled, the peak died off. We must conclude that *La Quinta del Buitre* did not have continuity because Real Madrid's youth academy did not have a coaching method to sustain its excellence.

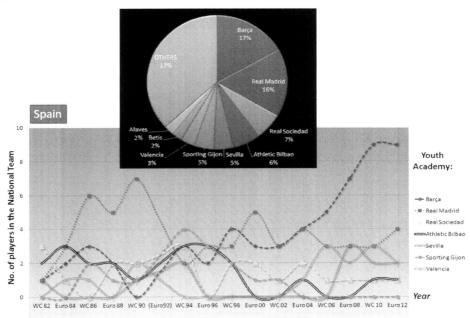

The graph depicts the number of players contributed by each youth academy to the Spanish National Team over the last 30 years in the two major international competitions (World Cup and EuroCup). The years that appear in parentheses indicate that the Spanish National Team did not qualify those years; the number of players was either obtained from qualifying games or extrapolated between previous and following years. The pie graph (inset) depicts the cumulative number of players (shown as a percentage of the total) contributed by each Spanish youth academy. For clarity, the graph only shows Spanish youth academies that contributed at least 3 players at some point in

185

Over 30 years, Real Madrid has contributed 55 players (16% of total), but the contribution is somewhat lower (14%) if we only count the last 10 years. Overall, 9 clubs contributed 2 or more players at least one year during the 1982-2012 period considered; these 9 clubs contributed 63% of the 335 youth players to the National Team (only 37% of the contributions were from "weak" youth academies that contributed at most one player at any given year). The 7 youth academies that had contributed 3 players (or more) in at least one same year during the 30-year period (shown in the time graph), overall accumulated 59% of the contributions.

D) The second largest feature in Spain is the increase of FC Barcelona youth academy players by 2004-2006, a tendency that has not stopped: presently (2012), the contribution to the national team is at record-high of 9 players. Interestingly, the rise of the youth academy dates from well after the tenure of Johan Cruyff (1988-1996), who is widely credited for a radical change in style (both of the first team and of the management of the youth academy). This latency only reflects the large amount of time that it takes to educate a soccer player: Xavi and Iniesta joined the club at the tender ages of 11 (in 1991) and 13 (in 1997), respectively, and became part of the starting first-team squad at around 18 (in 1998) and 20 (in 2004) years old, respectively – that's 7 years of soccer education. In the histogram of FC Barcelona for 2010, the 9 players' ages are very sparsely distributed between 21 and 32 (21, 22, 23, 23, 26, 27, 28, 30, and 32). This wide distribution is a strong proof that, unlike Real Madrid's *Quinta del Buitre*, the rise cannot be due to a coincidence of birthdays but rather is the result of a coaching method that will likely keep producing more elite players. The rise at the right end of this graph also offers a strong hint about the origin of the Spain's National Team's string of stellar performances lately. The graph suggests that the work done at FC Barcelona's youth academy is now paying off on a national level, since the skeleton of the team is FC Barcelona's and the players, who have played together since they were kids, play on an "auto-Barça-pilot" when they are playing in *La Roja*. Over the last 30 years, the FC Barcelona youth academy has already contributed 57 players (17%) of all the players in the Spanish National Team, and this percentage increases to 27% (almost 1/3) in the last 10 years (since World Cup '02).

E) In Germany, 11 clubs contributed 2 (or more) players at least one year during the 1982-2012 period considered; these 11 clubs contributed 45% of the 358 youth players to the National Team (55% of the contributions were from "weak" youth academies that only contributed at most one player at any given year). The 5 youth academies that had contributed 3 players (or more) in at least one same year during the 30-year period (shown in the time graph), overall accumulated 25% of the contributions. The distribution of excellence among youth academies is more fragmented in Germany than in Holland and Spain. Bayern Munich has learned the historical Ajax-Barça lesson and has been taking care of its youth academy patiently and steadily. As a result, its players are now contributing to the German national team in increasing numbers (a record-high of 6 in the World Cup 2010 and *EuroCup* 2012). Over the last 30 years, Bayern's contribution to the national team (9%) is about twice as high as the other strong youth academies (VfB Stuttgart, Schalke 04, FC Köln, Stuttgart Kickers, Hannover 96, and Karlsruher SC), but over the last 10 years Bayern dominates by far (17%), with an also higher presence of VfB Stuttgart (8%), Hannover 96 (7%), and Schalke 04 (7%). Bayern Munich is also a financial horsepower: for the first time in its 112 years of history, in 2012 the club presented €373 M in benefits, a European record-high. Unlike other teams which raise money by making shady deals with politicians or millionaires that made fortunes in areas of the economy unrelated to soccer, Bayern follows the Barça model and raises money entirely through TV contracts, sponsorships (a line-up of the strongest German companies: Adidas, Audi, Telekom, insurance giant Allianz, Lufthansa, Hypo Vereninsbank, and Paulaner beer), and the fees paid by their loud and loyal fans – 187,865 of them, which pack the stadium every weekend and buy 600,000 shirts per year. There is a sense of family in how the team is managed: legendary Bayern player-coaches (among them, Franz Beckenbauer, Karl-Heinz Rummenigge, and Uli Hoeness) serve as presidents or are on the board (this also tends to keep the big egos of the coaches in check); even though the team finished second in all three competitions in 2011 (*Bundesliga*, Cup, and Champions), the fans reelected President Hoeness by 97% of the votes. If there is a team that can dethrone FC Barcelona in the long term, this is it.

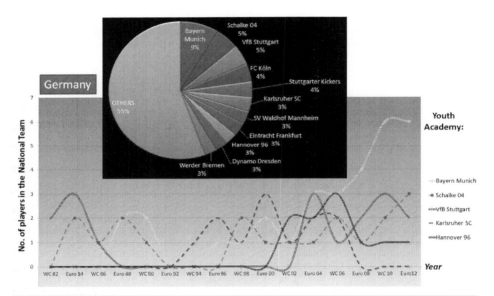

The graph depicts the number of players contributed by each youth academy to the German National Team over the last 30 years in the two major international competitions (World Cup and EuroCup). The years that appear in parentheses indicate that the German National Team did not qualify those years; the number of players was either obtained from qualifying games or extrapolated between previous and following years. The pie graph (inset) depicts the cumulative number of players (shown as a percentage of the total) contributed by each German youth academy. For clarity, the graph only shows German youth academies that contributed at least 3 players at some point in the last 30 years; the pie graph only includes the German youth academies that contributed 2 or more players at some point in the last 30 years.

The combined ascent of Bayern Munich, Schalke 04, and VfB Stuttgart cannot go unnoticed – Germany is on the rise as a whole. In just over a decade, Germany has spent more than €700 M in soccer youth programs, all coordinated and supervised by the German Soccer Federation (*Deutsche Fussball Bund* or DFB) while Spanish and Italian clubs are in critical debt and the *Calcio* and the *Premier League* are flooded with foreign players (both close to 50% in 2011-2012 – in Spain and Germany it is around 40% and in France 30%). Included in the first batch of young homegrown stars produced by this program are Bayern Munich's Thomas Müller, Bayer Leverkusen's André Schürrle, and Borussia Dortmund's Marco Reus – not at the level of Xavi, Iniesta, Fàbregas, Busquets, and Thiago, but excellent players that could give Spain a big surprise on any given day.

Anyways, these are just the first of the batch, the tip of the iceberg. The first players that came out of *La Masia* were not as good as Xavi and Iniesta either. It is so obvious that a change is coming, that the immutable old style of the German national team, based for decades on Panzer-type players – Stielike, Rummenigge, Schuster –, has changed: it is now refreshingly dynamic and joyful. For the 2006 World Cup, Germany invested €1,300 M in building or renovating soccer stadiums that are now filled to the top: a record 13.8 million tickets were sold during the 2011-2012 season. The DFB, which has its own program of 366 centers (comprising 1,000 coaches and 25,000 kids), imposed on every club the creation of a high performance center to help promote its youth program, among other functions. It is important to note that Germany has strategized this huge investment in soccer at a moment where the rest of Europe – including the soccer clubs – is in deep crisis. As the soccer clubs of weaker economies get debilitated, they are progressively forced to sell their best players while German clubs are slowly but wisely reinforcing their most durable asset: the homegrown talent. The coaches are mostly German, too. (Recent signing of Pep Guardiola for Bayern Munich will be an exception.)

Germany has shown many times in history that it knows how to invest its Deutsche marks, so the soccer industry should not be an exception. All they need to do is crank up their gold-digging mines until they, too, find gems like Messi, Xavi and Iniesta. I would not be surprised if in 10 years from now Germany has at least 10 centers with an output as strong as *La Masia*. With *La Masia* competing alone against a large pool of German youth players, it's only a matter of time before Germany takes over Spain's throne. (Many of my German friends are already celebrating based on well-deserved losses by Barça to Bayern and by Real Madrid to Borussia Dortmund in the semifinals of the 2012 *Champions League*, but I cautiously tell them to hold off their beer-popping because, as I argued above, in those games we were not able to see our beloved Barça for several unfortunate reasons.)

F) England invented the sport of soccer, so logically England is a country with a deep history of soccer youth academies and where we should expect more competition. In England, 14 clubs contributed 2 or more players at least one year during the 30-year period considered; these 14 clubs contributed 66% of the 291 youth players to the National Team, the largest fraction of the pie in the six countries studied (just 34% of the contributions were from "weak" youth academies that only contributed one player maximum at any given year). The 8 youth academies that had contributed 3 players (or more) in at least one same year during the 30-year period (shown in the time graph), overall accumulated 49.5% of the contributions. The most notable features of England's graph are the rise-and-fall of Manchester United (the generation of "Fergie's Fledglings", with Giggs, Beckham, the Neville brothers, and Scholes) and the ascent of West Ham United, appropriately nicknamed "The Academy of Football" by its fans, who are very proud of the club's long-time service to the national team. Previous illustrious national-team "graduates" of the Academy who did not make it into this 1982-2012 period study are Bobby Moore, Geoff Hurst, and Martin Peters. West Ham United has greatly benefitted from the increase in transfer fees, which allows the team to be well funded by the transfers from its youth academy, but has raised the question of whether retention of talent might be a much wiser long-term investment: the club, founded in 1895, has never won the *Premier League*. While it is obvious that the West Ham United contribution took the place of the Manchester United contribution to the English National team, the quality of the pool of players that have come through the Academy of Football is nowhere comparable to Fergie's Fledglings.

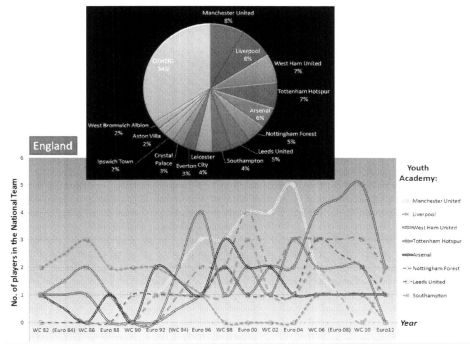

The graph depicts the number of players contributed by each youth academy to the English National Team over the last 30 years in the two major international competitions (World Cup and EuroCup). The years that appear in parentheses indicate that the English National Team did not qualify those years; the number of players was either obtained from qualifying games or extrapolated between previous and following years. The pie graph (inset) depicts the cumulative number of players (shown as a percentage of the total) contributed by each English youth academy. For clarity, the graph only shows English youth academies that contributed at least 3 players at some point in the last 30 years; the pie graph only includes the English youth academies that contributed 2 or more players at some point in the last 30 years.

Again, the rise-and-fall of Manchester United obeys to a poor management of its youth academy: after an accumulation of great players due to birthday proximities, the youth academy did not have a method to follow up on its own success; in recent years the first team technical staff has preferred to use the influx of cash from TV and merchandising to purchase outside players, at the expense of depressing the development of perfectly able players from their own youth academy. Notoriously absent from these charts are Chelsea and Manchester City, with 7 (2.4%) and 2 (0.7%) contributions to the National Team by their youth academies in 30 years, respectively, despite their huge expenditures in signings for the first team; neither of them have ever been able to place two players from their youth academy on the National Team on a given year.

We can also see in the graph hints of Liverpool's recent glorious path and troubled history. Between 1975-76 and 1989-90 (a span of 14 years), Liverpool won 10 *Premier Leagues*, 2 *FA Cups* (in 1986, it was a "Double"), 4 *League Cups*, 4 *European Cups* (1977, 1978, 1981, 1984), a *UEFA Cup* (1976), and a *UEFA Super Cup* (1977) – one of the most prolific runs of all times. In 1985, Liverpool reached the *European Cup* final again, this time against Juventus, at the *Heysel* stadium. Only two players from the Liverpool youth academy were in that squad, and they did not play (they were substitutes). Before kick-off, a group of violent Liverpool fans jumped over a fence and charged against Juventus *tiffosi*, indirectly causing a human avalanche that killed 39 supporters, mostly Italians. The game was played despite the ongoing tragedy and Liverpool lost 0-1 by an unfair penalty. Upon British government's request, FIFA banned the participation of all English clubs in European competitions indefinitely. The ban lasted five years; Liverpool was banned for an additional year, until 1991. The team has not won another *Premier League* since then. Yet in 2001, perhaps reflecting a generation of excellent players from the youth academy (4 contributions to the National Team in 2000: Steven Gerrard, Michael Owen, Steve McManaman, and Robbie Fowler), Liverpool won a "treble" (*FA Cup*, *League Cup*, and *UEFA Cup* – in fact, it also won the *FA Community Shield* that year).

G) England's situation is similar to Italy's, where a few rich clubs buy most of the elite Italian players but whose youth academies do not contribute proportionally to the elite pool. Juventus, for example, once contributed a record 8 players from its first team squad to the 1978 World Cup (off the graph), yet its youth academy only contributed two players.

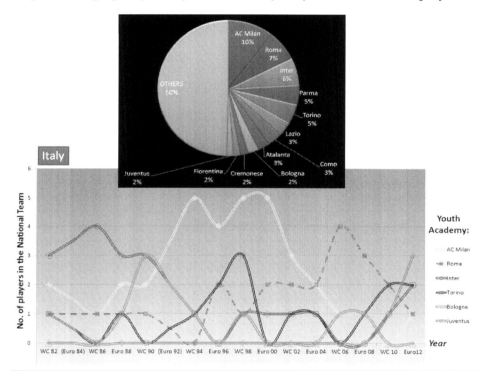

The graph depicts the number of players contributed by each youth academy to the Italian National Team over the last 30 years in the two major international competitions (World Cup and EuroCup). The years that appear in parentheses indicate that the Italian National Team did not qualify those years; the number of players was either obtained from qualifying games or extrapolated between previous and following years. The pie graph (inset) depicts the cumulative number of players (shown as a percentage of the total) contributed by each Italian youth academy. For clarity, the graph only shows Italian youth academies that contributed at least 3 players at some point in the last 30 years; the pie graph includes only the Italian youth academies that contributed 2 or more players at some point in the last 30 years.

We also see notable peaks, like the one contributed by Inter in WC'86, the generation contributed by AC Milan through WC '94-Euro'00, and the Roma peak of WC '06 – but they have all died off, similarly to the extinguished Manchester United (Euro '04) and Real Madrid (WC'86-WC'90) peaks. In Italy, 12 clubs contributed 2 players (or more) at least one year during the 1982-2012 period considered; these 12 clubs contributed 50% of the 314 youth players to the National Team (50% of the contributions were from "weak" youth academies that contributed only one player or less at any given year). The 6 youth academies that had contributed 3 players (or more) in at least one same year during the 30-year period (shown in the time graph), overall accumulated 34% of the contributions.

H) In France, the distribution of the pie is similar to England's. Here, 14 clubs contributed 2 players (or more) at least one year during the 1982-2012 period considered; these 14 clubs contributed 57% of the 290 youth players to the National Team (43% of the contributions were from "weak" youth academies that contributed only one player or less at any given year). The 8 youth academies that had contributed 3 players (or more) in at least one same year during the 30-year period (shown in the time graph), overall accumulated 39% of the contributions. As in most countries surveyed before, there is little correlation between the excellence of the youth academies and the number of titles won by the corresponding first team. The two teams that have won the *Ligue* most times (10), the St.-Étienne (founded in 1919) and the Olympique de Marseille (founded in 1899), have contributed 12 and 6 youth players, respectively, to the National Team in the 30-year period of 1982-2012; however, in this period, Olympique won the *Ligue* 5 times and St-Étienne none. Of note, Paris St.-Germain, a club that is owned by a Qatar prince and spends large sums in buying players for its first team, has – like Olympique – contributed only 6 players to the National Team in the last 30 yrs but, contrary to Olympique, has won just 2 *Ligues* since it was founded in 1970.

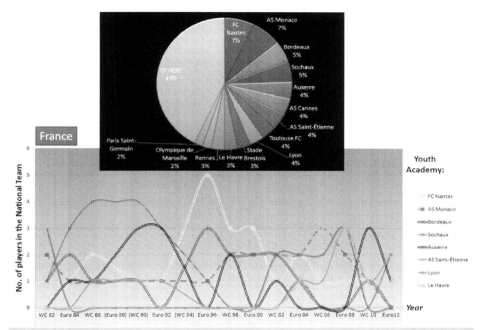

The graph depicts the number of players contributed by each youth academy to the French National Team over the last 30 years in the two major international competitions (World Cup and EuroCup). The years that appear in parentheses indicate that the French National Team did not qualify those years; the number of players was either obtained from qualifying games or extrapolated between previous and following years. The pie graph (inset) depicts the cumulative number of players (shown as a percentage of the total) contributed by each French youth academy. For clarity, the graph only shows French youth academies that contributed at least 3 players at some point in the last 30 years; the pie graph includes all the French youth academies that contributed 2 or more players at some point in the last 30 years.

Seeing these graphs, one very simple revelation comes to mind: Why didn't FC Barcelona and Bayern Munich copy the Ajax model sooner? Why don't *all* clubs copy it?

A worldwide phenomenon

After FC Barcelona's onslaught against Manchester United by 3-1 in the *Champions League* final in 2011, *Newsweek* magazine wondered in its cover: "Is Barcelona the best soccer team ever?" In the article, renowned soccer author Jimmy Burns reported that "all soccer people turned instantly into ballet critics to applaud a style of play that had an aesthetic dimension as well as being admirably, if not lethally, suited for the purpose of attaining victory". Sir Alex Ferguson, the highly respected *ManU* coach for the last 25 years, said that this was the best team they had ever faced. This time *ManU* star Wayne Rooney was on the field and had to personally suffer the humiliation. In 2009, as he was watching a Barça-Real Madrid game, according to his own words he stood up to clap, although he was alone in his living room; prompted by his wife what he was doing, he said he was watching the best performance he had ever seen. That 5-0 victory of Barça against Real Madrid is still considered worldwide one of the best games this team ever played: the French newspaper *L'Équipe* offered 275,000 free DVDs of the game to their readers despite the fact that neither team was French. As a testimony of FC Barcelona's global media attention, the day that Guardiola resigned as Barça coach, the Chinese social network Tencent Weibo registered 1.03 million messages referring to him. Similarly, the FC Barcelona stadium is now the second most-visited tourist attraction in Barcelona, only behind the unique and exotic cathedral Sagrada Família, ahead (sadly) of any museum or any monument.

The images above were obtained from social media and cannot be reproduced as single images elsewhere without permission. They are displayed here in a triptychal format as a historical document of the high media impact that FC Barcelona has had in recent times, which complies with fair use of images under U.S. copyright law.

The perception that FC Barcelona is one of the best teams (if not the best) is now a worldwide phenomenon, undoubtedly thanks to global reach of TV and the Internet. As of 2013, Barça is the soccer team with most followers in social media such as Facebook (42 million fans) and Twitter (15 million fans, counting its six Twitter accounts in English, Spanish, Catalan, French, Arab, and Japanese). Surprisingly, the country where Barça has the largest number of Facebook followers (with 3.8 million) is Indonesia, although since Indonesia has more than 240 Million people, these fans only amount to 15.8 people for every 1,000 Indonesians. Spain, by comparison, has a total ~1.6 M fans (in fifth place, with Mexico, USA and Brazil ahead of Spain) and about 33.8 fans per 1,000 Spanish people. Argentina has very similar numbers (33.3 M fans per 1,000 citizens and 1.3 M total fans, surely due to Messi. However, if Facebook fan number is a good measure of a club's popularity, then the country where Barça is, by far, most popular (with 43.7 M fans/1,000 people) is ... Chili – even more popular than in Spain! (The Chilean boom is likely due to the signing of Chilean star Alexis.) It would be interesting to find out, from the Facebook fan numbers of other large clubs, whether the distributions simply reflect a general passion for soccer in these countries.

Even in countries where sports are followed but soccer is not that popular (a.k.a. the United States – a recent Women's *European Cup* final, where the U.S. women were finalists, was not broadcast), now FC Barcelona has reached mainstream media: on January 2013, Barça and its thriving youth academy were featured in CBS' prime-time TV program *60 minutes* (which is the most successful program in U.S. television history based on ratings and the highest-rated TV news magazine). It was the first time that a soccer team had ever been featured on *60 minutes*. On February 2012, Messi was featured on the cover of *Time* magazine announcing his new title: "King Leo" – also the first time ever that a soccer player is featured.

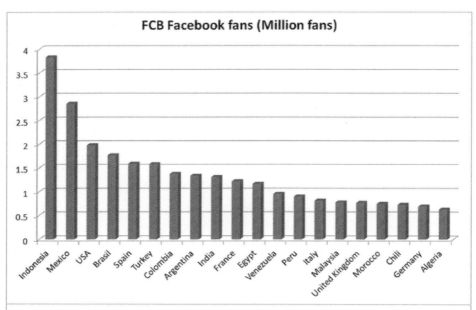

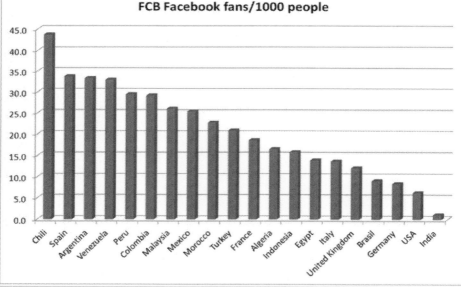

Popularity of FC Barcelona in various countries measured in number of Facebook fans (top graph). Facebook fan data is from April 2013 (source: sport.es). To normalize the data to the population size of a given country (bottom graph), approximate population data corresponding to 2010-2013 was obtained from Wikipedia.

I have already mentioned that my FC Barcelona apparel raises cheery comments almost daily by unknown passers-by in Seattle, a rather remote city by European standards. I'm not exactly alone wearing Barça apparel, as you might have noticed. Journalist Carles Salmurri of Barcelona newspaper *La Vanguardia* has collected more than 200 images where people from all over the world are wearing FC Barcelona merchandising. This includes the image of an Iraqi shielding himself from the sun with a Barça umbrella (published on the cover of *The International Herald Tribune* in 2008), a Libyan guerrilla fighter or a handcuffed Salvadoran teenager dressed in Barça gear, and a Palestinian adolescent reading the Quran with a Messi shirt. (My friend and writer Jaume Subirana, who has traveled often to Israel, has observed that the only point of agreement between Palestinians and Israelis seems to be that they are both huge Barça fans.) Also dressed in Barça shirts are sub-Saharans who leave Africa on precarious boats to land in the Canary Islands hoping to get a job in the European Union and members of the Kayapo tribe in the Amazon going for a doctor check-up in the north of Brazil. Even the son of David Beckham, perhaps the biggest soccer icon on Earth after Messi, an ex-Real Madrid and ex-Manchester United player, was seen innocently wearing a Barça outfit (instead of a "Beckham" shirt) with his mom – the photos appeared in every newspaper in the world, which I suspect must have been a bit humiliating for daddy. A number of celebrities have put on a Barça shirt to pay homage to the colors, such as Nelson Mandela, Spike Lee, Bruce Springsteen, Simon Peres, or Bill Gates. While I'm sure that a similar collection of photos could be produced of just about any major team, what is remarkable about FC Barcelona's presence is its *rise*. This popularity was unthinkable ten or even five years ago.

Best team *ever*?

Very few people question that the FC Barcelona squad led by Pep Guardiola was the best team in the world – mostly Real Madrid fanatics, and even so, I doubt they were being serious and that they held the same opinion in their most private confessions. (The "Barça envy" by Real Madrid fans has a name in the Spanish soccer jargon: "*Barcelonitis*".) In

February 2013, however, Real Madrid President Florentino Pérez pompously declared that "we are the greatest club in the world" – and since then many of his directors, coaches and players have repeated the motto, as if by sheer repetition they might be able to convince the world. There are about half a dozen clubs in the world that are just as qualified as Real Madrid to issue similar statements. To avoid these types of unproductive chest-thumping wars, the International Federation of Football History and Statistics (IFFHS) was founded in 1984. They are the ones who produce objective measures of "greatest" and "best" in soccer.

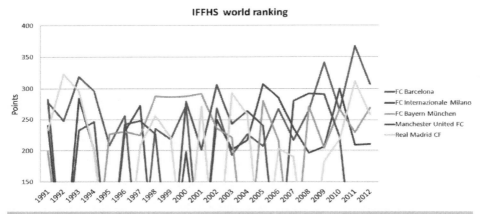

Rankings published by the International Federation of Football History and Statistics (IFFHS) on January 2013, which includes performance points through 2012.

Pérez must have missed the reports by the IFFHS that January 2013. Interestingly, about a week before Pérez's words, *Marca*, a sports magazine close to Real Madrid, published the monthly update on the IFFHS, which put Real Madrid on a "third place". (I found strange even the third place, so I looked it up.) Since 1990, the IFFHS started compiling objective performance statistics and assigning values to results based on their difficulty, for ex. 14, 7, and 0 points for a win, a draw or a loss (respectively) in a UEFA *Champions League* or *Copa Libertadores* match but only 8, 4, and 0 for the same results in all Asia, Africa and CONCACAF continental competitions, etc.; the points are distributed equally to teams in matches decided by penalty-kicks. IFFHS issues the statistics every month based on the previous 12 months' performance. The statistic is noisy, to be sure, as shown in the graph above that only depicts the five clubs that have been listed more often in the "top 25" world ranking list in the 22-year period between 1991 through 2012: Barça, Inter, Bayern, *ManU*, and Real Madrid. If we believe this measure, it is already apparent that Real Madrid is *not* the greatest club in the world: it has been listed at the top only twice, and it is most often below all the other four.

% times listed in the Top 25 IFFHS World Ranking (1991-2012)

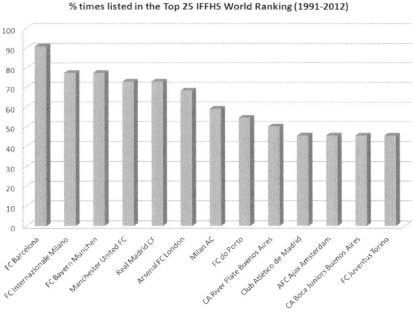

This graph depicts the number of times that a club has been included in one of the Top 25 rankings of the IFFHS list, expressed as a percentage of the total. For example, FC Barcelona has been included ~91% of the times (20 out of 22 times) in the period 1991-2012. Inter and Bayern have both been included 77% of the times (17 out of 22 times), and ManU *and Real Madrid have both been included 73% of the times (16 out of 22 times).*

There are ways to clean up the information contained in the IFFHS graph. One way is to count how many times a given club has been short-listed in the "top-25" IFFHS world-ranking list. As it turns out, FC Barcelona has been on the list 20 out of 22 times (91% of the times), followed by Inter and Bayern (17 times, 77%), *ManU* and Real Madrid (16, 73%), and Arsenal (15, 68%), among others, as shown in the graph above. Real Madrid is in a *tied* fourth place (by this measure).

If we count the number of times that a given team has been ranked #1 on the list, the comparison becomes more dramatic. FC Barcelona has been ranked #1 exactly 52 times (19.7% of the months!), followed by AC Milan (37 or 14%), Manchester United (33 or 12.5%), Inter (23 or 8.7%), Liverpool (19 or 7.2%), Sevilla (17 or 6.4%), Juventus and Real Madrid (both 16 times or 6%). In any case, even if these formulas are not a perfect measure of soccer performance, we see that Real Madrid is not even close to tying with FC Barcelona at the top by any measure, and it is lower in #1 counts than *ManU*, its "partner-in-fourth-place" in the "top-25" graph (see above). Unless by some evil twist of mathematics, the IFFHS formulas happen to do a disservice to Real Madrid and a favor to Barça, I think it is clear that Florentino Pérez is still speaking in his dreams.

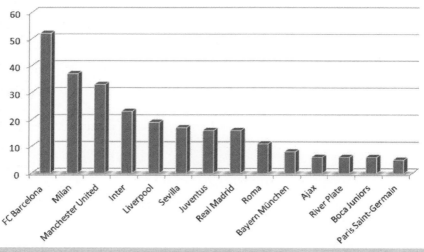

 # times ranked #1 by IFFHS (Jan 1991-Jan 2013)

This graph shows the number of times that a club has been ranked #1 by the IFFHS. For example, FC Barcelona has been ranked the top team 52 times over the period 1991-2012.

There are many other measures of Barça's performance. In 2012, the team scored 121 goals in 39 *Liga* games (3.1 goals/game), a total of 175 goals in 63 games counting all competitions (2.78 goals/game). Messi scored a record 91 goals. Of all the shots (469), 60.5% were on goal and 6.4% were on the post or cross bar. The precision in the passes reached an average 89% across all competitions, and possession was at 69.3% on average (74.6% for *Champions League* games). In the first round of the 2012-2013 *Liga* (19 games), under Tito Vilanova's management, the performance even improved and broke a historical record of points, winning 55 of 57 possible points. FC Barcelona led the statistics on goals in favor (64), biggest scorer (Messi, with 28), goal assists (41), minutes of possession (690, second was Real Madrid with 498), and fewer lost balls (1601, second was Valencia with 1678).

A somewhat more academic question is whether this Barça is the best team *ever*. I personally have my strong doubts, from the bit of history of soccer I know (see below). The question is academic because this team will never face the old teams and what we have left of the legendary teams of Uruguay, Hungary and Real Madrid from the 50's are blurry black-and-white movies from which it is hard to extract meaningful comparisons. So we will never find out. Also, even if we could analyze those movies in great detail, the comparison (and the imaginary challenge) would be unfair, because present training methods result in much stronger and faster athletes – so necessarily today's soccer is faster and more technical. Yet, since this team has broken so many records, a number of comparisons have been brought up with other great club teams that are now imprinted in the collective memory. What follows is a small homage to their heritage (I have skipped the many great national teams, to keep the list brief!), so that you can judge for yourself:

Arsenal 1930: the WM
Coach Herbert Chapman modified the classic 2-3-5 tactical scheme of the beginnings of soccer as a way to counteract the modified rule of offside (as it is today). His 3-4-3 placed more midfielders and prioritized the

defense, giving rise to lethal counter-attacks in a time when disordered attacking was the norm. Chapman gave Arsenal three big titles, died suddenly of pneumonia in 1934 and was succeeded by Shaw and Allison, who won four more titles. *Typical squad*: Preddy (goalie), Parker, Seddon, Hapgood (defenders), Baker, John, Jack, James (midfielders), Hulme, Lambert, Bastin (forwards). *Titles*: 2 *FA Cups* (1930 and 1936) and 5 English Leagues (1930-31, 1932-33, 1933-34, 1934-35, and 1937-38).

River Plate 1941-1945: "La Máquina" ("The Machine")
In the 1940s, Argentinian team River Plate won four Argentinian leagues with such superiority that a sports journalist nicknamed them "The Machine". The core group was formed by the forwards Juan Carlos Muñoz, José Manuel Moreno, Adolfo Pedernera, Ángel Labruna, and Félix Loustau. *Titles:* 4 Argentinian Leagues (1941, 1942, 1945, 1947).

Budapest Honvéd 1949-1955/Hungary 1954: the 3-2-3-2
In 1943 both Ferenc Puskás and József Bozsik made their debut for *Kispest FC*. The club's golden age began in 1949 when Hungary became a communist state and *Kispest FC* was nationalized, renamed to *Budapesti Honvéd SE*, and taken over by the Hungarian Ministry of Defense under the management of Gusztáv Sebes, the coach of the national team. The word *honvéd*, which literally means *defender of the homeland*, is also used to refer to an army private. Honvéd won the Hungarian league in 1949-50, 1950-51, 1952-53, 1954-55, and 1955-56. Coach Gusztav Sebes evolved on the WM and used very technical players mostly from the Honvéd to build the dynamic Hungary team of "Mighty Magyars" that swept Europe and played in the final of the 1954 *European Cup*. Hidegkuti was the first "false *nine*". Sebes also invented the concept of highly offensive fullbacks, so that the team could transform his tactic mid-game from a 5-3-2 to a more offensive 3-2-5 – a precursor of Total Football. *Typical squad*: Grocsis (goalie), Buzansky, Lorant, Lantos (defenders), Bozsik, Zakarias (midfielders), Budai, Kocsis, Hidegkuti, Puskas, Czibor (forwards). *Titles*: Five Hungarian leagues in 7 years.

Pelé's Santos (1957-1974)

Pelé made his debut at age 16 in 1957 for Santos, an already successful team coached by Luis Alonso Pérez ("Lula") that had won the two previous leagues (1955 and 1956), and immediately became the top scorer of the league. The next year Santos won the *Campeonato Paulista* with 58 goals by Pelé, a record that still stands today, massacring rivals by goal differentials as large as 10-0 or 12-1. Santos' most successful season was 1962, when it won the *Campeonato Brasiliero*, the *Taça Brasil*, the *Copa Libertadores* (the equivalent of the *Champions League* for South America), and the *Intercontinental Cup* (now renamed *Club's World Cup*). In 1963, the club won again the *Copa Libertadores* and the *Intercontinental Cup*. *Typical squad* (1962/1963): Gylmar (goalkeeper), Lima, Mauro, Calvet, Dalmo (defenders), Mengálvio, Zito (midfielders), Dorval, Coutinho, Pelé, and Pepe (forwards).

Manchester United's Busby Babes (1952-1968)

Matt Busby was appointed coach of Manchester United after World War II ended in 1945. He believed in developing his team from his youth players, which would be called "Busby Babes" by the press. *ManU* won the league in 1952, 1956, and 1957 (with an average age of 22!). In 1958, the airplane transporting the team suffered a crash at the Munich airport, killing 23 people, including eight players. Busby was badly injured but survived, along with Bobby Charlton and several others. Busby rebuilt the team by adding young talent such as George Best and Denis Law. This team won the 1963 *FA Cup*, the 1964-1965 and 1966-1967 English league titles, and the 1968 *European Cup* – after which Busby retired as coach and became club director (and later president). *ManU* fans nicknamed their three best players (Best, Law, and Charlton – all three winners of a *Ballon d'Or*) the "United Trinity". *Typical squad* (1968): Alex Stepney (goalkeeper), Tony Dunne, David Sadler, Bill Foulkes, Shay Brennan (defenders), Nobby Stiles, Bobby Charlton, Pat Crerand (midfielders), Denis Law, Brian Kidd, George Best (forwards).

Real Madrid in the 1950s: 1956-1960

This is the beginning of Real Madrid's greater glory. President Santiago Bernabéu was able to snatch Di Stéfano away from Barça (with the help of Dictator Franco) and filled the forward line with foreign stars, depleting their European rivals at the same time: Kopa from Stade Reims (their rival in the first and fourth *European Cup* final) and Puskas from Honvéd. Real Madrid had no rival in Europe for five years. *Typical squad*: Alonso (goalie), Marquitos, Santamaría, Atienza (defenders), Santiesteban, Zárraga, Di Stéfano (midfielders), Kopa, Rial, Gento, Puskas (forwards). *Titles*: 5 consecutive *European Cups*, one *Intercontinental Cup*, 3 *Liga*s.

Eusébio's Benfica in the 1960s

Benfica broke Real Madrid's dominance in the *European Cup* by winning (3-2) the 1961 final against the legendary Barça side of Luis Suárez, Hungarians Kubala, Kocsis, and Czibor, and Catalan goalie Ramallets. Next year, reinforced with Eusébio (nicknamed the "Black Panther" and generally identified as the best Portuguese player of all times), it would also win the 1962 *European Cup* final against Real Madrid. During the 1960s, the team reached the final three more times (1963, 1965, 1968). In this decade, the club won 8 Portuguese leagues (1960, 1961, 1963-65, 1967-69), and three Portuguese Cups (all of them "doubles", in 1961, 1964, and 1969). *Typical squad*: Alberto da Costa Pereira (goalkeeper), Mario João, Germano, Angelo Martins (defenders), Domiciano Cavém, Fernando Cruz, Mário Coluna (midfielders), José Augusto, Eusébio, José Águas, António Simões (forwards).

Real Madrid in the 1960s: The Yé-yé team

Coach Miguel Muñoz, who had been European Champion as a player in a Real Madrid full of foreign stars in 1956 and 1957, built a team entirely with Spanish players. They would be collectively called "*Los Yé-yés*" after sports magazine *Marca* published a photo of four members of the team dressed in Beatles wigs, in reference to the chorus in the Beatles' song "She Loves You" – *Yeah, yeah, Yeah*. Between 1960 and 1972, they won 9 *Liga*s (5 of them in a row), two *Copas del Rey* (the 1962 title was a "double"), and one *European Cup* (1966 – the only title that year). *Typical squad*: José Araquistáin (goalie), Manuel Sanchís, Pedro de Felipe, Ignacio

Zoco, Pachín, (defenders), Manuel Velázquez, Ramón Grosso, Pirri (midfielders), Francisco Gento, Amancio Amaro, and Fernando Serena (forwards).

Inter 1964-1965: the *"catenaccio"*

The highly defensive tactic *"catenaccio"* (translated as "bolt" or "latch"), very popular among Italian teams in the 1960s through the 80s, was actually invented by Swiss Karl Rappan as a variation of the WM (3-4-3). Rappan conceived a 1-3-3-3 system introducing a man at the back "closing" the defense – hence the name. Since the last defender is free of mark, he is usually known as *libero*. These defensive tactics have been criticized by many as a mindless accumulation of men in the back: "It's not that the Italians defend well; it's that they defend with many", as Argentinian coach César Luis Menotti pointed out. The most successful implementation of the *catenaccio* was a 4-4-2 by coach Helenio Herrera of Inter, no doubt due to the presence of great players like Luis Suárez. *Typical squad*: Sarti (goalie), Picchi (libero), Burgnich, Guarneri, Facchetti (defenders), Suárez, Bedin, Mazzola, Corso (midfielders), Jair, Peiró (forwards). *Titles*: 2 *European Cups* (1964, 1965), won against Di Stéfano's Real Madrid (1964) and Eusébio's Benfica (1965); 2 *Intercontinental Cups* (1964, 1965), won against Pelé's Santos both times; and 3 Italian Leagues in 4 years (1963, 1965, 1966).

Celtic 1967: the *Lisbon Lions* win the first "quintuple"

Based on Glasgow, Scotland, in 1967 this team won the *Scottish League Championship*, the *Scottish Cup*, the *Scottish League Cup*, the *Glasgow Cup*, and the *European Cup* (played in Lisbon) – all the five competitions they could possibly enter that year. The first British team to win a *European Cup*, they became known as "the Lisbon Lions". It was also the first time a "quintuple" had ever been achieved and only two more teams (Ajax and FC Barcelona) have equaled it later. From 1966-1974, coach Jock Stein guided Celtic to a world-record 9 *Scottish League* wins in a row, in addition to 6 *Scottish Cups* (1965, 1967, 1969, 1971, 1972, 1974), and 5 consecutive *Scottish League Cups* (1965-1970; these add two "trebles" in 1965 and 1969 to the 1967 "quintuple"!).

Ajax 1971-1974: Total Football

Inspired on Sebes' work (Hungary '54), Rinus Michels at Ajax departed from the catenaccio by proposing attacking football with a dynamic 4-3-3, where very technical defenders helped in attack and fast forwards such as Cruyff were able to retreat fast and help in midfield as well if needed, exerting "total pressure". Physical fitness was key. *Typical squad*: Jongbloed (goalie), Suurbier, Haan, Rijsbergen, Krol (defenders), Jansen, Neeskens, Van Hanegem (midfielders), Rep, Cruyff, Kaizer/Rensenbrink (forwards). From 1965-1973, Ajax won 6 Leagues, 4 Cups, 3 *European Cups* (1971, 1972, 1973), two *Supercups* (1972, 1973), and one *Intercontinental Cup* (1972). Note that in 1972 Ajax won all the five competition they could possibly enter that year, a feat only done previously by Celtic in 1967 and repeated later by FC Barcelona in 2009 (with 6 trophies).

Bayern Munich 1971-1976: The Hat Trick

Ex-Bayern player Udo Lattek set up in the early 1970s the basis of one of the most powerful teams in soccer history, formed almost entirely by German players. They started by winning an unprecedented three *Bundesligas* in a row (from 1971-1974) and ended by winning three *European Cups* in a row (1974-1976, dubbed "The Hat Trick" by Bayern fans). In 1974, Bayern contributed 6 players to the German national team that became World Champion. *Typical squad* (1976): Sepp Maier (goalie), Johnny Hansen, Udo Horsmann, Hans-Georg Schwarzenbeck, Franz Beckenbauer (defenders), Franz Roth, Bernd Dürnberger, Jupp Kapellmann (midfielders), Gerd Müller, Uli Hoeness, Karl-Heinz Rummenigge (forwards).

Liverpool 1975-1985: The King Kenny decade

No other club in the world can boast to have won 7 leagues and 4 *European cups* (1977, 1978, 1981, 1984) in the span of a decade; before 1990, Liverpool would add 3 more leagues to the count. The success of the team coincided with the tenure of Scottish player Kenny Dalglish (1977-1990), who scored countless goals by combining a fine touch with a devil-like speed. *Typical squad* (1978): Ray Clemence (goalkeeper), Alan Hansen, Phil Thompson, Emlyn Hugues, Phil Neal (defenders), Ray Kennedy,

Graeme Souness, Terry McDermott, Jimmy Case (midfielders), Kenny Dalglish, David Fairclough (forwards).

Real Madrid 1985-1990: the "Quinta del Buitre"

This is really, in my memory, the *great* Real Madrid – the one that was a pleasure to watch, knowing that it was safe as a Barça fan to envy: these were a bunch of exceptionally talented kids from Madrid and, if they could do it, so could the Barça kids do it in time. I vividly remember the elegance of Míchel's long curled balls, the electric dribble of Emilio Butragueño *"El Buitre"* – most ending in a goal or in a penalty –, and the galloping of Martín Vázquez down the left wing: an unstoppable team. Technically speaking, the "Quinta del Buitre" refers to the five players that came up from the Real Madrid youth academy (the above three, plus Manolo Sanchís and Miguel Pardeza) around 1983-1984. Together they won 5 *Ligas* (1985-1989) in a row, a *Copa del Rey* in 1989 (which was a "double"), and two consecutive *UEFA Cups* (1985 and 1986, also "doubles"). *Typical squad* (1989): Buyo (goalie), Chendo, Gallego, Sanchís, Solana (defenders), Martín Vázquez, Schuster, Gordillo, Míchel (midfielders), Butragueño, Hugo Sánchez (forwards).

Hiddink's PSV Eindhoven: the 1988 "treble"

A remarkable pattern is immediately apparent when we look at the list of former managers of PSV Eindhoven. When former PSV player Guus Hiddink took over as coach in 1987, PSV started dominating Dutch soccer (ending the decade-long Ajax domination), winning three Dutch leagues in a row (1987-1989), three Dutch Cups in a row (1988-1990, so two were "doubles"), and the 1988 *European Cup* (a "treble"). *Typical squad*: Hans van Breukelen (goalkeeper), Jan Heintze, Ronald Koeman, Ivan Nielsen, Eric Gerets (defenders), Berry van Aerle, Søren Lerby, Edward Linskens, Gerald Vanenburg (midfielders), Wim Kieft, Hans Gilhaus (forwards). This team would win two more Dutch leagues (1991 and 1992) under coach Bobby Robson. Guus Hiddink would return in 2003 to win the 2003, 2005 and 2006 league titles, as well as the 2005 Dutch Cup.

Milan 1989-1990: Pressure and offside trap

Coach Arrigo Sacchi used the quick mind of *libero* Baresi to narrow the field of play to a small band where rivals where choked under pressure. The perfectly orchestrated movement of the Milan defense (at Baresi's call of "Milan!") to trap the opponent's forwards in offside, repeated over and over, is one of the most spectacular collective plays I have ever seen: so clever that AC Milan didn't even have to touch the ball. The opponents looked like fools every time over and over, caught in the offside zone, but Baresi would surprise them again and again – and again! It might have been *dozens* of times *per game*. Milan's formation was a rather classical 4-4-2. *Typical squad*: Galli (goalie), Baresi (*libero*), Tassotti, Costacurta, Maldini (defenders), Donadoni, Rijkaard, Ancelotti, Evani (midfielders), Gullit, Van Basten (forwards). *Titles*: 2 *European Cups*, 2 *European Supercups*, and 2 *Intercontinental Cups* (all in the same years: 1989 and 1990), but no Italian Leagues.

Cruyff's *Dream Team*: 1990-1994

This is the Barça side that won 4 *Ligas* in a row and the 1992 *European Cup*. It revolutionized Spanish soccer by showing that the old principle "the best defense is a good attack" is not only fun but also very effective. Compared to Guardiola's team, this team did not have a Messi, but it had three magnificent forwards (Romário, Stoichkov, and Begiristain) which were equally impossible to mark; the *Dream Team* did not have Busquets, Iniesta and Xavi, but on the other hand Guardiola could make passes at first touch just like Busquets, and Michael Laudrup was even better at passing than Xavi (imagine!) and had that Iniesta-looking dribble – the "croquette" (a move that Iniesta claims to have learned from Laudrup). In the back, the team had in Ronald Koeman a slow defender that could be at times a liability and the next moment an asset – nobody in the *Liga* (not even Cristiano Ronaldo) has shot free kicks like him in the last 20 years, and he could set 40-meter passes with the precision of a tennis player. As Johan Cruyff put it: "If you can deliver a pass of forty meters, you don't need to run them". *Typical squad*: Andoni Zubizarreta (goalkeeper), Sergi Barjuán, Ronald Koeman, José Ramón Alexanko, Albert Ferrer (defenders), Michael Laudrup, Josep Guardiola, Eusebio Sacristán (midfielders), Beguirisitain, Romário, Stoichkov (forwards).

Manchester United 1999: Sir Ferguson's "treble"

In 1999, Manchester United, coached by Alex Ferguson, won the *Premier League*, the *FA Cup*, and the *Champions League* – the first "treble" in English football history. The victory over Bayern Munich in the 1999 *Champions League* final was considered so epic that Alex Ferguson was even knighted. It *was* epic, everything about that final was. The day of the final would have been the anniversary of Matt Busby, the former coach of *ManU* who had survived the tragic plane crash where 23 people, among them eight players, died at the Munich airport in 1958. Before the game, which was played at the *Camp Nou*, opera singer Montserrat Caballé performed a live song while the late Freddie Mercury sang on the screen. Both teams had an impeccable pedigree: they were both winners of a "double" in their countries, both opting for the coveted, once-in-a-decade "treble". *ManU* midfield stars Roy Keane (captain) and Paul Scholes were missing out on the final due to suspension, and Bayern forward Lizarazu was out due to injury. The best referee in the world, Pierluigi Collina – the tall, bald referee with a quick whistle and a menacing look that all players respected – was appointed for this game. Bayern scored from a free kick in the 6th minute and the 1-0 trailed into the 90th minute, when the fourth official showed that three minutes of injury time remained. As *ManU* won a corner, goalie Peter Schmeichel risked into Bayern's penalty area. The rebound fell on Gigg's feet, who flicked the ball over to Sheringham, who then shot the ball straight into the net. Equalized! Right after the kick-off, *ManU* won another corner. It was the 92nd minute. Beckham swung the corner in, the ball was headed downwards by Sheringham, and Solskjaer shot the ball up into the roof of Bayern's net. Unbelievable! Collina said that it was one of the most memorable matches in his career, likening the crowd's cheer at the end of the game to a "lion's roar". *Typical squad*: Peter Schmeichel (goalie), Phil Neville, Ronny Johnsen, David May, Gary Neville (defenders), Ryan Giggs, Roy Keane,

Paul Scholes, David Beckham (midfielders), Andy Cole, Ole Gunnar Solskjaer (forwards).

Bayern Munich (1998-2004): Hitzfeld's era

The legendary coach Ottmar Hitzfeld, "The General", twice elected World Coach of the Year, had previously coached Borussia Dortmund (1991-1997) before coaching Bayern Munich (1998-2004 and 2007-2008). He had transformed Borussia Dortmund from a small team that had not won a major title in the last 30 years to a club that won two *Bundesligas* in a row (1994-1995 and 1995-1996) as well as a *Champions League* (1996). He is one of three coaches to have won the *Champions League* with two different clubs, and he is remembered at both for the respect with which he treated every player and employee. At Bayern, he won a total of 14 titles in his 7 years at the club, including five *Bundesligas* (1998-99, 1999-00, 2000-01, 2002-03, 2007-08), three Cups (1999-00, 2002-03, 2007-08, all "doubles"), a *Champions League* (2001), and an *Intercontinental Cup* (2001). Engraved in this team's memory is one of the most devastating losses in football history, in the *Champions League* final of 1999, when Bayern – having hit the post and the crossbar – was leading only 1-0 at the 90th minute and Manchester United scored two goals in injury time. *Typical squad* (1999): Oliver Kahn (goalkeeper), Lothar Matthäus, Michael Tarnat, Thomas Linke, Samuel Kuffour, Markus Babbel (defenders), Steffan Effenberg, Jens Jeremies (midfielders), Alexander Zickler, Carsten Jancker, and Mario Basler (forwards). If we take into account that Kuffour was born in Ghana but raised through the ranks of Bayern's youth system, the squad was almost entirely German.

Real Madrid 2000-2003: *Los Galácticos*

This is the team that was put together by Real Madrid's President Florentino Pérez right after his friend the Madrid Mayor rezoned the club's training ground, which allowed the club to sell it for hundreds of millions of euros, cancel the club's €270 M debt, and buy all the *Galácticos*. Without that shady operation (which required the cooperation of corrupt politicians), Real Madrid would not be the club that it is now. Still, those that only care about the football (and less about the fairness) argue that the circus was worth it, although they won less than was expected of them: by summer of 2003, they had conquered two *Ligas* (2000-2001 and 2002-2003), a *Champions League*, and an *Intercontinental Cup* – so coach Vicente del Bosque was sacked. *Typical squad*: César (goalkeeper), Roberto Carlos, Fernando Hierro, Iván Helguera, Míchel Salgado (defenders), Santiago Solari, Claude Makélélé, Luís Figo (midfielders), Zinedine Zidane, Raúl, Fernando Morientes (forwards). Excellent players on the bench were Iker Casillas, Guti, and Steve McManaman. David Beckham was signed in 2004 and Robinho and Sergio Ramos in 2005.

*   *   *

Aside from their glory, all these teams have one thing in common: a somewhat brief existence – with the exception of Manchester United, the only one who has had a powerful youth academy. FC Barcelona is having a similarly shiny winning streak as all these teams – but will it last?

The FC Barcelona youth academy has contributed to the club not only in large numbers of players but also in changing soccer coaching methodology and tactics *worldwide*. Soccer coaches from all the corners of our planet – including professional as well as youth and children coaches – have learned three crucial lessons from watching FC Barcelona play: that technical ability is much more important than physique (because so many of Barça players are quite small), that pressuring the opponents causes them to make mistakes (a non-obvious expenditure of energy), and that going through efforts to keep the ball pays off in the end (a non-obvious tactic – many coaches still repudiate it). Some of these concepts were cooked at the Ajax youth academy, as explained elsewhere in this book, but it is the refinement of these methods by *La Masia* and the success of the FC Barcelona youth academy that have been widely noticed by coaches and fans alike. These stylistic legacies will surely remain in the retinas of soccer fans for decades to come. However, as Guardiola has pointed out, it is easy to defend a winning style; the day that Barça starts losing – and we already see signs that the team is becoming weaker –, he has warned, the old critics of possession soccer will come back to tell us they were right.

The final conclusion of this chapter, and this book, is that paying for soccer education and tying it to the club's style of play is a much more prolific investment than buying soccer stars. The recent string of victories by FC Barcelona has brought the youth academy and the first team's winning style – possession soccer – to the center stage of global media. While many youth academies around the world are now using possession soccer as their favorite teaching method, no doubt due to FC Barcelona youth academy's success, other teams with great youth academies (e.g., Manchester United) have also dominated world soccer for large periods of time playing a different style. Then, a corollary of our conclusion is that what matters is not so much the style of play but that strong links should be formed between a team's youth academy and the first team – that visionary connection that Jack Reynolds established for the first time at Ajax more than 100 years ago.

The importance of relationships in team-building: lessons from "La Roja"

Can that link be all that explains the success of teams such as the old *ManU*, Barça, and now Bayern? As a scientist, I like to find other explanations, and I see at least another plausible one. Every team that has been built on the furnaces of a great youth academy has had another key advantage: their players had developed close friendships because they had been playing soccer since they were early teenagers. I'm not speaking of the fact that, as players, they develop a keen sense of each other's movements, tactical preferences, and physical weaknesses from a very early age: that is the precise *objective* of youth training. I'm speaking of an added value. Friends are more likely to run for their friends, forgive their mistakes, support them through hardship, and cheer from the bench – there are no egos in a team of friends. It's all about the fun surrounding the ball.

Spain's national team provides a good example for my point that team relationships are crucial in soccer. *"La Roja"*, as it has become known (due to its red-shirt uniform), is not an easily-managed team. It is not a club so it does not have its own youth academy, but almost: the players, at least the best ones, have known each other for a while from belonging to the youth versions of the national team (the sub-17, the sub-19, the sub-21, etc.). For the most part, it is a team that works pretty much on auto-pilot because they do not train together every day during the year; as a way of connecting with each other, international friendly games are organized once in a while. In Spanish, "coach" is translated as "entrenador", but the national team's coach position is called "seleccionador" – the "picker" or "chooser", the person who picks or chooses – because in his task he lacks the daily influence on the players of a normal coach. Vicente del Bosque, an ex-Real Madrid player who is the "seleccionador" since 2008 (right after *La Roja* had won its first *EuroCup*), has seized the opportunity of building the *La Roja* skeleton around key FC Barcelona players (Xavi, Iniesta, Busquets, Pedro, Fàbregas, Piqué, Puyol, Valdés, Jordi Alba), which are all from Barça's youth academy; the team also has players from the FC Barcelona youth academy but no longer play at Barça (Reina) and players that play at FC Barcelona but did not come from the academy (Villa). Using the same large nucleus of players (seven from FC Barcelona and three from Real Madrid), Spain has won, for the first time in history, the last three major international competitions (two consecutive *EuroCups* and one World Cup) – a feat unmatched even by Pelé's Brazil (who won two consecutive World Cups in 1958 and 1962 but failed to win the *Copa América* in between) and Beckenbauer's Germany (who won the *EuroCup* in 1972 and the World Cup in 1974 but lost the *EuroCup* final against Czechoslovakia in 1976, after the famous penalty cleverly scored by Antonín Panenka).

At first sight, *La Roja* plays in a characteristic Barça style, using long possessions with short, precise triangulations to tire – some say "hypnotize", others "bore" – the opponent and constant team-coordinated pressure to force ball losses by the opponent. Del Bosque, following Guardiola's example at FC Barcelona, often prefers to field an excess of quick-feet midfielders, playing with a "false 9" to confuse the opponents' defenders. (The "fake center forward" or "false 9" is an old tactic invented by the Hungarians in the 1950s: the "false 9" comes out of the box, creating a void in the box if he is followed by the central defender, or creating a numerical superiority in the midfield if he is not followed.) Instead of re-inventing the wheel, del Bosque has wisely opted for getting a free ride from Guardiola's legacy; in del Bosque's own words, "We do our very best to emulate Barcelona's *tiki-taka*. We or I lack coaching ability so to make up for this, I force the players to watch Barcelona play". Spain has, indeed, successfully imitated Barça's possession soccer style and Total Pressure tactics; at the 2010 World Cup, Spain always had the largest possession percentages (ranging from 73% against Switzerland to 57% against Germany) and the two players in the tournament that had made most passes were from *La Roja* (and from Barça: Xavi and Busquets). Even Germany and Italy, Europe's traditional soccer heavy weights, have changed their soccer style of play in light of FC Barcelona's positive influence onto Spain's national team. Germany's players in the 1970s (the decade dominated by Germany) were all *über*-strong and tall, the *panzers* of soccer. In the 1980s, Italy spread – rather successfully – its infamous ultra-defensive *catenaccio* theory according to which the first and foremost task of a footballer is to avoid getting goals, rather than scoring them. Now Germany is a fast-attacking team based on the Bayern Munich squad and Italy is an even more creative team based on Juventus' squad. These two "cultural revolutions" have authors: Joachim Löw (Germany's coach) and Cesare Prandelli (Italy's coach), who both happen to be admirers of – yes, you guessed it – FC Barcelona and Josep Guardiola.

Vicente del Bosque has his critics too – Cruyff amongst them. On a closer inspection of del Bosque's tactics, we see that he does not quite place his players in Barça formation. He always insists on playing with two "pivots", rather than one as Barça does (the "pivot" is the player that acts as the liaison between the defense and the midfield – usually only

Busquets at FC Barcelona). In defense formation, the double "pivot" becomes in practice a hidden six-man defense that depletes the attack of manpower, slowing down the reaction time. As a result, Spain's national team almost never receives a goal but has very low scoring averages because their line-up is a low-risk one – their most frequent win result at the 2010 World Cup was 1-0, and they conquered the World Cup with a shameful lowest goal-average in history. Del Bosque did not re-invent the wheel, and that's fine, but why put spokes in such a well-greased engine? Possession soccer and Total Pressure were were designed precisely to avoid over-crowding defensive tactics. "A lot of love, but it lacks sex", said the French international ex-soccer player Lizarazu, to describe Spain's style of play. As a Barça fan, I always wondered, in amazement, how much better this team *could have* played: indeed, some Barça fans refer lightheartedly to *La Roja* as "Barça B".

I was also an initial critic of Del Bosque but I slowly learned to appreciate the intelligence of his methods. First one needs to realize that, unlike Real Madrid, *La Roja* has no incentive to improve its performance to match up to FC Barcelona: these are two teams that will never cross their paths. More importantly – and herein lies the genius of Del Bosque, an elegant character who has never even bothered to defend his tactics publicly – one must take into account that *La Roja* always plays in elimination-type of competitions (never in leagues), so it cannot afford to lose *a single game*. Soccer is a game of errors – as Cruyff observed –, and if Spain had conceded a single error in one of the games that led to one of its three titles, perhaps now the world would not be praising *La Roja* so much.

As the results suggest, Del Bosque is a key piece in this team. It suits him: as a player, he was an elegant midfielder and a key piece of the Real Madrid of the late-1970s that won 5 *Ligas* and 4 *Copas del Rey* in 8 years (1974-1982) alongside captain "Doctor" Pirri, electric dribbler Juanito, and effective goal scorer "Puma" Santillana. When he retired, he worked for the Real Madrid youth academy for 15 years, as a scouter and as a coach. There he inherited the legacy of Luis Molowny, ex-player of the legendary Di Stéfano team of the 1950s and the first director of the Real

Madrid youth academy, who had envisioned the key ingredient to youth coaching: "Treat the player with affection". By the time he was first asked to be Real Madrid's first-team coach, in 1994, Vicente Del Bosque had seen half of the players grow up and knew that the best way to treat them was with his usual warmth. He would use the same methods later with *La Roja*. He is a reasonable man, a father of a Down syndrome kid, always respectful and considerate, full of dignity and common sense, who has made it his priority to keep his team a haven of camaraderie. It was not a simple task. It must not have been easy to ask the Real Madrid players to adopt the same possession soccer tactics that their own coach, José Mourinho, would scorn publicly as futile. Some of the players from Real Madrid were not in good terms with those of FC Barcelona after a series of bitter rivalries during their regular competitions. However, del Bosque made it clear that those conflicts had to be left behind, and minimized their impact by diplomatically deflecting the attention of the media towards more important problems. Against the whole country's opinion, he has even been supportive of players who were going through difficult moments at their clubs, making the national team a therapeutic home for them. Every time a dissenting opinion was raised by a journalist or a player, he listened and simply said something along the lines: "Good point. We did what we thought was the best for the team at that moment. There are many ways to achieve victory, but what is important is to be here, celebrating it." Cruyff has summarized in a few words the light that he emanates: "He is a *señor* [gentleman]". In a revealing example, the 2012 *EuroCup* semi-final against Portugal ended 0-0 and had to be resolved by a penalty shootout. The coaches designated Cesc Fàbregas (an excellent penalty taker) as the second shooter, since logic dictates that the best shooters should go first to relieve the pressure for the other shooters. However, Fàbregas refused to go second because he had the hunch that the fifth and last would be the deciding shot. Many coaches would not have tolerated childish superstitions to take over cold calculation in a moment of high tension, but most coaches are not del Bosque. "We were not going to quarrel over such a petty detail", was del Bosque's humble explanation about how he solved the crisis. Stepping out of the limelight to irradiate his calm over the whole group when the group needs it the most, is what del Bosque has always done best: another inch to the left, and Fàbregas' shot would have not gone in. The fifth shot indeed became the deciding one and Fàbregas dramatically sent the ball ricocheting from the post into the net after whispering a few words to the ball, like a furtive accomplice: "We are going to make history".

The players have also said that another cohesive factor has been the good karma between their families – their parents and children have been together for many years in this journey, forming relationships that give stability to the players. This is a team without egotistical stars, only comrades having fun. In sum, as a result of del Bosque's management, the relationships in *La Roja* have been very positive and the team spirits have always been very high – a winning recipe: after the 2012 *EuroCup*, he held the world record for the biggest percentage of victories of any other national coach in history, at 85%. This is not the first time either that this remarkable man achieves such heights. In the four-year period (1999-2003) when he coached a Real Madrid full of stars (Figo, Zidane, Ronaldo, Beckham, etc.), he won seven titles, including two *Liga*s, two *Champions Leagues*, and a Clubs' World Cup. The day after winning the last *Liga*, he was sacked by Real Madrid's incompetent management, in five minutes and by a second-level director, on the grounds that his coaching methods were "obsolete" (!). Never again (or before) Real Madrid has achieved that string of titles. He is now the only coach in history to have won a *Champions League* (twice!), a World Cup, and a *EuroCup* (did I forget? add to that a *Liga* and a Clubs' World Cup as well). He will never boast about it.

The lesson to be learned is that perhaps even the team tactics are somewhat secondary. It is not a coincidence that the two heroes of this story – Pep Guardiola and Vicente del Bosque – both paid great attention to youth soccer and both developed a keen sensitivity to how kids develop their different needs and abilities. And they both applied this sensitivity to successfully manage a team of adults. What really matters, in order to build a great team, is to have skilled, cooperative-minded players and an intelligent, patient and kind coach that safeguards the "team spirit" like a *pater familias*: the players' relationships and their love for the ball.

Summary

This book tells you the story of how FC Barcelona has managed to build one of the best soccer teams in the world using primarily the players from its youth academy (nicknamed *"La Masia"*). Messi, Iniesta, and Xavi have dazzled soccer fans around the world with their ballet-like positioning and passing skills and ended up sharing the podium as top, second, and third best players of the world in the *2010* ranking. When compared to all the other great teams in history, a feature that makes this Barça unique is that it is backed by a youth development program of unprecedented scale and strength: most of the squad has been playing together since they were teenagers. During the 2013-2014 season, 17 of the 25 players of the first team were from *La Masia*, a historical record. *La Masia* now trains kids from all continents, including American boy Ben Lederman, and even puts them through college (three of the newest youth academy recruits, Montoya, Bartra, and Sergi Roberto, are all in college). This book reveals that this accumulation of talent is the result of a 30 year-long plan, set in motion by the brilliant mind of Dutch coach and ex-Barça player Johan Cruyff.

It all started in 1972, when a modest youth development program fell in the hands of Laureano Ruiz, a visionary coach who (against contemporary trends) decided to give priority to ball exercises rather than physical training and established that all teams in the youth academy would play with the same tactics (4-3-3). Under Ruiz's tenure, the *juvenils* (despite being a different team every year) won the Spanish Championship for five years in a row (1973-1977). When Ajax coach Rinus Michels became Barça coach, he brought the attack-minded, scientific coaching methodology of the Ajax school; he immediately spotted Ruiz's talent and put him in charge of the whole youth academy in 1974. At that time, Barça also signed up the Dutch star Johan Cruyff and the fans fell forever in love with the Dutch soccer style known as Total Football. Cruyff and Ruiz left, but a number of excellent youth coaches continued to teach Total Football to the kids. In 1979, President Josep Lluís Núñez remodeled an old farmhouse next to *Camp Nou* and made it a residence for young footballers now known as *La Masia*.

When Johan Cruyff came back as a coach in 1988, he found Michels' heritage: a youth academy in full swing thriving with young, creative midfielders such as Milla, Guardiola, and Iván de la Peña. Cruyff put the kids in charge of the ship and converted Barça fans to a new religion: possession soccer. He mandated that every team in the youth academy played with the same attacking style and formation as the first team, for consistency – an old Ajax method pioneered by Jack Reynolds, Ajax's first coach. Ruiz's innovative techniques finally met the Dutch fertile methodological framework – somewhat inspired in cloning technology – which slowly weaved a nest for all the future eggs. FC Barcelona started scoring handfuls of goals, winning titles like sausages, and producing clonal players. Most importantly, people had fun at the stadium (Cruyff's team was nicknamed the *Dream Team*), won four *Ligas* in a row and a *European Cup*, and saw a decades-old tendency reversed: presently Real Madrid – managed by an incompetent board of directors that prefers to buy foreign stars with the profits of shady real estate deals than to take advantage of their excellent youth academy – spends several-fold more in player signings but typically ends second in *La Liga* and they have seen steep declines in their worldwide rankings and popularity.

Now FC Barcelona enjoys a long hegemony in *La Liga*, largely because the model is no longer challenged – only developed: everyone at the club rows in the same direction. In 2008, twenty years after Cruyff's arrival, Guardiola – one of the first and most brilliant of Cruyff's pupils – was signed as a coach and implemented a gentle management style based on the same rules of respect that he had learned to observe at *La Masia*. The team took off like a rocket with a young Messi, Xavi and Iniesta, plus Valdés, Piqué, Busquets, Pedro, and later Cesc Fàbregas, Thiago Alcántara and a long list of others that are coming up. This homegrown

Pep Team would win three *Ligas* in a row (2008-2009 through 2010-2011) and two *Champions Leagues* (in 2009 and in 2011). Importantly, the youth academy players have been playing together for so many years that they are close friends. As soccer is fundamentally a team sport, perhaps *La Masia* has inadvertently found soccer's most coveted secret: a key ingredient to building a perfect team is to create a respectful environment where (skilled) teammates can solidify their friendships. With the explosion of *La Masia*, FC Barcelona's slogan, "More than a club", crafted a long time ago to remind fans that FC Barcelona would stand against centralist Madrid forces (dictator Franco shamelessly favored Real Madrid), suddenly has acquired a renewed meaning: This club not only tries to play the best soccer, it also provides a model for education and social values.

This book also reveals data gathered from public databases to show that the strategy followed by most rich clubs to be at the top (purchase top players and sell their homegrown) is unsustainable in the long term because the investors that support these clubs did not raise their riches from soccer. Financing soccer with the proceeds of different industries (e.g. in Spain, the real estate sector) has been the cause of major "soccer bubbles" in Europe. The MLS should learn this valuable lesson and promote its youth academies before American soccer falls in the hands of big businesses that are not interested in the development of youth players. How many Ben Ledermans might American towns have in store for the future?

Appendix: Teaching Barça-style soccer to children

"Play is the highest form of research"
        Albert Einstein (1879 – 1955)

Technically speaking, FC Barcelona does not teach soccer to children – the (free) academy teaches Barça-style soccer mostly to *teenagers*. (For younger kids, from 6-9 years old, FC Barcelona runs the *FCBEscola*, a fee-based soccer academy that teaches the same principles as – but does not guarantee the entrance into – the youth academy.) It is important to emphasize that the scouts who decided that those kids had the appropriate characteristics for developing into a Barça player did not teach them to play Barça-style in the first place: these teenagers were taught to play soccer elsewhere when they were children. Is it possible to teach younger kids to play Barça-style *before* they enter the youth academy? Provided the group of kids is motivated to learn, I think it is possible.

Once in a while a coach will have the opportunity to manage a team of highly talented and motivated players. Even at these children-age leagues, as well as in the Select Soccer leagues, the world of soccer coaching is full of arrogant coaches that believe that the high performance of the team is solely their merit. This is usually the same type of coach that, given a group of less talented players, will often lose his temper and blame the players for the poor performance of the team. I'm the first to acknowledge that I would not have been able to obtain the fantastic results that I obtained in my four years of coaching – I don't recall losing a single game – if the players had not been fantastic. Having said that, I believe the methods (which were not mine) did help.

The first thing one notices about the FC Barcelona methodology is that it is very scientifically structured, as I have explained elsewhere in this book. When you read Dutch coaching manuals you see that this rational approach has, with all certainty, a Dutch origin. As a scientist, I'm very drawn to this approach. As a player, I was never formally coached but I was lucky to play in the intramural league of the University of Barcelona, where a lot of ex-soccer players (looking for a second career) ended up playing. Our Physics soccer team was led by Prof. Javier Tejada, a Quantum Magnetism world expert and ex-player of Zaragoza (a First Division club in *La Liga*) who had an incredibly accurate left foot. Other departments (such as Physical Education) had many more ex-players. One of these teams had a short, stocky striker who had scored more than a 100 goals in his 9 or 10 years at local club Espanyol. When we played against his team, I was always in charge of marking him (he played midfield at the time, like me). Even though I was 18 years younger and obviously a bit faster, the guy had so many tricks in store that he was very hard to stop. I enjoyed every minute of the game; this was the equivalent of a private lesson for me. I observed the way he protected the ball, or suddenly turned around on his heels and went in the opposite direction, completely fooling me. Marañón had been a great shooter and an even better header when playing against First Division defenders. We didn't know what to do to defend against their corner kicks, because Marañón jumped so high. Then my physicist mentor, Javier Tejada, came to the rescue with a bit of scientific insight: "Marañón is always at the right place at the right time and he heads the ball perfectly, right? So forget about the ball; just pay attention to him. All you need to do is jump when he jumps, next to him, so that you displace him in the air and he misses his target". Tejada's strategy worked beautifully. From that day on, Marañón never scored again on corner kicks against our team, and I learned about the value of applying science to soccer.

I became personally interested in the question of how to teach soccer in Barça style to the youngest kids the minute my wife asked me to coach my son's kindergarten team and I saw my then-five-year-old son's expectant eyes begging for a "yes". It was not hard to convince me: I was looking forward to grow a soccer pal to my own, improved image. However, these kids were not kids from the FC Barcelona youth academy or Catalan kids familiar with Barça culture and Barça-style concepts. These were kids from a Seattle elementary school called Bryant. The team was formed of most of my son's best friends. I decided to include this appendix precisely to show that, in my experience, the methods of the FC Barcelona academy can be extrapolated to kids as young as 6 years old – something that is not obvious because, except for my son, they did not watch Barça regularly (or not at all). With the help of my friend Mehrdad Jazayeri, who is also a skeptical scientist like me, we started coaching them inspired by FC Barcelona coaching methods and I can report that this type of implementation works very well in the hands of neophytes. (The *FCBEscola* shows year after year that it works well in the hands of *professional* coaches.) Exercises were always designed to maximize the contact with the ball. The lesson that healthy relationships are a fundamental ingredient for the success of the team, as noted elsewhere in this book both for FC Barcelona and *La Roja*, was also evident at this early age. The following is an account of that personal experience, probably one of the happiest times of my life. If only I could keep coaching them forever.

Simple logics for children

As pointed out earlier, one of the most attractive features of the FC Barcelona style of play is its logical simplicity, since it can be taught to children (in all its complexity!) much earlier than other styles of play. Its No. 1 postulate, Possession Soccer, was explained once by Cruyff in the simplest terms: "While we have the ball they don't have it". Every kid understands this. I have always felt that children, who are naturally curious, need to be given an explanation for why they do the exercises that they are asked to do. Why should they stop dribbling and pass the ball? "To play at first touch is to play very well. To play with two touches is to play well. To play with three is to play poorly". Every kid knows how to count and quickly learns to associate that keeping the ball to himself (more touches) will result in loss of possession. Cruyff has also said that soccer is a sport that is primarily played with your brain. So I remind the kids that their brain is like a computer, and they should think about their team as a computer network. They all know about the Internet, and that a computer disconnected from the Internet has no access to Google, YouTube, and all these tools that they love so much. So when they dribble without passing they are like a computer that is disconnected from the Internet. On the other hand, when they pass to their teammates, their computing power gets amplified and they have access to their teammates' brains. Since many kids know how to play chess, another analogy that resonates with them is to compare them with chess pieces: if they dribble (one on one), they can only advance like a pawn; at most, if they dribble like Messi, they can advance like a horse, but even Messi sometimes he doesn't find a square to land on. If they learn to pass in all directions, they multiply their value as a piece: they can activate other pieces, become a queen and be much more lethal to their opponent. What would they rather be, a pawn or a queen?

Paying attention to details and communication

In my opinion, the most important ingredient for coaching kids is to pay attention to details. "I've never asked a player to do something he can't do", Guardiola has said. This commonsensical principle is extremely important for coaching kids, keeping in mind that each kid will have different needs, goals, and challenges. A kid needs constant guidance and positive reinforcement to properly learn to position his feet and body in the various soccer moves, such as passing, kicking, etc. This takes time and patience. An example: some young kids do not kick well because they do not position their feet with enough precision during running, so these kids should first improve their running skills, e.g. by stepping on or around ladders, cones or other obstacles, sideways, and backwards, as dancers learn in their floor exercises to precisely position their feet. Just watch their little feet and decide what is best for each kid. (I have found that this observation exercise that I had to do for my players has been extremely useful later for scouting players and, at games, for ranking the ability of our rival players: it sufficed to watch their little feet for a few minutes; soccer is a sport that requires a high degree of feet coordination, so the ability of a player is most often already manifested in the dexterity of his running.)

Another important aspect of teaching soccer to kids is that communicating soccer concepts that are obvious to adults is a challenge. Concepts like "control" or "triangulation" are met with a blank stare when you try to convey them to a six year old. It's very nice when journalists distil Barça's style into "position, pressure, possession, circulation, definition". But how do you convey these concepts to a group of kindergarten kids that chase the ball all at once? You have to use different words to switch their minds away from playing "bumblebee soccer" (their first instinct). If you (the coach) get mad at the kids for executing some drill wrong at a game, think twice: you are probably having a bad day. I have seen many coaches that scream with angry voices when kids miss shots, when they are not covering well their marks, or when they are not being aggressive enough, not realizing that it only points to two failures as a teacher: first, that coach is letting the parents know that he did not succeed in teaching that to the kids in the previous months of training; and second, he is showing that he does not have a good grasp of basic child psychology: why is the coach mad at me, the kid thinks, if I haven't had time to learn it? I have always felt that, for young kids, it is extremely important that the coach be an example of conduct and that he love every minute of the game, lose or win, rain or shine: that's what the kids are going to learn to love.

At this very young age, soccer has two very different components that (following FC Barcelona methods for older kids) can be worked out separately: position and technique. By "position" I mean the ability of a player to know where he (or she) has to be. It's a tactical ability that has to do with his ability to read the game and the positions of the other players and has nothing to do with his ability to kick the ball. The norm here in the Seattle leagues is not to specialize kids in any given position (the league gives you pamphlets encouraging rotations), so we have tried to rotate them in all positions – a philosophy with which I agree for this age group. (Needless to say, equal playing time is mandatory.) By "technique" I mean the ability to handle the ball (mostly with the foot, but also with the chest, head and knee), to pass it, protect it, and to pass it or shoot it to the intended place. The rest – what I would call "soccer intelligence" — is most effectively taught simply by showing soccer games to the kids (which also provides role models for them). As I explained above, one of the problems we encounter is that most of our kids do not watch soccer games, so soccer intelligence is a bit sluggish in American kids at this early age, relying mostly on an innate capacity to read the game.

Do not confuse the above paragraph to mean that kids should take turns to play randomly in all positions. I have seen parent-coaches that do just that simply to satisfy the parents that are watching and want to see their kid "play up front". I always looked at the games as the "performances" where the parents come to see what we learned at practice. I told the parents that the kids do not really learn anything at the games, so it does not matter much where they play. At practice, each has a ball and kicks it many times per second, so their brains are constantly learning. At games, the ball is shared by a dozen kids so the average frequency of contact between their little feet and the ball is reduced to less than once a minute, at best. Most kids, if asked, will tell you that they want to play forward and score lots of goals, but it is the job of the coach to make them see that it is not a reasonable expectation for everyone. Kids that are placed in a position for which they do not have enough skill will not get to touch the ball and will suffer. A teammate that does not perform a good function will not be respected by his teammates and the team karma will hurt. On the other hand, good forwards respect good defenders and vice versa. I always made a point that our starting line-up had to reflect our strongest team possible (no preferences between "starters" and "non-starters" are made at these ages), and when/if we had a clear advantage, then we could rotate around. I put a lot of thought into the line-ups and never, ever listened to the parents. In the end, my strategy worked for everyone:

in most games we did win a clear advantage and, by the second half, I was able to introduce rotations that made everyone (players and parents) happy. The important stuff, though, still happened at practice.

Improving the technique

In soccer, good positioning skills give you order (the opposite of chaos). For me (I have a "Barça bias"), proper soccer starts with good positioning. However, if the players can only play with their brains, and their feet are useless, the passes and the shots will be too imprecise to get anything done. I have seen very intelligent kids, with very smart sense of space, who could not handle the ball well because of lack of technique. Technique comes with practice, practice, and practice. Nobody has been born with the ability to play something as unnatural as soccer. Kids that practice the most on their own are the ones that have the finest touch. Generations of players have improved simply by repetitively kicking the ball against a wall, as Guardiola has described in his memoirs. A flat wall offers immense possibilities because it returns the ball with almost the same momentum and angle that it got impacted with. Play up close to test your reflexes, or far away to practice your shot. Cruyff has explained how, as a young lad, his favorite exercise was to run next to a wall, "pass" the ball to the wall, and work on controlling the return at full run – no wonder he developed such a fine control! Learning to juggle at an early age is also a great way to acquire a good technique. If it serves as a benchmark, I know that Guardiola could juggle the ball 1,000 times by age seven (and probably most other great soccer players). Start your practice with a bit of juggling – one minute or so should be enough, more as a motivational tool and for you to correct mistakes (the ball should not be kicked higher than the head for the youngest kids that are still doing one or two touches; for older kids that can juggle a few times, the upper limit should be the hip; later, when a kid can juggle 20 times or so, the threshold is knee). The important point is that they look forward to improvement and practice on their own – juggling can be done almost everywhere, indoors, while waiting in line at school, etc. By the way, I have found that, perhaps in contrast with their regular homework, children love "soccer homework" – the homework should be explained to them at practice and then sent by email to all the parents as a reminder; parents generally do not mind, on the contrary, it shows that you are involved with their children's soccer education and they are usually very grateful.

As a coach, one needs to always think of ways to improve the technique of the players – the technique is the basic tool from which everything builds up (keeping in mind that if they don't know how to position on the field, they will be useless players). In the case of very young kids, you are starting from scratch – that's the bad and good news: all you need is patience, and time. When you start with 6- or 7-year olds, who inevitably kick the ball with their toes and place the opposite foot too far back, you will first need to teach them how to properly kick the ball. I started with a simple exercise: the kids had to be three steps away from the ball, take steps towards the ball, place the support foot next to the ball, and place themselves in shooting position, with the foot in the air – but not shoot – and come back where they were at the beginning, as if they were rehearsing a dance movement in front of the static ball; I know all about the theories that say that shooting needs to be practiced with a moving ball (which I believe to be true for older kids), but if a kid cannot complete this very simple exercise, that means (s)he does not have the basic coordination to learn to shoot and the assignment to shoot will be to hard for him/her. As soon as they had learned this "dance", I told them to pay attention to their arms (opposite arm forward and same arm backward) for best balance, and finally I introduced the "shoelace kick". At this point, if they had the balance right, they all did it correctly. Week after week, we trained and designed exercises (most of them very common) to improve their technique. Kids don't have the same motivations for learning for the sake of learning as adults, so often we would build in extra motivational tactics (such as contests – they are very competitive!). For example, we would have shooting contests (against a target, the goal far away, to kick over one of the goals, etc.) and divide the kids in two groups and count which group would win – no need to offer any prize: they hate to lose. As far as physical exercises go, kids this young don't need to stretch or warm up, but we tried to start them with some running (simple races across the field, usually with the ball) just to burn some calories, specially on days where the practice was more static (shooting, rondos, etc.). (Some coaches might disagree and make them stretch as an educational tool, to get them in the habit for later; that's good too, but it takes time.) Once in a while we would make races of various distances without a ball to keep a mental tally of who our fastest runners were.

Basic positioning skills: Teaching children to separate

The most defining statistic about FC Barcelona's style of play is that its players pass the ball much more often and with higher precision than the other teams. (I believe the precision statistic has been exaggerated, because the precision is simply a result of Barça's strategy of choosing not to execute long passes precisely because they are less precise; in the start of the 2013-2014 season, when central defenders Piqué and Mascherano started experimenting with frequent long passes, we saw that their precision was not very desirable either.) Barça's strength is that it conceives soccer as a passing game; Messi might be a dribbling super-star, but he graduated from this "passing university" with honors. How can one even start teaching these passing concepts to kindergarten-age kids that all really, really want is to kick the ball?

When we first started working with kindergarten children, we encountered the very well known problem that all the kids tended to cluster around the ball, making it impossible for the ball to circulate. This is what we term "bumblebee soccer". We tried explaining to them that they needed to separate, but someone needed to get to the ball, right? These kids were too young and excited about the ball to understand. The first thing to teach is very counter-intuitive to a young kid: to separate from the other kid that has the ball, rather than cluster. (Hey, I want the ball too!) I designed an exercise called "non-contact soccer" whereby two teams of three kids were defending their own kiddie goals but were not allowed to cross the midline. The fields were very short, 6 meters long (or the size of the goalie's small box in a FIFA-size field), to make it possible to score from past the midline. There were two defenders and a goalie. Since one of the three attackers was always free, the challenge was for the three attackers to pass the ball fast until they saw a hole through the two defenders, and as soon as the attackers lost the ball they had to quickly get back into defensive position. This exercise allowed the kids to learn basic positional skills and lose their tendency to play "bumblebee soccer".

Basic positioning skills: Tactical formations

Another defining feature of FC Barcelona and its youth academy teams, inherited from the Ajax school, is that their tactics emerge from their position on the field. Rather than spending too much energy in unnecessary, predictable long runs, they fool their opponents by moving around them, like dancers following a choreography only known to them. Then, a second later, they go back to the same initial position, like magnets on a self-reset mechanism.

In my opinion, teaching soccer has to start by teaching fundamental footwork and then add basic positioning skills *before* you introduce the concept of passing. Assigning positions provides a structural framework to develop passing skills. The above-explained exercise to prevent "bumblebee soccer" worked wonders. On the field, in their first 3 vs 3 competitions (6-year olds), we set up a player to defend the goal and one player on each wing. This defines a triangle, which is very easy to grasp. Having two forwards on the "wing" positions has two advantages: 1) when the back-defender (position #1) has the ball, he has two clear pass options – either to the right (position #2) or to the left (position #3)–; and 2) the two wingers are naturally drawn towards the goal (where the action is), so it's best to tell them that their position is away from it to avoid clustering – indeed, most likely you'll need to remind them to return to their positions at every play. The tasks are then simple to enumerate: there is one player on position #1, one on position #2 and one on position #3, which makes it easy to call a player back into position when they are off position ("remember you are playing in position #2"). There is no need to have more than one player to defend the goal, because at this age players are too clumsy to dribble anyways. The attacks need to converge towards position #1 anyways, and (s)he is instructed to boot it towards one of the wings. Most importantly, as soon as the players assimilate the formation, each player forms an expectation of having a teammate in the other positions (or their vicinity) and passing is much more likely.

Teaching tactics to kids is tricky, because I might be speaking words that have very rich meanings to me (I have used them most of my life) but they are meaningless to them. I remind myself, when giving tactical instructions to kids, to speak simple. For the youngest ones (U6 through U8), the purpose of good positioning is mostly to avoid "bumblebee soccer", so we simply rehearsed our formations like dancers would rehearse a choreography: moving up and down the field all together – until I saw that, in scrimmage games, they would stay in their assigned zone. For U9 and older kids, the most important instructions that I give them are separated in two groups: when we have the ball and as soon as we loose the ball. When we have the ball, I tell them that I'm happy if 1) the player that has the ball looks up and passes fast; and 2) everyone else moves to an empty spot – specially the forward wings. As soon as we loose the ball, I tell them that I'm satisfied if I see them running to the nearest opponent in order to 1) force him to boot the ball or try to dribble; or 2) block the most likely pass. I can't think of a simpler way of explaining soccer to kids. If they do both things right, our possession is overwhelming and we end up scoring most of the goals.

The *rondo*

To improve the precision of the pass, the *rondo* or "piggy in the middle" – the stellar exercise of the FC Barcelona and Ajax youth academies – is an excellent choice. In its adult form, the rondo is too complex for kindergarteners who are still learning to aim. It was difficult enough without the "piggy" in the middle, so we started by asking them to concentrate on finishing a whole turn: achieving ten short passes sideways can be challenging at this age. We also wanted them to understand that the most effective (less risky) pass in a rondo is the pass to the next man, not through the middle where the "piggy" is. It requires learning a "scissor pass" (90 degrees to your side) as opposed to a pass to your front (easier), and also using both the inside and outside of your foot. (The kids named the exercise "washing machine" and it stuck.) At eight years old, some can do rondos (with the "piggy" in the middle) well and some are still lacking skills, so we keep on practicing them. It can be played in many flavors, adapting it to players of various skills: only two touches allowed, at first touch, naming a "piggy" in an adjacent rondo before they receive the ball (to teach the players to survey their surroundings), etc. – but in all cases the players should either not move or only be allowed to move along a line (imaginary lines tend to promote imprecise passing).

The *rondo* is a very technical exercise but it has its disadvantages. First, it does not give a quantitative feedback to the kid about how much more accurate his pass needs to be. How much is his aim off by? The recipient of the pass usually corrects the error and the exercise goes on. For this reason, I complemented the *rondos* with an exercise where pairs of players had to pass the ball to each other along a line, separated by 20 or 30 meters, and tell the other player aloud the distance (more or less) by which they had missed the perfect pass.

Another disadvantage of the *rondo* is that it does not favor learning looking over the shoulder prior to receiving the pass because the players do not have opponents behind their backs trying to steal the ball from them. In this regard, there exists a variation of the *rondo* where the players are organized in two teams in a small square field and the objective of the exercise is to keep the ball away from the other team (without goals) – a "possession game". Possession games are very dynamic and players must be very alert about their surroundings at all times.

Teaching them to look up

The success of the "non-contact soccer" experiment made me realize that the best way for kids to grasp the intricacies of the game is not by means of explanations (like an adult would), but rather through the introduction of artificial rules in their practice games. That's because rules carry a punishment: a foul, the loss of ball possession if the rule is not followed. Only then the rule, I found, was invariably learned very, very quickly. Another example: one of the biggest problems in youth soccer is to make kids distinguish between "pass" and "kick", specially because the former requires that the player looks up first (very difficult) and the latter doesn't. When we would scream "pass", they would "kick" the ball to nowhere because, in the haste, they had not made the effort to look up first and aim at a person. You see kids as old as nine or ten years old doing this sometimes. We knew that we better correct this soon or they would acquire a bad habit. The solution? Screaming "look up" had not worked, as you might have guessed. So in our practice games, I introduced the rule that a "kick to nowhere" was punishable as a foul, and possession would change for the other team. So our kids very soon learned, without us having to scream "look up" all the time, that they better look up before passing. With time, they have acquired the good habit of looking up and passing quickly as soon as they receive the ball – an imperative for a quick exit of the ball in defense and a healthy circulation of the ball in midfield: the goals come naturally.

Teaching them to look up before they receive the ball: the "Radar"

If the other team has learned to put pressure, you will notice that your kids don't have time to look up even if you have taught them to: as soon as they have received the ball, they have a player on them and they don't dare to get the eyes off it for fear of losing control of the ball. The only way out of this negative loop is to teach the kids to look around them *before* they receive the ball, when they are less marked, in order to gain time – a skill I introduced to our third-graders (8-9 year-olds or U-9) with great success. First, I introduced the skill, which I call "Radar", in a controlled setting: one player ("player A") was placed 10 meters away from me and the rest of the players in a line (taking turns to be "player B") 10 meters behind player A. I placed one cone 10 meters to my right and one 10 meters to my left. Player B was instructed to start running to either cone (his choice) as soon as he saw me pass the ball to Player A. Player A had to pass the ball at first touch to the running player B – in order to do that successfully, they quickly figured out that they had to turn around while the ball was coming to them. (Player B passes the ball to coach upon receiving the ball and occupies the space of Player A.) The exercise can be made more complicated if Player A has to guess whether Player B is friend or foe by looking at whether Player B runs towards a cone or towards him (if Player B runs towards him, he has to protect the ball or pass it back to coach), and more challenging by increasing the speed of the ball. The "Radar" skill was then introduced into scrimmage games; here I constantly reminded them to "Radar" and challenged them to increase the number of successful "Radars" per game. They first need to learn to activate the "Radar" when they are not under pressure, but the key concept they have to learn is that, the tighter the space, the more they have to gain by activating the "Radar" – the "Radar" is what will allow them to circulate the ball out of difficult situations.

Playing in silence

Not all coaches agree with me on this and will teach young players to "call for the ball" ("here!", "pass!"), a habit that has two negative drawbacks: 1) it acoustically signals the position of the caller to the opponents, and 2) it biases the teammate that was carrying the ball from making his own decisions. I have seen that my players have improved as a result of implementing a "playing in silence" rule, and I benefitted from it myself. (I love it when, playing as a defender, the attackers yell past me – they are much easier to follow.) When we accepted a few kids from another team that had not been training with us, we noticed that they were used to call for the ball all the time, I explained that it's better to play in silence so you stay stealth, but they kept on doing it out of habit. I figured I better come up with another rule (for scrimmages only) before it's too late. This time the rule was that if you call someone's name or say "here", etc., your team loses possession too. They learned to play in silence in a couple of weeks. (Yelling is a good defensive weapon for defenders and goalies to help each other, but I thought it would be easy to introduce that later.) Whenever a parent or another coach argues with me on this, I always refer them to go watch a Barça training session: you hear the footsteps and the ball slipping on the ground.

Dribbling skills

Every exercise has to be done twice: once for each foot, the good foot and the bad foot, or coming from the right side and coming from the left side. I'm a big fan of the classic exercises: dribble four cones and shoot, for example. I have read the theory of other coaches that say that it's best to practice dribbling other kids because that's what they face in games, but for very young kids, if you can't dribble around a cone you won't dribble a kid. The cones will allow you to see what's wrong in the way the kid places the feet, and then you can correct that. Some kids can't even run very well yet at six years old, they are not that well coordinated. I have them run down the field and touch the ball at every step with each foot – a difficult skill! Another great exercise is to dribble and play games with a tennis ball, a trick used by young Andrés Iniesta and his friends at *La Masia*, to gain finer control. (If they whine about how difficult it is, try getting them excited with the story that this is how they, too, can become as good as Iniesta.) The kids will have plenty of opportunity to practice "real dribbling" during the scrimmage game at the end of practice.

The hardest thing to teach is, by far, the dribble, because it comes in so many forms and shapes, and depends on each situation and each player's physique and technique. From what I have seen, the dribble appears naturally from fine ball handling and fast feet, so I've insisted in always teaching good foot skills first. The dribble is very much a self-learning process, so in fact we don't go beyond teaching a few tricks such as "Cruyff's turn", the Zidane step, or the scissors. At this age, having played three or four years of soccer, the kids have already developed their own style of dribbling, and every practice ends in a game where they get to play and develop all these skills.

Control skills

One of my favorite sayings in soccer says that "a good control is half a goal". It also speaks for the consequences of a bad control – you will miss the goal. So we have spent many practices throwing balls high up in the air and the kid has to trap the ball with the inside of his foot, and even return it at first touch. A common misconception in youth soccer is to teach kids to stop the ball by stepping on it, which is easy to learn but actually slows down the control in a real game situation because it is not compatible with stopping the ball while running. Proper control should be taught with the inside of the foot, and advanced control with the shoelaces or the outside of the foot. This is an exercise that requires a lot of dedication (one on one), so the coach's work needs to be complemented by parents' "homework". In order to make it a fun exercise, I gave different controls different names: a perfect one that gets stuck next to the foot is a "Messi", one that separates from the foot by a few centimeters is an "Iniesta" or a "Xavi", the worse ones are a "Keita" or a "Pinto", and if he doesn't even touch the ball then I use Real Madrid defender names with poor technique such as "Coentrao" or "Arbeloa". (Feel free to invert the villains if you are a Real Madrid fan or use your own ones, the point is to have fun with your kid while you are giving him/her marks without upsetting him/her if he/she misses a control.) I have spent so many hours doing this with my son in the backyard that at eight years old, he would nail controls just as well as me – it's ridiculous how fast kids can learn. However, my favorite exercise of all is tennis-soccer (a kids' version of volley soccer whereby 2 vs 2 kids play with a tennis net in between, and have to kick it over, only one bounce allowed between touches). It is the fun version of juggling, very good for developing a fine touch with all sides of the foot. And better yet, the coaches often get to play too.

Learning how to kick the ball

A most important exercise is to teach the kids how to kick on goal. It helps the coach to start with a static ball, so that the position of the feet can be quickly corrected (the most common mistake is to not place the non-striking foot next to the ball). However, as soon as this concept is grasped, kicking should be practiced always on rolling balls and with both legs, as this is the situation that will be encountered in real games.

I have learned that the ball matters. Sizes 3 and 4 (size 5 is the professional soccer ball) are not really very well engineered, because the materials have not been scaled to produce the same bouncing experience and elasticity as adults feel for size 5. A size 3 ball is horribly tough for the foot of a kindergartener or first grader. I taught my son to shoot with a volleyball, which has the same weight but produces a nicer feeling. When he was eight, with thin legs, he had a cannonball shot that I've never had (so it's not in his genes). Size 4 balls, the one that was mandatory for 8 year-olds, had the right weight for him, but have a "flat" bounce, so he would prefer the experience of size 5, which has the "right" bounce – but did not have the right weight for the biomechanics of his muscles and bones: after a while, his legs would hurt.

At soccer practice, we emphasize ball lifting because at ages below eight or nine they almost never pass or kick by lifting the ball, but our team gains a clear advantage by doing it. So we have a high target on the wall and for 5-10 minutes they have to hit it as hard as they can from a distance, or they have to shoot over a goal that is taller than them. Here also, you have to spend a lot of time correcting the position of their body and both of their feet, player by player. As a result, many of the kids in the team – ahead of what you see in their category – can easily score over the goalie (since these kids do not reach the top of the goal, we have two kids that have higher scoring averages on free kicks than the best professionals!).

Simple drills that will give the team a lot of mileage

Most teams up until U-11 and U-12 fail to train basic drills that are actually very important for a game. The most important one is how to keep possession of the ball after your team takes a throw-in. This requires a sequence of well-orchestrated moves to fool the opponents, but with a good repertoire of them, the opponents do not stand a chance. For the youngest kids, who are all fixated into marking their opponents in a basketball-like fashion without much running, the easiest to teach is "give me an L". The receiver of the pass has to run orthogonally to the thrower and turn 90 degrees (describing an "L") towards the opponent's goal; when the receiver makes the turn, the thrower does the throw-in. There is always a hole in that direction. For older kids, it just suffices to make them realize that the thrower is free and should receive a return pass at first touch. So the receivers can pretend to go away (the defender will follow) and then return a safe pass. There is really no excuse to not rehearse the throw-ins: this is a situation that happens more than once a minute during a game – that can be more than 50 throw-ins. If you don't rehearse it, your players won't be well prepared and will lose possession about half of the times. Most coaches encourage their players to "throw it down the line", which is very easy to defend and very hard to control for the forward: the ball is then so close to the line that any slight mis-control (for example, because the defender makes a legal contact with the forward at the instant that the forward touches the ball), and the ball goes out of bounds. (I have a name for this lack of desire for maintaining possession at throw-in situations: "throw it down the garbage".)

A similar thing happens with corner kicks. You can complain as much as you want that your players are too young to reach the goal (when they start playing on big fields), but that means that you are not offering tools to execute the set piece. If your players can't reach the goal comfortably, have them *pretend* to take a corner kick, but instead at the moment of execution of the corner kick by player A, one of your players (player B) that is closer to player A runs towards him to receive his pass, passes it back while player A (who is unmarked) gets closer to the goal. He should be able to shorten the distance by at least 10-15 meters at least, and by the same token add some extra lift to the ball thanks to the extra momentum of player B's pass. When the players have done this a couple of times in a game, and/or are very comfortable with this play, a nice variation is when player B *pretends* to touch the ball and lets the ball go through so that someone in your team can put the ball into the net.

Teaching respect

The FC Barcelona youth academy emphasizes respect almost above all the other teachings – respect for the opponent, the referee, the teammates, the coach, even family and friends. I know that this is not unique to FC Barcelona, but I also know that not all clubs emphasize this teaching. The local Seattle youth soccer leagues, with an emphasis on recreational soccer, also insist on this aspect which I have always greatly appreciated. Kids are rarely physically violent on the pitch (unlike adults), but sometimes they can be mean to other kids if allowed. For example, they might make fun of an opponent after they have scored a goal or to one of their teammates for missing a pass. We have never tolerated it in our team under any circumstance: if persisting, the kid is substituted immediately for some time, and usually that kid has learned the lesson for ever. In general, however, I'm not in favor of punitive actions: most kids do things wrong because they do not know any better, and a clear explanation of why that is wrong is usually sufficient. (I suspect that it helps that the explanation takes places while the game goes on and they anxiously miss play time, but at least I do not become the threatening teacher: I prefer to be seen as an advisor-friend figure, to whom they can turn when they are in doubt, than to be feared.) When we saw that a player had criticized another one for missing a shot or a pass, we favored encouragement amongst teammates ("good effort!") rather than punish the player because we are educators, not policemen. On the pitch, criticism (to teammates, the referee, etc.) is destructive to the team. Strengthening positive-reinforcement is a self-management attitude that helps them leave behind mistakes and other crises, which ultimately benefits the team, making them better teammates and also better citizens.

As for respecting the coach: I'm not running a large school so discipline is not very important (I don't see the need of coming to shake my hand, like they are taught to do at Barça, and my kids are all very courteous to me anyways). The only discipline that we have found necessary to impose is on the bench during game days, because they were all pestering us "Can I go in?" literally every minute and we could not think about substitutions or the game. We needed silence, so I put a new bench rule: if you asked "Can I go in?", then you would have to go back to the end of the line (they take rigorous turns). Now we all watch the games and they help cheer, it's much more fun.

We will never really know whether I taught these kids to play in FC Barcelona-style, and it doesn't matter. As I said above, there is not one "true way" of teaching soccer. The biggest strength of the team might perhaps be as much their passing abilities as the strength of their friendships – they have that in common also with the great *ManU* team of Giggs, Scholes and Beckham and this continuous string of youth teams produced by Barça. Teams are not simply an ensemble of players: there are also the parents who cheer and help organize barbeques, the siblings who play with each other on the sidelines, the medical personnel, the staff in charge of the gear, the administrative staff, the players' agents (for more advanced ages), and the coaches who care for them all. I see a soccer team as a community, a large family with the common goal of enjoying the game. I have experienced this warm feeling as a player, as a fan, as a coach, and as a parent.

Perhaps soccer is even simpler than we think. We coaches try to plan every detail. But maybe soccer is less about planning and more about empathy, about feeling the flow and the astuteness of your friends around you. What matters the most to me, as a coach and a father, is that they remember these friendships around the pitch, all this love around the ball.

Visiting Pep at Munich

Coaching the Bryant Blasters at Arena Sports, Seattle

"The cells of soccer"
(homage to Xavi, Iniesta, Messi, and Busquets)
By Aileen Wu and Albert Folch (FolchLab Art)

Each soccer ball is a collage of images of muscle cells taken with a microscope. The original images were digitally cut in hexagon shapes and their negatives were cut in pentagon shapes. The brown appearance of the cells in the white images indicates that the muscle cells have been stained with a dye that binds to their acetylcholine receptors, which the cells use to communicate with neurons.

Bibliography

Below are listed the books from which I have extracted information for this book. I chose not to show the long list of hundreds of newspaper articles because it would have added at least ten more pages to this book and I'm sure most readers would not have bothered to read them. The sports journalists from whom I have used most material have been Martí Perarnau (*Sport*), Oriol Domènech (*Mundo Deportivo*), Santiago Segurola, José Sámano, Ramon Besa (*El País*), and Alfredo Relaño (*As*).

BarçaEternal – The book that all Barça supporters should have. Authors: **Toni Closa and David Salinas**. Publisher: Ediciones B (2012). Language: Trilingual (Catalan/Spanish/English). Summary: This 1000-page mini-book contains all the conceivable statistics (including the rosters and results of all the games!) of FC Barcelona throughout its history (from 1899 through 2012). The data on the number of youth academy players used to build the graphs in previous pages was obtained from this book. For obsessed fans only.

El camí dels campions – De La Masia al Camp Nou. Author: **Martí Perarnau.** Publisher: Columna Edicions (2011). Language: Catalan. Translated title: *The path of the champions – From La Masia to the Camp Nou.*
Summary: Ex-Olympian and sports journalist Martí Perarnau has gathered the most authoritative source of information about the structure, coaching methods, and scouting procedures of FC Barcelona's youth academy. The book includes a memorable list and characteristics of the best 50 players (among a total of 255) born between 1989 and 1996 that were playing in *La Masia* in 2011. Arguably the best analysis on the FC Barcelona youth academy ever published.

Fórmula Barça – Viatge a l'interior d'un equip que ha descobert l'eternitat. Author: **Ricard Torquemada.** Publisher: Cossetània Edicions (2011).

Language: Catalan. Translated title: *The Barça Formula – A journey to the inside of a team that found eternity.*
Summary: Sports journalist Ricard Torquemada explains in clear terms the foundations of Pep team's style of play and analyzes Guardiola's tactics.

Futbol – La meva filosofia. Author: **Johan Cruyff.** Publisher: Ediciones B (2012). Language: Catalan. Translated title: *Football – My philosophy.*
Summary: In this book Cruyff writes with his usual simple language about his visionary soccer philosophy, explaining what it takes to play offensive, beautiful soccer. The book is full of great tactical advice for coaches and precious observations on player development.

Me gusta el fútbol. Author: **Johan Cruyff.** Publisher: RBA (2002). Language: Spanish. Translated title: *I love soccer.*
Summary: This is a delightful book where Cruyff explains his philosophy about soccer, expresses his witty and enlightening opinions about the soccer world, and helps us better understand and enjoy the game.

Ajax Barcelona Cruyff – The ABC of an obstinate maestro. Authors: **Frits Barend & Henk van Dorp.** Publisher: Bloomsbury (1997). Language: English.
Summary: Dutch sports journalists Barend and van Dorp published a compilation of their own interviews of Cruyff over a period of over 30 years. A great resource to better understand the man behind Cruyff.

Escoltant Cruyff – La seva vida i el seu futbol en 150 frases. Author: **Edwin Winkels.** Publisher: Cossetània Edicions (2010). Language: Catalan. Translated title: *Listening to Cruyff – His life and his football in 150 sentences.*
Summary: Sports journalist Edwin Winkels offers a very complete collection of the most memorable quotes by Johan Cruyff. Each quote is dated and commented in its historical context.

Brilliant Orange – The neurotic genius of Dutch soccer. Author: **David Winner.** Publisher: The Overlook Press (2000). Language: English.

Summary: A freelance journalist, David Winner gives a great account of the great Dutch soccer exploits and tragedies by framing them within Dutch politics and the Dutch society. This book is a must-read for soccer fans who want to understand why Holland lost against Germany in the 1974 World Cup final and how the loss has impacted Dutch soccer ever since. The book also helps grasp the immense stature of Cruyff in Dutch soccer and his contributions to Total Football.

El auténtico método del Barça. Author: **Laureano Ruiz.** Publisher: Lectio Ediciones (2013). Language: Spanish. Translated title: *The authentic Barça method.*

Summary: As stated in this book, Laureano Ruiz is one of the pioneers of youth coaching in Spain and the coach that President Agustí Montal hired in 1972 to revamp the FC Barcelona youth academy, around the same time that Rinus Michels was signed from Ajax to implement his Total Football ideas. Nobody at FC Barcelona has ever questioned his contributions, and he has had his share of recognition. You will not find much new information in this poorly-written book, except for the revelation that Laureano feels so insecure about his immense contribution to youth coaching that he needs to congratulate himself at every paragraph. A few random examples of his lack of modesty: "I believe I have pioneered the style of play based on positioning, fine-touch, and intelligence to comprehend the game"; "I invented the *fantasy-play* [4-3-3] in the 60s"; "our tactic was so spectacular that Michels took it to the Dutch national team"; "I have stood out in five fundamental facets: player, coach, writer, teacher, and researcher"; and so on. He even devotes a whole box to explain the source of his insecurity and pretentiousness: "Life has taught me that if we wait for others to praise us, the praise will never come".

Coaching soccer – The official coaching book of the Dutch Soccer Association. Author: **Bert van Lingen.** Publisher: Reedswain (1997). Language: English.

Summary: Despite being a tiny country, the Dutch are a soccer super-power thanks to their coordinated coaching effort on a national level:

Dutch coaching is a sophisticated scientific method – explained in this book – that is applied uniformly to their thousands of soccer academies. This book is a must-read for people who want to learn to coach more effectively, covering all ages. It includes drills and great advice on all the aspects of the game, from technique and tactics to behavior management.

Teambuilding – The road to success. Author: **Rinus Michels.** Publisher: Reedswain (2002). Language: English.

Summary: Dutch coach and Total Football architect Rinus Michels dissects what it takes to build a successful team, from youth team development to professional teams. The book is very interesting in that all the concepts that Cruyff has preached to the Barça choir are there, almost verbatim. Nobody challenges the fact that Cruyff brought them to Barcelona from the Ajax school, where both Michels and him had learned (and helped develop) these concepts in the 1970s as a coach-player duet. In the book one finds what might well be Michels' contributions to Total Football's theoretical framework, something that Cruyff was not interested in. However, Michels was never able to implement Total Football again successfully without Cruyff on the pitch (and was able to repeat its success *with* him – at Barça!), whereas Cruyff's *Dream Team* had already been shining brightly in TVs across the globe (and Cruyff's legacy of "team building" from a youth academy was a well-solidified paradigm at FC Barcelona) when Michels published this book in 2002. So who first conceived Total Football, and who taught it to whom? It is interesting that Michels never reflected on this point.

La última hora del último día. Author: **Jordi Soler.** Publisher: RBA (2007). Language: Spanish. Translated title: *The last hour of the last day.*

Summary: This fascinating book is an autobiographical novel that tells the story of Jordi Soler's grandfather, who exiled from Franco's dictatorship and started a colony in the depths of the Mexican jungle. Jordi grew up there. The relevance to this book is his hilarious account of how Johan Cruyff became to be worshipped by the local Indian population.

Els secrets del Barça – El que no t'han explicat mai del millor club del món. Author: **Lluís Canut.** Publisher: Columna Edicions (2010). Language: Catalan. Translated title: *Barça's secrets – What you have not been told about the best club in the world.*

Summary: Sports journalist Lluís Canut reveals some behind-the-scenes secrets about FC Barcelona.

Els nens de La Masia. Author: **Albert Masnou, Javier Miguel, Jordi Gil & Ivan San Antonio.** Publisher: Grupo Z (2011). Language: Catalan. Translated title: *La Masia's children.*

Summary: A commented photo-album of the players of the FC Barcelona team that were raised at *La Masia* – i.e., most of the squad. The pictures depict the players when they were kids as well as teenagers during their *La Masia* training and celebrating youth trophies. A book that brings us closer to the players.

La meva gent, el meu futbol. Author: **Pep Guardiola.** Publisher: Grupo Zeta (2001). Language: Catalan. Translated title: *My people, my football.*

Summary: Guardiola's autobiography. Written in a somewhat informal style, each chapter focuses on a different person from the soccer world that had an influence in his career.

Pep Guardiola. Author: **Jaume Collell.** Publisher: Columna Edicions (2009). Language: Catalan.

Summary: Guardiola's most complete biography to date, covering from his childhood to his first year as manager of the first team.

Pep Guardiola: Another way of winning: The biography. Author: **Guillem Balagué.** Publisher: Orion Books (2012). Language: English.

Summary: Guillem Balagué has had the unique opportunity to interview Guardiola at length for the first time since he became manager, so this new biography provides an enlightening glimpse into the inner workings of the Pep team (with its good and bad moments) that had never been offered before. The brief chapter on his childhood and adolescence, by contrast, does not add much to what was already known.

Paraula de Pep. Author: **Santi Pedró.** Publisher: Ara Llibres (2009). Language: Catalan. Translated title: *Pep's word.*

Summary: A compilation of Guardiola's most memorable quotes extracted from press conferences Since Guardiola never gave interviews (to avoid favoring one media against another), this book is a good source to grasp his philosophy and management style. The book was made after a TV program that was aired on the Catalan channel TV3; the program can be watched on YouTube by searching "Paraula de Pep".

The Making of the Greatest Team in the World: Barça. Author: **Graham Hunter.** Publisher: BlackPage Press (2012). Language: English.

Summary: This is a great book about the best years of Guardiola's era and its main actors, even the behind-the-scenes ones that you might not have heard of. Graham Hunter is a journalist who has lived in Barcelona and has enjoyed close access to Barça players (he was even next-door neighbor with Thiago Alcántara), which shows in the level of detail of the text.

Barça: A People's Passion. Author: **Jimmy Burns.** Publisher: Bloomsbury (1999). Language: English.

Summary: A journalist who usually focuses on the economy, and the son of a British spy assigned to Madrid after the Spanish Civil War, Jimmy Burns provides an objective overview of the first 100 years of history of the club, the passion of the Barça fans, and the machinations of the Franco junta, framing it all against the backdrop of Catalonia's political struggle within Spain.

Kubala!: L'heroi que va canviar la història del Barça. Author: **Frederic Porta.** Publisher: Edicions Saldonar (2012). Language: Catalan. Translated title: *Kubala!: The hero that changed the history of Barça.*

Summary: This book is a biography of Lázsló Kubala, the legendary Hungarian player from the 1950s that made FC Barcelona a winner again, and in doing so, lifted the spirits of Barça supporters and the Franco-repressed Catalan society.

Sunyol, el president afusellat del Barça – Crònica política i humana d'un dirigent excepcional. Author: **Carles Llorens.** Publisher: Ara Llibres (2011). Language: Catalan. Translated title: *Sunyol, the Barça president who was executed by firing squad – A human and political report of an exceptional leader.*

Summary: The story of FC Barcelona president Josep Sunyol, who was shot by a Franco militia firing squad on 6 August, 1936, during the Spanish Civil War, in which Sunyol (as did most Catalans) joined the Republican side against Franco.

La Roja – How soccer conquered Spain and how Spanish soccer conquered the world. Author: **Jimmy Burns.** Publisher: Nation Books (2012). Language: English.

Summary: A good connoisseur of Spain and its many complexities, Jimmy Burns writes about the history of the Spanish National team since its inception, along with its many ups and downs and political turmoils.

Barça – Revista oficial FC Barcelona, Núm 54 (Desembre 2011-Gener 2012). Publisher: FC Barcelona (2011). Language: Catalan. Translated title: *Barça – Official magazine of FC Barcelona, No. 54 (December 2011-January 2012).*

Summary: The Barça magazine is sent to all *Camp Nou* seat subscribers. This issue, titled "The most admired model", featured an inside look at the new *Ciutat Esportiva* (the youth academy fields and facilities that will substitute *La Masia*, as well as an article on Paulino Alcántara (1896-1964), the all-time top goal scorer of FC Barcelona if we include friendly games (142 goals in official games and 227 in friendly games, totaling 369 goals). Messi will most likely beat Alcántara soon, but he will never beat Alcántara in a different field: Paulino Alcántara, while he scored so many goals, managed to study Medicine and became a respected doctor!

Barça – Revista oficial FC Barcelona, Núm 57 (Juny-Juliol del 2012). Publisher: FC Barcelona (2012). Language: Catalan. Translated title: *Barça – Official magazine of FC Barcelona, No. 57 (June-July 2012).*

Summary: This special issue of the Barça magazine, titled "Guardiola's legacy", featured a rare insider's view of the dressing room (commented by Guardiola himself) and is a good source of statistics on Guardiola's great four years of coaching.

Barça: Our best year ever. Author: **Miguel Ruiz & Jordi Finestres.** Publisher: Angle Editorial (2009). Language: Tri-lingual (Catalan/Spanish/English).
Summary: Photographer Miguel Ruiz had exclusive access to the players (even inside the dressing room) during Pep Guardiola's tenure and the result is this exceptional 200-page book of the best photos of the period. For proud fans.

Dearest Barça. Author: **Lluís Canut.** Publisher: Columna Edicions (2009). Language: Tri-lingual (Catalan/Spanish/English).
Summary: This photobook includes a very complete, 184 page-long collection of photographs that cover the whole history of FC Barcelona. The pictures are thoughtfully commented by sports journalist Lluís Canut. A good gift-book for someone interested in FC Barcelona and its history.

Avui patirem – El retrat més autèntic de l'afició del Barça. Author: **Joan Maria Pou.** Publisher: Ara Llibres (2006). Language: Catalan. Translated title: *Today we will suffer – The most authentic portrait of the Barça fans.*
Summary: The title alludes to a the traditional stereotype of the FC Barcelona fan, but please understand that FC Barcelona did not use to win so much as it does now. The Barça fan base has been accused of being pessimistic – when a tough rival was visiting the *Camp Nou*, one would hear in entering the stadium (I remember it!): "Today we will suffer". This book leaves behind that stereotype and describes (somewhat humorously: Joan Maria Pou is an expert, funny radio show host) at the various types of fans and their behaviors.

Ronaldinho: la màgia d'un crac. Author: **Toni Frieros.** Publisher: Grupo Zeta (2004). Language: Catalan. Translated title: *Ronaldinho: the magic of a crack.*

Summary: A short and simple biography of Ronaldinho, meant to be given away with newspaper Sport, but that contains some interesting accounts of the hardship that Ronaldinho had to endure during his childhood.

Estimat Rijkaard. Author: **Armand Carabén van der Meer.** Publisher: Empúries (2005). Language: Catalan. Translated title: *Dear Rijkaard.*
Summary: Rijkaard's biography told by sports writer Armand Carabén. The book speaks very highly of his successes as manager, but was written before the decline of FC Barcelona in the 2007-2008 season, which is attributed to Rijkaard's soft hand with the stars.

Leo Messi: El tresor del Barça. Author: **Toni Frieros.** Publisher: Grupo Zeta (2006). Language: Catalan. Translated title: *Leo Messi: Barça's treasure.*
Summary: A short and simple biography of Leo Messi by the Sport newspaper, with a few remarkable stories of Messi's childhood.

Messi: La historia del precoz ganador de tres Balones de Oro. Author: **Luca Caioli.** Publisher: Grup 62 (2012). Language: Spanish. Translated title: *Messi: the story of the precocious winner of three Ballons d'Or.*
Summary: Luca Caioli's over-300 page-long book is the most authoritative and detailed account of the first 24 years of Leo Messi's life.

La força d'un somni – Els camins de l'èxit. Author: **Albert Puig.** Publisher: Plataforma Editorial (2009). Language: Catalan. Translated title: *The strength of a dream – The paths of success.*
Summary: Albert Puig, who is now one of the directors of the youth academy, was the coach of one of the *infantils* (U12) team when this book was published. Here he shows us what it takes (the good and the bad) to become a professional soccer player by gathering rare testimonies from ex players, active players, and coaches that have been through the Barça system. The book also gives frank advice for players (and parents!) to stay out of trouble.

Ara parlo jo. Author: **Carles Rexach.** Publisher: Ara Llibres (2008). Language: Catalan. Translated title: *Now it's my turn to speak.*

Summary: With a sincere style, ex-player Carles Rexach tells about his days at FC Barcelona since he was a 12 years old, including his long-time friendship and (later) quarrel with Johan Cruyff. A nice book for fans who (like me) admire this Barça legend.

Un any al paradís: El meu diari del triplet. Author: **Andrés Iniesta.** Publisher: Ara Llibres (2009). Language: Catalan. Translated title: *One year in paradise: My diary of the treble.*

Summary: Iniesta wrote this delightful book about how he lived the year 2008-2009, one of the most successful of the Guardiola era. The book is told in eight episodes "because eight is my number".

Andrés Iniesta: 8 Grandes Historias. Authors: **Jordi Gil & Javier Giraldo.** Publisher: Sport (2012). Language: Spanish. Translated title: *Andrés Iniesta: 8 Great Stories.*

Summary: Eight great stories about Iniesta told by soccer players or coaches such as Michel Platini, Louis Van Gaal, Víctor Valdés, Frank Rijkaard, Bojan Krkic, Fernando Torres, and Xavi Hernández.

Força Barça! – Còmic oficial del Barça. Authors: **Pepe Caldelas & Jorge Santamaría.** Publisher: Ulst Sports (2009). Language: Catalan. Translated title: *Força Barça! – Barça's official comic.*

Summary: The history of FC Barcelona, in comic. Light reading for curious teenage fans.

Quan no perdíem mai. Edited by: **Antoni Munné** (multi-author book). Publisher: Alfaguara (2011). Language: Catalan. Translated title: *When we never used to lose.*

Summary: This book is a compilation of 15 short writings by various writers that reflect on the most important moments of Barça's history and its present string of victories. Good literature written exclusively for Barça fans – a growing literary genre nowadays.

Viaje al corazón del fútbol – Conversaciones desde la pasión o la admiración sobre el gran Barça de Guardiola. Author: **Juan Cruz Ruiz.** Publisher: Editorial Corner (2011). Language: Spanish. Translated title: *A journey to the heart of*

soccer – Conversations from the passion or the admiration about Guardiola's great Barça.
Summary: In this book, 26 intellectuals talk with Juan Cruz Ruiz about the various ways in which they have been enjoying watching Guardiola's Barça play.

Los grandes – Diálogos con hombres de fútbol. Author: **Danilo Díaz.** Publisher: Ediciones B (2012). Language: Spanish. Translated title: *The great – Dialogues with men of soccer.*
Summary: A compilation of interesting interviews to a sparkly set of soccer coaches and players performed by Chilean sports journalist Danilo Díaz.

Soccer Men – Profiles of the Rogues, Geniuse, and Neurotics Who Dominate the World's Most Popular Sport. Author: **Simon Kuper.** Publisher: Nation Books (2011).
Summary: Bestselling coauthor of *Soccernomics* provides valuable testimonies of the worse behaviors of famous soccer players on and off the pitch. The book is well-written but it fails to analyze the underlying reason for these behaviors (the lack of involvement by the clubs in the players' education) and, in my opinion, the same stories could have been told with the respect that these soccer legends deserve. By casting a negative light on the players, Simon Kuper only emphasizes that, contrary to the players, he had the privilege of being educated at Oxford and Harvard while the players had to invest their time on learning soccer – and most of them ended up achieving soccer pinnacles much higher than the one that Kuper has reached in literature. Worse, Kuper's condescending tone is the writer's equivalent of the "rogue" and "neurotic" behaviors that he describes in soccer players. Overall, the book is tainted with a clear bias for English soccer that produces some rather farcical lines: "The route through the middle, guarded by Nicky Butt and Paul Scholes, looks daunting even for Rivaldo and Ronaldo". The same bias makes Kuper turn off the simplest fact-checking, as when he states (referring to Manchester United) that "No club in Europe has won more trophies in the past decade". How about checking Barça's record, since

ManU lost two *Champions League* finals against Barça, in 2009 and 2011? In the period 2001-2011 that he is alluding to, Manchester United has won 5 *Premier Leagues*, one *FA Cup*, one *Champions League*, and one *FIFA Club World Cup*, whereas FC Barcelona has won 5 *Ligas*, two *Copas del Rey*, three *Champions Leagues*, and two *FIFA Club World Cups*.

White Angels – Beckham, Real Madrid & The New Football. Author: **John Carlin**. Publisher: Bloomsbury (2004).
Summary: To write this book, John Carlin had unprecedented access to Real Madrid players and directors, traveling with them to matches. The book cleverly uses the figure of superstar David Beckham to unfold the stories of the other Galácticos and present the reader with an X-ray of the whole club.

A Beautiful Game – The World's Greatest Players and How Soccer Changed Their Lives. Author: **Tom Watt**. Publisher: HarperOne (2010).
Summary: This coffee-table book consists of gorgeous photographs and candid interviews of great soccer players (Messi, Casillas, Ribéry, Donovan, and Beckham, among others) looking back at their childhood and the beginning of their careers.

Ward's Soccerpedia – The Lore and Laws of the Beautiful Game. Author: **Andrew Ward**. Publisher: Anova Books (2006).
Summary: An outstanding collection of soccer trivia, filled with the most bizarre soccer anecdotes.

The World is a Ball – The Joy, Madness, and Meaning of Soccer. Author: **John Doyle**. Publisher: Rodale Books (2010).
Summary: This book from cultural critic John Doyle is an account of various soccer matches (mostly World Cup games) as an excuse to tell us how soccer and its colorful circuses of fans surrounding it evolved together in various parts of the world.

The World's Game – A History of Soccer. Author: **Bill Murray**. Publisher: University of Illinois Press (1996).

Summary: Sports historian Bill Murray has written a lucid account of the growth of soccer since its invention as a sport by the British until the present day. The book is rich in allusions to geopolitical conflicts that have surrounded or affected soccer at any given moment.

The ball is round – A global history of soccer. Author: **David Goldblatt.**
Publisher: Penguin (2008). Language: English.
Summary: Everything you need to know about the genesis of soccer since ancient times, its modalities, and how it is played around the globe. Many readers will wonder why the same amount of information could not have been summarized to less than 900 pages.

Printed in Poland
by Amazon Fulfillment
Poland Sp. z o.o., Wrocław